An Amazon and a Donkey

An Amazon and a Donkey

Natascha Scott-Stokes

CENTURY
London Sydney Auckland Johannesburg

Copyright © 1991 by Natascha Scott-Stokes
All rights reserved

First published in Great Britain in 1991 by Century
Random Century Ltd
20 Vauxhall Bridge Road, London SW1V 2SA

Century Hutchinson Australia (Pty) Ltd
20 Alfred Street, Milsons Point, Sydney, NSW 2061, Australia

Century Hutchinson New Zealand Ltd
PO Box 40-086, 32–34 View Road, Glenfield, Auckland 10, New Zealand

Century Hutchinson South Africa (Pty) Ltd
PO Box 337, Bergvlei 2012, South Africa

Natascha Scott-Stokes' right to be identified as the author of this work
has been asserted by her in accordance with the Copyright, Designs and
Patents Act, 1988.

Set in Linotronic Palatino by CentraCet, Cambridge
Printed and bound in U.K. by Mackays of Chatham Ltd, Chatham, Kent

British Library Cataloguing in Publication Data

Scott-Stokes, Natascha
An Amazon and a Donkey
1. Peru. Amazon River Basin. Description & travel
I. Title
918.110463

ISBN 0-7126-3452-5

For Pam Gawler-Wright
and in memory of P.J.G.

Contents

4: Amazonia

Appendices

Bibliography

Acknowledgements

Thanks to all the people along my route who offered me their help and hospitality. To Mark Booth and Gail Rebuck for opening the door of publishing to me. To my parents, German grandmother, and aunts, for giving me very generous financial support even though they thought my project risky. To my mother especially, for never trying to stop me, and for encouraging my writing efforts. To my friends who believed in me and gave me a send-off without sentiment. To Pam, for inspiration, support and affection. To Charity Scott-Stokes, Pam Gawler-Wright, Martin Hubbard, and Patrick Campbell, for valued criticism. To Jo Pelly, for a beautiful place to write in.

For practical help and advice in England, I would like to thank Dr John Hemming, Robin Hanbury-Tenison and Shane Winsor of the Royal Geographical Society (RGS); Dr François Odendaal; John Harrison; Tanis and Martin Jordan; Peter Salisbury of the Long River Canoe Club (LRCC); Dennison Berwick; Anne-Marie Barret of STA Travel; Jack Holland of Rough Guides; Nick Dalziel of the Writers' Guild of Great Britain; Stephen Corry and Virginia Luling of Survival International (SI); Oswaldo Vasquez of the Catholic Institute of International Relations (CIIR); the former Consul-General of Peru, Mr Miguel Pons; the Cultural Attaché of Peru, Dr Carlos Zavaleta; Carmen Granda-Byrne of the Peruvian National Tourist Board (FOPTUR); Louisa Gillett, Sarah Austin.

For the same in Peru, thanks to Naomi Fukuda Suzuki of FOPTUR in Lima, who assisted me beyond the call of duty, and without whom many vital factors would have been impossible; Guillermo Rocca Paredes of FOPTUR in Trujillo, and Mauro Granados Maglino of FOPTUR in Huaraz; Americo and family; the South American Explorers Club (SAEC); Jim Bartle; Ellie Griffis, editor of the *Lima Times*; Justin Gilbert of the British Council; Paul Martinez of the British Embassy; Padre Pancho of the Society of Jesus; Hector M. Alva Narvaez of the Interior Ministry; Colonel Luis Lazarte of the Immigration Office; Carolyn Williams of CIIR: Terry Pennington of the Royal Botanical Gardens at Kew.

I consulted the following organizations and thanks go to them and their staff: Medical Advisory Service for Travellers Abroad (MASTA); RGS; the Writers' Guild of Great Britain; CIIR; SI; SAEC; Mountain Medicine Centre; STA Travel; Hi-Peak Leisure; Standford Maps; the Survival Shop; FOPTUR; Latin American Bureau (LAB); Asociacion Interetnica de Desarollo de la Selva Peruana (AIDESEP); Instituto Geografico de Peru.

Note: some names of people and places in Huaraz have been changed.

Introduction

'But why do you want to go alone?' they kept asking. Why not? was my reply. Still the question came again and again. My mother even offered me ten sessions with a psychiatrist, at one stage, convinced that my dream to travel down the Amazon was really an obsessive fixation (I remember wishing she would offer a mosquito net instead).

However, after a while I myself began to wonder whether there was not something strange about wanting to travel alone. This pervasive question soon became an embarrassment, asked persistently by all kinds of people in tones ranging from the incredulous to the suspicious. Was my determination to travel alone really so strange? To me it seemed like an excellent way to discover South America: I would begin in the Peruvian Andes and walk through some of the world's most stunning mountain ranges, before heading north along the Marañon river, and eventually arriving at the rainforests to travel on the great Amazon itself, exploring along the way and perhaps even staying at a native settlement.

Exciting prospects such as these seemed to pall in other people's eyes when the idea of my going alone came into play.

'I've always travelled alone,' I would say, beginning to feel like a freak.

'I'm not a "group" kind of person,' I would explain; 'Anti-social,' they murmured.

I believe that a person is much freer travelling alone: unconstrained by the need to compromise with others all the time, more likely to meet people, and more likely to be invited into private homes and families. One can be a guest; more is often an imposition or a threat. Good arguments these, but people would then throw in my face that I am a young, five-foot-one-and-a-half

1

female, who would inevitably be the target for all kinds of trouble: 'You'll get robbed, raped and shot – probably in that order.'

The questions and shakings of the head were endless, and eventually I got fed up with arguing and justifying, and contented myself with being very calm and determined about my intentions, my tone brooking no discussion of my solitary journey.

I first thought about travelling to South America when I was seventeen or eighteen. I would spend hours poring over maps, plotting grand treks around the entire continent; studying climate charts and seasons in order that I might see every destination at its best; calculating costs – what I would need in terms of equipment and guide books and how long I would stay in each place. I have always been rather good at making plans; I especially love timetabled plans, which neatly date when, where and by which date I will have achieved my goal. I would do this kind of thing for days, conveniently putting off essays or any other work, and instead constructing a dream.

At last I had a year to spare between school and the beginning of my degree course and I was firmly decided on heading across the Atlantic. But it was not to be: I spent six miserable months on the dole and even a short spell trying to sell vacuum cleaners didn't make me enough money for a grand tour of South America. At that time I spoke no Spanish, and it was this, and my age (I was then only twenty) that decided the question. Instead, I got enough money together to spend three months in the eastern Caribbean, as close as I could get to my dreamland, and a delicious consolation for the time being.

Five years of college went by and, as far as I was concerned, I was always on my way to South America. I read anything to do with that part of the world and spent my summers learning Spanish in Barcelona.

It was in October 1986 when my ideas about what I was going to do in South America and where exactly I was going to go crystallized. I went to see a film by François Odendaal about kayaking down the Amazon, and I think it was then that I first became fascinated by the idea of a journey down that river. The one and only time I had ever been in a canoe was as a young

2

teenager, so I decided the kayak was not for me. I would just have to walk the first part until the river became navigable.

My dream took shape and I finally knew what I was going to do. I began to buy walking boots and other things I thought I might need. My planning went into top gear, and I wrote to everyone I had ever heard of who had been to the Amazon. Surprisingly, almost everyone wrote back, some at great length, packing their letters full of vital details: such as whether or not I needed a gun, or what to do about altitude sickness. I was so busy planning, I rarely had time to consider the consequences of what I was setting out to do, and if I ever did, I quickly shoved disconcerting thoughts to the back of my mind.

In September 1987 I was all set to go, or would have been if I hadn't been offered a contract to write a travel guide instead. On a personal level it took almost unbearable self-control to put my departure off for at least another year. On the other hand, I had to think ahead, and this was an opportunity too good to be missed.

It was 1989 and nearly ten years since I had first dreamed of leaving. My work on the guide was coming to an end and the last spurt of planning for my Amazon journey was underway. I decided to travel from the Marañon source of the river because it began north of Lima and seemed to be beyond the immediate sphere of *Sendero Luminoso* (Shining Path) terrorists. As the shortest of the three sources of the Amazon, it has been neglected by the organizers of expeditions and only a handful of people have ever journeyed down it. Certainly, no one has ever walked the length of the Marañon, and the Andean region it flows through is virtually unknown to outsiders, making it all the more attractive to me. In contrast to the mountains and the Maranon, the journey along the Amazon was going to be a time to discover life in the rainforest and, ideally, life among the Indians. Years of reading about the forest and its people made me yearn to discover it for myself and, although I had made little progress with contacts for arranging a visit to a tribal village, I had a few addresses, and so some hope of achieving this.

The steadily worsening situation in Peru was something I could not, nor wished to, ignore in the plans for my journey. The

3

country's downward spiral of economic decline, political and social chaos, and violent battles between state forces, terrorists and narcotics traffickers, seemed to make the possibility of a military coup or a civil war a very real danger. I had been following the situation closely for some time and, in spite of the obvious threat to my own plans, I was eager to travel to Peru at such a crucial time in its history: at last I would get a chance to experience at first-hand issues which, so far, I had only read about, and in particular my proposed journey would take in the Andean region, where many of the country's most crucial issues are being fought out.

As a state Peru is characterized by macroverticality, that is, the country's climate, vegetation and culture are separated into and defined by three distinct zones; *costa* (the coast), *sierra* (the mountains) and *selva* (the jungle). From the beginning, civilization in Peru has been moulded by this division, each zone engendering very different societies. The people from each region have not only developed different lifestyles and cultures, but different languages and socio-political systems too, and this is an important key to the understanding of Peru's problems today. It is not a unified country with a homogeneous culture. There are powerful political and cultural prejudices and divisions between each zone which are further complicated by an important racial aspect. The coast is predominantly peopled by *mestizos* (those of mixed Spanish-Indian descent), and by a minority of Spanish and European descent, the latter forming the ruling elite; the Andes are also inhabited by *mestizos*, but a large proportion of the population is formed by Quechua Indians or by those of predominantly Indian descent; the *selva*, on the other hand, is inhabited mainly by descendants of the Indian hunter-gatherer tribes of the rainforest.

Communication and co-operation have, understandably, always been problematic between these various groups, not least because of the physical difficulties of travel and access in Peru. In recent years, Amazonian development and settlement, and mass migration to the coastal cities, in particular Lima, have blurred, to a degree, the racial and geographic divisions. However, it remains true to say that there is no such person as a Peruvian: people refer to themselves rather as *de la costa*, *serrano* or *de la selva*. The logistic difficulties of administrating a country like Peru are staggering even without the added burdens of the colonial

4

legacy, institutionalized corruption, economic collapse and political and social disarray. The combined effect of all these factors has created an impossible situation: a country paralysed by seemingly irreconcilable internal divisions, its progress, if any, hobbled by a foreign debt that in 1989 topped $16 billion.

The *Sendero Luminoso* and other guerrilla factions thus have a perfect setting for their activities. Self-styled Maoist 'freedom fighters', the *Senderos* have been trying to mount a civil war since the early 1980s. The group was founded by a local university professor-turned-revolutionary in the Andean town of Ayacucho and, until recent years, its influence was very much focused on and around this area. However, since forming an alliance with the rich narcotics cartels, the military and technological resources of the *Senderos* have dramatically improved and its power base has expanded. Peru has nothing with which to defend itself: the army doesn't even have enough boots for all its soldiers.

The people who pay the price for the government's impotence are the poor – the city slum dwellers, the peasants and the Indians – who make up the majority of the population. The *campesinos* (Andean peasants), in particular, have become hostages of terror and deprivation. They are caught between the combined forces of the military and the police ranged against those of the terrorists and the narcotics traffickers. Each group roams the highlands, conscripting young men and boys, eating the food of the *campesinos* (already in short supply), and shooting those they suspect of supporting the other side. Vast areas of the central, southern and northern Andes have now been abandoned by officialdom: no police, no army, no school teachers, doctors or law courts can operate there; no public transport exists even where there are roads, and no supplies of any kind from the commercial world beyond reach these regions. The inhabitants there are left to their own devices without any help or protection. It is a nightmare without any end in sight.

This was my destination; and the beginning of a journey which was the realization of a dream that I had to try and follow, or else live with regret for the rest of my life. In the days leading up to my departure I rushed round, organizing last-minute details and trying to keep calm about the increasingly disturbing news coming out of Peru. One headline in a newspaper read 'Khmer Rouge in Peru'; most people continued to question my journey, doubt turning to disbelief and concern. My friends, however, never doubted me and, in the moments when I doubted myself, they were the ones who reminded me that I could do it. I thought about the possibility of never coming back but finally came to the conclusion that I would at least go out chasing my dream, and that has got to be the best way to go.

1
Lima

Headlines

This book is a personal story, but no one can travel without becoming aware of a country's own story, and during the seven-month period of my journey, Peru went through a time of drastic decline. To give at least some idea of the complexity of the country's problems, I will preface my account of the first three parts of my journey with facts and statistics drawn from the news headlines that were current when I was there. No analysis is offered; for anyone interested in finding out more, I have listed the sources in the bibliography.

The economy

At the beginning of March 1989 the government launched the second phase of its economic programme for the year, which included the following measures. The official base rate was devalued by thirty per cent, with the value of the Peruvian Inti against the US dollar going from I/920 in February to I/1,200 in March. Accumulated inflation for the first two months of 1989 was 109.9 per cent according to the National Statistics Institute; price increases from March 1988 through to 1989 therefore stood at 2933.1 per cent. Interest rates went up by 25 per cent and the monthly minimum wage was increased by 30 per cent, from I/42,000 to I/55,000; daily minimum wages were set at I/1,633 which, at that time, would have bought two cups of coffee in a café in the wealthy suburb of Miraflores. The price of gas went up by 30 per cent, electricity by 40 per cent, water by 80 per cent. Basic products such as bread, sugar, milk, cooking oil, pasta, rice, margarine, frozen fish, diesel oil and kerosene, although subject to price control, increased between 20 per cent and 50 per cent.

The International Monetary Fund (IMF) considered lifting Peru's 'ineligible' status, but the Inter-American Development

Bank (IDB) then declared Peru ineligible for further credit as a result of the government's failure to come up with $12 million in overdue debt repayments. Payments on a further $60 million debt were due in April of that year. President Alan Garcia responded by saying that the government was not prepared to sacrifice Peru's reserves for minimum gain (the IDB had promised $100 million in fresh credit if Peru paid off its $75 million arrears); according to the president, the gain of $25 million just wasn't worth it. Meanwhile the Peruvian Treasury pointed out that they were unable to pay even the overdue $12 million. At this time, Peru's total debt to the private banking sector alone was $8 billion and its total foreign debt stood at $16 billion.

Death toll related to political violence

The total death toll for January and February in 1989 was 794, of which around 352 were killed during clashes between terrorist groups *Sendero Luminoso* (Shining Path) and *Tupac Amaru* (MRTA), and the armed forces.

The minister for the interior, Armando Villanueva, introduced a new anti-terrorism plan, which included setting up an anti-terrorist fund to which businesses and other interested parties would be invited to contribute, to help provide the fuel, food and transportation needed by the government and armed forces in waging its war against terrorism.

Confusion

I've always been very good at talking. But now was the time to stop talking and start acting. The closer my departure came the more terrified I felt. All those years I had spent dreaming about my great adventure and wondering about the physical and mental challenge were suddenly in the past. What if it had all been just talk? I had told people my plan so many times that it had lost its meaning; I could form the familiar sentences but they had become empty of significance. I was no longer sure if I knew what I was talking about where my journey was concerned. Fear and uncertainty whispered, 'You can still back out. Your friends won't love you less. Who cares what anyone else thinks? Forget it. Get married to the sensible chap who's been trying to save you from yourself for years. Are you really going to be so stubborn as to get yourself killed just because you couldn't admit you didn't want to go . . .?' I decided that if any of these thoughts were true, I was not going to admit it. I was going to go, and if it turned out to be a horrible mistake then that was just too bad.

It was very sad leaving England, my friends, and my family. Would I ever see them again? I was treated and pampered like a sacrificial lamb, invited to last suppers by friends, and my mother said she would go and plant a cross in the jungle if I did not return. The atmosphere was one of melodrama and throughout the day of my departure, I cried frequently.

In the morning I sat down to paint a watercolour for my mother. I wanted to give her something to make my journey more real to her so I painted a picture of myself dragging my stubborn *burro*, the donkey I planned to buy as a travelling companion, through the Andes. This exercise made me aware of her anxiety and of the selfish quality of my ambition. This uncertain venture would inflict worry and strain on the people I cared most about. Could I justify it?

11

Finally, I came to the conclusion that, above all, my driving force in this enterprise was something much more positive than mere ambition, pride, or a need to prove myself. It was quite simply chasing a dream. It was the impulse towards discovery: meeting new people and learning new ways, seeing places previously only read about or seen on TV. I was keen to experience a new world and also to discover things about myself. How would I cope with travelling alone for seven months? Would I crack under the pressure of potential danger and discomfort? Would I be brave? I could not wait to find out.

Danger in the Air

On arrival in Lima it seemed that death and fear were never far away. It was my first night, I was strolling around and getting a feel for the city: the scene was a loud and bustling street, vendors shouting, money-changers waving wads of cash, beggars holding out their hands to a forest of passing legs; suddenly the sound was cut, voices dropped away, the street became an ominous place and people began running. Running from what? I had neither seen nor heard anything frightening and, as unexpectedly as the rush began, just as quickly was it over. The experience was like moving through a herd of nervous antelope, constantly twitching at some dangerous scent, or an unusual noise. I felt like a new player who doesn't know the rules.

It was the same down at the beach in the posh suburb of Miraflores. The crowd of glistening young bodies suddenly jumped up and ran as one to the water's edge. Again, I was bemused and reminded once more of my newness. Everyone's attention was focused on a line of rocks leading out to an exclusive pier and restaurant. One of the guards from the restaurant surveyed the scene from the rooftop, swinging his machine-gun round to free his hands for the binoculars, and other guards held back the crowd of jostling bodies below. Three men swam out against the incoming tide towards the rocks, periodically thrown back by huge waves, while another tried to pick his way across the sea-whipped boulders. What was going on? I asked another bystander.

'*Un muerto*,' a washed-up corpse, he replied laconically, as if it happened all the time, and maybe it did.

In Lima, all is well one minute, and the next you can find yourself caught up in a riot, held at knife-point, or worse. Volatility is in the air, and while threatening, it is also exciting. It gives that extra edge to walking down the street.

The police are useless. Everyone will tell you that they are as likely to rob you as anyone else. A favourite scam is arresting *gringos* for purchase or possession of drugs, and then demanding large sums of money to drop the charges. It is difficult to know whether it is just the police or other *ladrones* (any kind of robber) involved; whatever, the scam continues to be successful. A poor Spanish boy staying at my hostel was subjected to this trick, and lost not only all his money, but his passport too, not to mention his nerve. He foolishly bought cocaine in a café and, within minutes of the purchase, the police had arrested him: they were in cahoots with the dealer.

Picking pockets is a particularly inventive rip-off. There is the game of smearing sauce on a hapless tourist, only to wipe it off helpfully while emptying the grateful innocent's daypack. Money is dropped on the ground; someone will tell you it is yours in the hope that you will bend over long enough for them to get at your pockets. Best and most effective are the gangs of small children, the piranhas. These children, usually under ten years old, over-whelm their prey by virtue of numbers: even a grown man can be defeated when faced with three boys hanging on each leg and arm, while others pull off anything they can, from his clothes and shoes to his watch and camera. Just like the dreaded fish, they can strip a victim in seconds.

My awareness was soon tuned to a fine pitch, yet moving around Lima was far less nerve-racking than I had at first expected.

In my experience, Peruvian thieves are the most gutless crooks there are. It is almost a game: they follow you, try to unzip your bag on the bus, and overcharge you in the restaurant; but if you turn and confront them, they give up immediately. They have no fear or shame. Caught in the act, they will shrug their shoulders and grin, or maybe say something like *lo siento gringita* (sorry little tourist), but it is obviously a meaningless gesture.

This is almost harder to cope with than the attempted crime itself; Western cultural givens like fairness and standard rights and wrongs are made to seem irrelevant, and it's this, as well as the crime, which poses a threat. Corruption is the norm. It is so normal that even to call it that seems churlish, like complaining about losing just because you don't know how to play. There is a darker, more violent underside to this game, of course, and every now and then it manifests itself like *il muerto* at Miraflores. However, after a day or two, I felt quite au fait with the city.

The *collectivo* vans, crammed to breaking point, soon held no terrors for me and, when I met a Scottish poet who had been hiding in taxis throughout his visit, I felt reassuringly superior. (He was about six foot, which made trying to squeeze into the little Toyota vans a daunting prospect.) Once inside, you were likely to be sitting on someone's lap, and any chance of escaping thieving hands was impossible. The breakneck speed of the traffic and a system of only stopping if someone shouted *'Baja!'* (Get down!), made it impossible for a newcomer to get off at the intended destination. One just has to guess, or ask the other passengers, who are surprisingly friendly: they try not to embarrass newcomers by showing that they cannot understand a word of their Spanish, and earnestly tell them where to get off; unfortunately, it usually turns out to be the wrong place. Practice soon evens up the gamble, and the ride is then fun: like jumping on and off a rollercoaster.

Lima is not an attractive city. Locked in grids, its blocks of streets spread out under a haze of humid cloud and grey pollution. Wrecks on wheels belch black fumes at pedestrians, and the parks are littered with dog-shit and the bodies of the drunk and destitute.

In the city the poor were as rampant and as pervasive as inflation. 500 Intis (about 20p in March 1989) and about a third of the daily minimum wage was enough to buy a meal if you knew where to go, however it was basic food stuffs like sugar, milk and bread – the staples of the poor – that inflation made inaccessible. In downtown Lima, I saw street children hovering at restaurant entrances, waiting for customers to leave their tables, so they could finish off the scraps. Sometimes a person would even leave a plate half-eaten and motion the child to come and eat. Waiters almost never intervened. Often the beggar would take the customer's place at the table; sometimes one would stand in the doorway, cleaning up with fingers and tongue.

Little of the colonial architecture seems to have survived, which considering that Lima was the capital of the Spanish-American empire, is a sad disappointment. Concrete dominates the scenery, with a style reminiscent of a dreary Los Angeles suburb and a corresponding lack of character; even swanky Miraflores is all concrete and high-rises, the few redeeming features including a slightly lower level of pollution and a couple of pavement cafés.

Barranco is the only quarter that evokes anything of the colonial past, its main square lined with houses in the traditional pastel colours and home to a grand old church. During the summer, live music gives the place the air of a *fiesta*, and I spent a couple of happy evenings here, digesting the city, getting drunk with new friends and listening to Peruvian salsa bands. Here painters and drug pushers mix with tourists and the self-consciously smart locals.

A few days separated me from England, but already it all seemed to belong to the distant past. This was my promised land and here anything could happen.

Chan Chan and Beach Boys

Abby and I were invited to spend a couple of days at Huanchaco, nine hours up the coast, and decided to go. I had met Abby on the plane; she had come over to study Spanish.

Huanchaco is a tiny fishing village outside the northern town of Trujillo and, on the road between the two, there lies one of South America's most famous archeological sites: Chan Chan, ancient city of the pre-Inca Chimu civilization.

We took the night bus, and hardly had we left the sprawling shanty towns of Lima, but it halted for the first of a series of interminable military checks. This was an opportunity never missed by the vendors; as soon as the wheels had stopped, a bevy of them – shouting men, women and children – would clamour at the windows and stream aboard the bus, hands, arms, and necks hung about with wares. Children as young as four or five were selling oranges, peaches, and fruit juices in the middle of the night, while the women lugged great baskets of festering sandwiches or fly-stuck cobs of corn down the aisles. The men seemed to prefer selling items like plugs, washers and batteries; perhaps there was more status to be had in the sale of batteries. *Helados, helados* (ice-cream), *agua de manzana, agua de manzana* (apple juice), *Coca-Cola, Fanta, Pepsi, Coca-Cola, Fanta, Pepsi!* Everyone shouted at once, an endless, repetitive litany to the one or two things they were selling. Again and again until it became a chant of desperation, a cry for pity. Much later, there was a man trying to sell plastic salad forks. At four in the morning? The persistence of these people shouting up and down the bus aisle, holding their goods inches from your face so that at least you have to look, is amazing only if one does not consider them as citizens of a country that offers no respite to the poor.

*

17

We arrived bleary-eyed at six in the morning. The town was only just coming to life, so we sat in the white dawn light and waited for the shutters to go up on the restaurants around the main square. Tramps were having their morning wash in the fountain, and the instant photo man was setting up his camera, ready for the tourists. An hour later, the square's shopfronts still had their metal shutters firmly closed. The only place that seemed to be open was the restaurant belonging to the five-star hotel and so, in spite of our crumpled looks, we decided to be decadent and have breakfast there.

We were dying to go to the loo and, after ordering, we both went off to the toilets, hoping there would also be somewhere to wash. Abby took her whole travelling bag with her, and the waiter eyed us suspiciously. It was only the fact that we were foreigners which had allowed us even to enter the place in such a state. After two strong coffees and a cigarette, we both needed to go to the loo again. The waiter became even more concerned. Abby had tried to have a bath in the sink, and the floor was now drenched in water. We left quickly, leaving what amounted to a Peruvian day's wage for a couple of coffees, orange juices, and two pieces of toast.

Huanchaco is a sand-blown fishing village, numbering a couple of hundred inhabitants. The guide books will tell you that the main point of interest is that the inhabitants, like the fishermen of Lake Titicaca, are the only people who still make and use reed boats. The other attractions are the massive waves crashing in from the Pacific; during the summer, hordes of surfers and fashionable *Limeños* descend on Huanchaco and its beaches like clouds of locusts.

For a few, subsequently painful days, we paid homage to the sun, and then we went to visit Chan Chan. From the road connecting Huanchaco to Trujillo, the famous site looks like a few crumbled mud walls in the desert, an old building site left abandoned, rather than the remains of one of the most sophisticated pre-Inca civilizations in South America. Rain and the damp atmosphere of the coast have slowly eroded the great, nine-metre walls that used to enclose the palace compounds. But since they were constructed out of sand and mud, it is incredible that there

18

are any remains at all. The secret of their longevity is the mixture of a certain kind of cactus juice in the adobe, which 'glued' the mud bricks, holding them together to this day.

We wandered around the dusty expanses, trying to imagine what it must have been like, while keeping an eye out for the notorious robbers that were rumoured to hide in the maze of walls, lying in wait for unsuspecting tourists.

According to Chimu legend, the kingdom of Chimor was founded sometime between AD 900 and 1000, when sea-borne invaders, probably from Ecuador, conquered the Moche Valley on Peru's north coast. The newcomers soon ruled a large coastal empire that stretched from present-day Tumbes, to Lima in the south. Chan Chan was their capital, and by the time the warring Incas came to conquer in the late fifteenth century, the city had a population of around 50,000, making it larger than any European capital at that time. The city centre alone extends over an area of six square kilometres, and it contains no less than ten separate palace compounds, each surrounded by tightly packed *barriors* (dwellings), which housed the clearly defined classes of Chimu society.

It seems remarkable that such a city could have flourished there, in this barren desert land; however, according to archeological records, large-scale irrigation had already been developed as early as 1800 BC. Long before the arrival of the Chimu, the Mochica civilization had formed sophisticated state structures and agricultural systems to sustain the population. The Incas, in comparison to such cultures were barbaric, warfare their only excellence. Their invasion of the north coast required little effort: they cut Chan Chan's water supply, and that was the end of that. The conquerors were impressed with what they found and many believe, although it has not been proved, that the admirable social and bureaucratic organization of the Incas was derived from the Chimu model.

It's sad that so little remains to give an idea of the splendour that must have been there; little decorative carving is to be found, and the graves and palaces have long since been looted of any art treasures. All that is left are the ramparts of sand, making Chan Chan a desolate and somehow absurd monument, an outsized sandcastle which the desert is slowly reclaiming.

*

It happened that our visit to Huanchaco coincided with the annual surfing convention. *Limeños*, indistinguishable from Californian beach bums, paraded through the village in fluorescent shorts with a surf board tucked under the arm, while fishermen mended nets by their reed boats, as they had done for thousands of years. I found this juxtaposition of culture, age and class depressing. The fishermen and the surfers shared a nationality but little else, and their differences were more complex than those between the city and the country. The surfers were as much strangers as any foreigner, and the fishermen aptly call them *gringos falsos*. I felt that the surfers' whole-hearted, uncritical love affair with TV-taught, American pop culture was a denial and even a rejection of their Peruvian identity. Perhaps I am being unfair: these were, after all, the young, rich elite; but since they will form the governing class of Peru it is disturbing how little they seem to care about the future of their own nation, its people and culture.

It is, therefore, one of the particular problems that Peru has to face, in that the very people who are best qualified – in terms of education and wealth – to invest in the country, seem to feel very little national loyalty or identity. They prefer to get out while they can, and leave Peru to be fought over by the *Senderos* and the military. Why do they see the United States as the promised land? There are, of course, the obvious attractions of material comfort, economic stability, and functioning public, and to a greater extent, private services. However, these considerations aside, I think the emigration of the Peruvian elite, or at the least, their indifference to the fate of their nation has more to do with the inheritance of traditional colonial attitudes: the Spanish-descended elite see themselves as keepers of a country whose wealth is extracted to finance the rich living and power structures of another world, or in this case, another class. Their attitudes are those of absentee landowners who, although born and brought up in Peru, identify themselves culturally with the West, and espouse Western aspirations and prejudices.

The surfers on Huanchaco beach seem to me to be symbolic of this cultural identification with the West, and consequent rejection of Peru, its people, its history, its arts and, of course, its problems. Television advertisements abound with images of white, Coca-Cola-swigging joggers, while the representation of Peruvian culture in the arts and media is, in contrast, marginalized

20

into quaint displays, brought out and dusted off for tourists, no more. It was explained many times to me in the cafés of Miraflores that Peruvians are 'plain lazy and no good'; that nothing works and nothing ever will. It is a widespread opinion, from Andean *campesino* to mine owner, and it does not bode well for Peru. For me, this was one of the saddest impressions I came away with: that Peru, a country so rich in natural and human resources, a nation so vital in cultural and creative power, should be so impoverished in terms of the commitment of one class to another, and of all to the future of their society.

The Bureaucratic Jungle

Before March 1989, and my arrival in Peru, the *Senderos* had concentrated their efforts in the southern highlands of Peru, with only the occasional foray made out of there to bomb Lima or one of the coastal towns. From then on, however, they began a high-profile campaign of violence, spreading their net to the northern Andes, as well as to important locations throughout Peru. The frequency of death due to political violence rose sharply, and for the first few months of 1989 the figure was estimated by the State Senate Committee on Violence to be 794, bringing the total number of such deaths since 1980 to 12,965.

A major change in their strategy took place as well, and this was the decision to target foreigners for attack, in an attempt to sabotage the tourist industry, one of Peru's most important sources of revenue. At first it was aid workers and journalists who were the victims of terrorism, but soon it became clear that any *gringo* was fair game if the killing achieved effective publicity.

I tried, therefore, to get the latest advice and information from as many different people as possible. Back in London, the Peruvian consul-general had shaken his head at me, told me he thought my plans very dangerous, and handed me their latest update on emergency zones and no-go areas.

On arrival in Lima, I was amazed to be welcomed by a representative from FOPTUR, the Peruvian National Tourist Board at the airport. I had only phoned their London office the day before, more for the sake of a sense of completeness than anything else: what could a tourist office possibly have for a real traveller like me, I thought arrogantly. I was soon humbled in my realization that I could not have coped without them.

Naomi Fukuda, a Japanese Peruvian lady, was the representative: delicate, perfectly groomed, she was to be my guiding light

22

throughout that two-week stay in Lima. She made appointments for me to see leaders of the missionary orders and other ministries, escorted me herself to meetings, and acted as interpreter in the stumbling conversations I attempted, making me appear rather more important than I was and, to my joy, ensuring that I and my journey were taken seriously. Although Naomi was sceptical about my route in the face of the recent *Sendero* activity, she was at least prepared to help me with things like letters of recommendation and extended visas.

When I outlined my proposed route to the British embassy staff, they too shook their heads and, after consulting with the Peruvian military attaché, they advised me that I should not attempt the journey. According to their sources, the northern reaches of the Marañon were lined by coca plantations, where I would most certainly be an unwelcome visitor; while the area through which the upper reaches of the Marañon flowed in the rainforest was one disputed by Ecuador, and therefore had a heavy military presence: a lone female traveller could not possibly hope to get through such obstacles unscathed.

The only person who thought I would survive was Jim Bartle, a well-known American hiking expert, who had been resident in Peru for many years. He was the only person I could find who had first-hand knowledge of at least some of the mountain ranges I was going to cross, and so I felt his advice was probably more reliable than that of other scaremongers.

'Obviously you're going to go whatever I say,' he observed correctly. According to him, I was very likely to cross paths with the *Senderos* in the Cordillera Huayhuash, but they were unlikely to do more than demand money and food.

Even though I had to admit that there was a strong chance of being held up in the mountains, I clung to the possibility that it might not happen and, that if it did, I would lose only material things. It would be all right, I thought, with what some might have felt was childish conviction. It had to be – I had gone too far to give up now.

My most immediate problem was to obtain a seven-month visa. Foreigners are usually given visas which last ninety days, after which they have a choice either of braving the Lima immigration

23

office, or leaving the country and re-entering in order to get another three months. In my case, both of these options were unrealistic; it made no sense to return to Lima or leave Peru in the middle of my expedition, and, in any event, I did not know whether it would be possible: I had no idea where I would be three months from now.

In London, the people at the Peruvian embassy had informed me that it was officially impossible to obtain such a visa and my contact at the immigration office in Lima confirmed that view; but in Peru, there is always hope that the impossible will become possible, and in this case Naomi and her string-pulling promised a chance that I would get what I needed. It was not until I actually had the stamp in my passport, though, that I believed I was going to get it, and when I did, it was like a miracle.

Things had not started off well. On the morning that I had arranged to meet Naomi before going together to see the immigration people, she phoned to say that she couldn't pick me up and would I meet her in town? We arranged a rendezvous outside a garage on the corner of Paseo de la Republica and 28 de Julio. This turned out to be an enormous junction of dual carriageways, with garages on a number of its corners and, after I had waited forty minutes, I gave up and went home hot, hungry and irritated. I had got up early (punctuality is not one of my talents) and even missed breakfast to be certain of making the appointment, and I was disheartened. Naomi phoned soon after, however, and we met later in the day to go for an interview at the Ministry of Interior.

This was an achievement in itself but also potentially risky: if my journey, and my motives for attempting it, were found suspect at this stage, the whole project would be off before it had begun. Driving into the heavily guarded compound was like venturing into the mouth of the dragon. Armed guards were everywhere, and I had to leave my passport at reception just to get through the front door – a disturbing experience in Peru, where they can throw you in gaol if you cannot show any ID. I entered the dragon with Naomi and climbed up bleak flights of stairs, walked down long, empty corridors lined with closed doors, until we came to the carpeted floors and the portraits on the walls of the *director gobierno*'s waiting room. There we waited for about an hour, and that was short by local standards.

Senor Alva's office was large and comfortable with the obliga-
tory enormous desk, but also a sofa, coffee table and armchairs.
We sat in front of the desk and I tried to gauge what kind of a
man I was faced with by studying his family photos. They looked
a well-fed collection of people, cosily gathered on a sofa, exuding
conservative values. A television, perched on the office window
sill, was blaring out an Argentinian soap opera, and the director's
attention was, every now and then, drawn irresistibly to it, his
eyes glancing back and forth, to keep up with the latest love
affair while we discussed my politics. He was suspicious of my
motives, wanting to know what I thought of the government's
Amazon project and what exactly I would write about Peru. This
man could open all the doors for me or close them firmly in my
face and it was imperative that I said the right thing.

His suspicions were well-founded: not long before my arrival
some British journalists had insinuated themselves into the
Amazon region disputed by Ecuador and proceeded to rubbish
the government's administration policies there. Clearly, such bad
press was undesirable from the government's point of view,
sensitive to the effect it might have on their foreign aid; particularly as the International Monetary Fund (IMF) was continuing to
declare Peru ineligible for further loans. The director was not
going to do me any favours if he believed I was another, similarly
motivated, journalist. I explained that I was not a journalist, and
even pointed out coyly that I thought Peru should be left to
conduct its own affairs without interference from the West.

I knew it was what he wanted to hear but it is what I believe.
It angers me that Europe and the United States, who have both
been, and continue to be implicated in the political and economic
exploitation of Peru and other countries in South America (as
well as other Third World countries), now assume a moral
superiority – especially in the areas of conservation and development. The rainforest, for instance, is now a political football, and
is at risk of being destroyed for quick cash, forever. It should, of
course, be used productively and studied for all it has to teach
us; but why should South Americans be any different from
anyone else? Where is there a government that will put ecology
and people before economic and political gain?

In any event I managed to convince Senor Alva that I was not
a troublemaker and, after about an hour, he agreed to write an

official recommendation for me to show to police or local prefectures whom I might bump into on my journey. This was invaluable: I could go anywhere I liked, emergency zone or not, with approval from the highest authority. Of course, local police captains or the army might still have their doubts about me, but they were less likely to act upon them, if I showed them this letter. Of equal importance and use was the phone call he made to the colonel in charge at the immigration office, advising him about my imminent application, and recommending that it should be granted. This was one time when being female and looking half my age was a definite advantage: machismo, albeit avuncular, wielded in my favour, and when we went to the immigration office the following morning, we were almost certain of success.

Getting into the colonel's office was a minor achievement: even at nine in the morning the place was full of people, pushing and shoving, shouting and knocking on closed doors, and a few who possessed status of some kind and just walked through. At the door at which we waited, a hard-faced secretary blocked the way, deaf to all pleas except to those from figures of authority or those in possession of an effective recommendation; everyone else had to wait outside, perhaps getting a chance to sneak in during a lull in the secretary's attention. It was a madhouse. I had a male FOPTUR representative with me for this battle, but even he seemed confused and ran back and forth, shouting after yet another deaf official. He was pleading sweatily at the colonel's door, opened just a crack, and it was with relief that I saw him turn, waving frantically at me to come over. I waded through the clustered bodies, and slid through the magic door.

It was only a fraction less chaotic inside than in the corridors without. The colonel was a handsome, silver-haired man in his early fifties, chain-smoking, and with the self-important air of a busy man, but otherwise calm and collected. Doors slammed, frantic knocks came from outside, three phones were ringing on every desk, but the colonel was in control and did not miss a trick.

He acknowledged my presence between flicks of his cigarette, and I smiled in the hope that I was conveying suitable deference while retaining an air of confidence. Would we catch this man's attention long enough for him to put his vital signature in my passport? It was luck and Senor Alva that squeezed us in between

26

phone calls. Semantics almost foiled us at the last fence: between myself, the FOPTUR man, the colonel, and his secretary, we somehow managed to get into a ridiculous tangle about what constituted seven months. Should the stamps be dated from my arrival in Peru or from the last day of my present visa? If they put three normal visas in, that would give me nine months: was this a good thing? Should the visa end on the last day of September or the first day of October? The colonel's suggestion that we should come back tomorrow seemed the last straw. Finally, it was decided, the small sum of forty dollars changed hands, and I had the impossible: permission to travel in Peru for seven, continuous months.

2
Huaraz

Headlines

The economy

Inflation for the month of March stood at over 22 per cent. By the end of the month, the street value of the dollar soared by nearly 40 per cent, from I/1,250 to I/1,700. Meanwhile, the devalued coinage, worth 0.0825 of a US cent at the time, was put to a new use by street vendors, who adapted them into washers for nuts and bolts, making the going rate for a kilo of coins I/360.

Inflation for the first quarter of 1989 was calculated to be 198.1 per cent and the new prediction for the year as a whole stood at 10,000 per cent. Inflation for the month of April alone topped 48 per cent. The value of the dollar against the Inti increased by a further 20 per cent in the first two weeks of April, a dollar buying I/2030. The price of public services, including gas, rose sharply at the end of April, less than a month after the latest increase. Only days earlier, the minister for the economy, Carlos Rivas Davila, had stated that devaluation of the official base exchange rate would not take place on a bi-weekly basis.

However, the Central Bank devalued the official base exchange rate by 10 per cent in the first week of May, the second devaluation in two weeks, and this just days after the minister for the economy had denied there would be bi-weekly, let alone weekly, devaluations. Economic analysts now calculated the prediction for the year's inflation to be nearer 20,000 than 10,000 per cent.

Death toll related to political violence

Over the five-week period from the middle of March to the first week in May, 187 suspected terrorists, at least twenty-two soldiers and policemen and ninety-three civilians were killed,

cause of death ranging from being caught in crossfire to assassination. The figures are estimates and are possibly much higher,
but the government's policy of declaring large parts of Peru
emergency zones results in a dearth of news. At this time, the
government admitted that at least 259 towns and villages
throughout Peru lacked local government because terrorists
had run them out, and that nine of the country's departments
were operating in a state of emergency: Apurimac, Huancavel-
ica, San Martin, Junin, Ayacucho, Pasco, Huanuco, Lima and
Callao.

Of all the many skirmishes and battles around the country, the
clashes in the jungle town of Uchiza, in the department of San
Martin, were some of the worst Peru had seen so far. The town
is at the heart of drug trafficking country, in the Huallaga valley,
and one of the main departure points for small aircraft heading
for Colombia. It is also an area where the *narcos* and terrorists
have formed a strong alliance: in return for guarding the coca
plantations and acting as strongmen for the *narcos*, the terrorists
receive financial backup and the latest weaponry. At the end of
March, an estimated 300 armed *Senderos* attacked Uchiza police
station. The toll was reported to be ten police dead and four
injured, and fifty terrorists dead. It was the second time the
police station had been attacked and, about two weeks later, the
army killed thirty-four suspected terrorists in the upper Uchiza
valley in retaliation.

Amid escalating violence and rising tension, police and army
units raided the university campuses of San Marcos and Enrique
Guzman y Valle at the end of April. The authorities claimed they
were carrying out an anti-subversive operation. Over 2000 heavily
armed soldiers and 600 police staged the surprise raid, closing off
all surrounding roads with tanks and troop carriers at 3 a.m.,
before storming the campus dormitories. Over 500 students were
arrested, and large quantities of arms, including sub-machine
guns and almost 300 sticks of dynamite, were reported to have
been found. Student leaders, however, claimed that most of the
arms found were planted by the police.

Also at this time, government authorities tested the herbicide
known as Spike, for possible use in the eradication of coca
plantations. Environmentalists protested that the defoliant wipes
out all plants, not just coca, and does lasting ecological damage,
including contamination of the food chain. Representatives of

twenty-one nations, including Peru, had previously condemned the use of defoliants to eradicate coca plantations at the conference of the Inter-American Drug Abuse Organization (CICAD).

Love and Fear

I fell in love with Huaraz as soon as I stepped off the coach. It was six in the morning, cold and drizzling, but birds were breaking the dawn silence, and the air was exhilaratingly pure. Men wrapped up to their noses in shawls and ponchos crowded around the arriving passengers, hustling for taxi fares.

I was so involved with the moment of arrival, of finding myself 3053 metres high in the Andes, that I hardly cared who took me where. I did have one address: I was going to stay at Hostal Huascarán, a name that had caught my eye in every issue of the *South American Explorer*; I had read somewhere that English was spoken there too, a comforting thought during these early days when my Spanish was still so inadequate. The cab bumped along for a short while, and soon I was there and found myself drifting off to sleep between fresh white sheets, overcome by exhaustion and a deep sense of happiness.

I awoke a couple of hours later, refreshed from the eight-hour night ride, and ready to explore my new base. Huaraz lies about 410 kilometres north-east of Lima, and is the capital of the department of Ancash, the heartland of the most popular hiking region in the Andes. It is situated in the middle of the rich agricultural valley known as the Callejon de Huaylas, and I thought it would be a perfect place for acclimatizing to high altitudes and getting fit for my journey.

The majestic contours of Huascarán cut into the cobalt blue horizon at a glorious 6768 metres, and all along the valley's eastern side stands the famed Cordillera Blanca, its glacial peaks and highland valleys making up one of the most beautiful mountain ranges in the world. The Marañon springs to life in a range directly south of the Cordillera Blanca, in the equally high, but more remote Cordillera Huayhuash.

I planned to spend about two weeks here, going on regular

34

short hikes, gathering more advice about how to organize my trek into the Huayhuash and, of course, arranging to buy a donkey. I would have to walk for about two months until the Marañon became safely navigable, and the donkey was to carry my provisions and equipment; when I reached northern Peru and regular boat traffic, I planned to sell him again. I had never had anything to do with a donkey before, and he would be my only companion during the first half of the journey: I was looking forward to meeting him.

On my second morning I was greeted at breakfast by Americo, son of the proprietor.

'*Buenos Dias*,' said a bear of a voice, and I looked up to see a man with black hair framing a face weathered by thirty years of sun and wind. He had black eyes and long eye-lashes, a sensual mouth, and a smile that revealed startlingly white teeth. I thought his looks were arresting but more magnetic still was the sense of kindness and calm about him.

'Are you travelling alone?' he asked.

'I am,' I replied.

'How long are you staying? If you need any help with anything, just let me know,' he said. I was mesmerized by his tone.

'Well, I'm planning an expedition along the Maranon. I'm going to walk its length, and then travel along the Amazon, all the way to the sea.' I said, knowing I sounded ridiculous.

'Hmm, that's a big project. Probably very dangerous.'

It was the kind of understatement that I would soon learn was typical of Americo. It was also characteristically unjudgemental. I do not know what his first impression of me was, but while I am sure he thought I was quite mad, he never said so. I was drawn to him almost immediately. He asked if I would like to join him taking photographs of a traditional Sunday procession: I quickly got my camera.

Easter was approaching and in Catholic Peru the traditional celebrations and processions were already being rehearsed. Indian peasants dressed in their best clothes were streaming towards one of the churches in an uphill quarter of the town.

The women wore embroidered skirts, one layered on top of another, and each a different colour. The men wore dark suits, topped with black *sombreros*. The women also wore hats, but cream coloured ones or brown, with a wide band stitched on that fanned out into a rosette on the right-hand side. Their blouses and shawls were as brightly coloured as their skirts, and it seemed the louder the colour, the better. Pink would cover bright yellow, poison green join orange and purple, and in between there were layers of other shades, all drawn in at the waist by a collection of cords and strings. Perched on the back of almost every woman and girl was a baby, wrapped tightly into a light, woven blanket, and held in place by a knot at the chest. A band played out of tune loudly as we joined the crowds, and we tried to find a wall to stand on and take photographs. No one seemed to mind our cameras.

Later, we walked to the outskirts of town and up a steep path leading to a cross, a couple of hundred metres further up, which looked out over Huaraz. Americo led the way, walking slowly so that I would not lose my breath; there was nothing difficult about the ascent, but my heart beat like a mad drum, and we had to stop more than once, the unaccustomed altitude was still getting to me.

As we rested in the spring grass, I tried to hold my own in Spanish, our conversation stupidly simple – or at least mine was. We chatted about our cameras and the view, and I caught myself wondering what Americo might look like without any clothes on . . . I tried to ignore my mind drifting and concentrate on the beauty all around me. I was here to begin my journey, not to fall in love with a man.

Viewed from the cross, modern Huaraz could be seen to fill almost the whole width of the valley, extending in grid-formation from the main square and the half-built cathedral. In 1970, most of the towns and villages of the Callejon de Huaylas were almost entirely destroyed in what was possibly the worst earthquake ever to hit South America. The main quake lasted less than one minute, but it measured 7.8 on the Richter scale, and killed 80,000 of the valley's inhabitants. Huaraz lost half its population, but other places fared even worse; most drastically, the small town of Yungay was completely buried underneath a combined land-slide and avalanche, which came off Huascarán's mountainside in the space of three minutes. All that remains is the hilltop cemetery, and the tops of four palm trees, which used to stand on the town's main square. The new Yungay is built next to this eerie sight; the inhabitants are recent migrants, brought in on a government incentive. Many of Huaraz's people are also new to the region, and the rebuilding is still unfinished, twenty years later.

'It was Sunday, and our family was walking home from the countryside, when suddenly the earth beneath our feet began to shake and shake. *Que passa?!* (What's happening?) we cried out. My mother was pregnant with my younger brother, and we were very frightened for her. It was terrible,' Americo said simply.

The next few days went by as in a dream. Americo enchanted me and I spent little time thinking about my expedition, let alone concentrating on getting fit for it.

Semana Santa (Holy, or Easter Week) in Huaraz is a great tourist event, and even *Limeños* come up in droves to watch the famous Easter processions, that culminate in a gaudy, symbolic re-enactment of Christ's resurrection. Hotel prices during this period increase eightfold or more, and therefore I moved in with Americo.

I had hardly used my room since my arrival but, none the less, when it came to the bill, I paid the father for the whole of my stay; in effect I had paid to spend the nights with Americo (which I thought was a bargain for $1.50 a night).

It was, of course, awkward: on the one hand I was a guest, and on the other I was obviously more than that, and whenever the family and I came across each other we exchanged embarrassed smiles. The mother was especially silent and wary, and I could sense her anxiety.

Fortunately, we went hiking for a couple of days, which gave us all a break and, when we returned, I was formally introduced to the family, barely two weeks after I had arrived at their guest house. Two weeks is fast going anywhere in the world, but in Peru a woman does not move in with a man's family unless marriage is imminent; Americo's family was showing tremendous good faith in accepting me into their home, and I was grateful for their generous spirit.

*

The bomb went off shortly after midnight. We had been drifting off to sleep and, at first, the significance of the great, booming thud did not register.

'What was that?' I asked stupidly.

'A bomb,' said Americo, and we lay in silence, our ears straining to hear more. After a short time we settled back to sleep. It was then that a second, third and fourth bomb exploded in rapid succession, and we were wide awake again. The explosions had been very loud, and sounded very near. I had never heard a bomb go off before, and this new, unreal experience generated a tense fascination in me, fear remaining momentarily intangible.

As soon as the other explosions had thundered out, Americo got his clothes on and went off to find out what was going on. Alone, I suddenly did feel scared and, as gunshots and police whistles pierced the silence, the seriousness of the situation finally dawned on me. Outside the hostel, the whole family was standing in shivery silence. The terrorists had tried to fell the electricity pylons situated on the rim of the valley, not far from us. Shouts and gunshots continued in the darkness, and police trucks screeched off nearby. After some time we all returned indoors, but sleep was gone. Americo and I went to sit with one of his brothers, and I tried not to stare when he loaded up a small pistol and put it under the mattress. Would he really use it? What if the gun went off in the middle of the night? I wondered, but said nothing.

The next morning, red flags marked the four electricity pylons the terrorists and their bombs had tried to destroy, but not one had fallen. The flags fluttered in the wind, a reminder of the night's fear, until the police removed them later in the day.

During the weeks that followed, electricity cuts and explosions became quite regular. Huaraz is an important hiking base and the campaign was clearly intended to scare off the tourists, who were expected to be arriving shortly for the beginning of the summer season. Bombs were planted in and around Huaraz, and nights became dark and frightening times. No one went out after dusk, and the tense evenings indoors were punctuated by the

38

sound of dogs barking madly, police whistles, shouts and gun-fire. A number of policemen and civilians were killed in various shoot-outs: one occurring quite near the inn. A man was walking home after dark when a police patrol asked him to stop: he panicked and ran away, only to be shot down before the police could verify that he was harmless.

Meanwhile, during the day, life went on. The Indian market was as bustling as ever, a couple of tourists wandered about town, and the shops and restaurants were open as usual. An air of unreality hung about the place; it was easy to feel that the nights were just bad dreams, if it were not for the used cartridges which lay in the dirt roads, to be gathered by children competing for the largest and most various collection.

The only other indication of trouble were the few demon-strations by the *campesinos* of the valley, protesting against food shortages and the drastic price increases. The cost of living had gone up by 42 per cent in March and, by April, accumulated inflation for 1989 stood at 343.1 per cent. Anti-government feelings were running high, yet the *Senderos* seemed to receive little support. The bombs were keeping away the only source of income the region had, the tourists. The terrorists were stirring up increasing resentment and talk at this time was of civilians taking up arms against them, rather than against the government.

Bombs were flying around the place, I had a donkey to buy, provisions to gather, and a journey to make, but all that seemed unreal: meeting Americo had thrown me completely off track. My commitment dissipated and I began to doubt my desire to go off tramping through the mountains by myself, when Huaraz and Americo beckoned.

Worst of all, I stopped writing: I had nothing to say. I was rapt with happiness, and yet frustrated with my capacity for dissatis-faction; I was having an affair with a wonderful man and enjoying family life in Huaraz, yet I resented the demands all this made on my writing and my expedition. It led me to reflect that most women who achieve anything, do it on their own: men get in the way or, perhaps more precisely, women let men get in the way of their own potential.

The temptation to stay in Huaraz was very strong, but my

ambition was stronger. Finally I organized myself and bought the provisions for my two months' walk. It was a long shopping list: two kilograms of rice, three kilograms of spaghetti, tins of tuna and tomatoes, packet soups, bread, tea, coffee, sugar, salt, dried fruit, and presents for the *campesinos* I would meet on the way. I enjoyed making plans about daily food rations and all the possible combinations of dishes I could make from limited supplies. The large seaman's bag I had brought from England was soon completely full and, with the rest of my equipment including pots, stove, tent, etc., packed, it weighed about forty or fifty kilograms.

Arrangements to buy a donkey were also coming along, but slowly. I decided that, for the first ten days (when the hiking would be toughest and it would be good to have company in case of injury), I would pay a donkey driver to accompany me through the Cordillera Huayhuash. I had excellent maps, but I had never been hiking, let alone here in these mountains, I had no experience of donkey driving, and neither had I camped before. The journey through the Huayhuash to the source of the Marañon would take about ten days, which I thought would be time enough to learn the basics of camping and donkey handling from the *arriero* (donkey driver). It would also ease the fear of departure, afford me some degree of protection in case of encounters with the *Senderos*, who were known to be in the Huayhuash area, and allow me time to build my confidence. Only the year before a Canadian expedition had been involved in a shoot-out in the Huayhuash and, although the *arriero* would be little use when faced with guns, two people had to be better than one.

The local FOPTUR office had found a man called Callupe, who was supposed to be an experienced *arriero* and familiar with the Huayhuash, so we arranged a time to meet and dicuss money and practicalities. He was a small man with a large, long nose, and small, shifty eyes, giving him an unfortunate, rat-like appearance. I was not hiring him for his looks, however, and we soon got down to studying my maps.

'So you know the area well?' I asked.

'*Claro*,' he said. 'I've been there many times. No problem.'

He knew the area well, he said, because he came from Chiquian, a town on the edge of the Huayhuash and our starting point for the journey. The situation with the *Senderos* was changing all the time, so I asked Callupe when he had last been in the mountains. His reply – that it had been last September – was not very encouraging; however, he insisted that there were no problems and, anyway, he knew the *compañeros* (the *campesinos* used this diplomatic term for the *Senderos*) personally, and he was sure that even if we met them, they would do us no harm.

'They are good people, my friends. They will do nothing to us,' he said confidently.

I was not so confident; I had found out that his brother had been a member of the Canadian party that had been engaged in the shoot-out the previous year. There were also rumours about the reputation of the Callupe family for dishonesty. But I was getting impatient to leave now, and if Callupe was all I could get, he would just have to do. He knew I had official co-operation behind me, and I had also told him that I was going to write about the journey, which he seemed to find an attractive idea. It seemed unlikely that he would try to rip me off. We haggled about money for a while, but soon arrived at a price I was prepared to pay, and we also came to an arrangement about the donkey. It seemed best to use an intermediary to buy him, as prices were sure to rocket if I, as a Western woman, showed up as the prospective owner. My inability to tell one donkey from another was another factor. For the tough journey ahead it was essential to get a strong and resilient animal, preferably a five- or a six-year-old male. We therefore arranged that Callupe would travel ahead to Chiquian, buy the donkey, and that I would meet him there on 13 April.

'You will pay me all the money now?' he asked.

I paid him half of our arranged fee, and then half the amount a good donkey would cost, and we said goodbye. I had his signature on a receipt and a contract of employment, but these things mean little here, and I just had to have faith that Callupe would be in Chiquian when I got there, *and* that he would have bought a good donkey. Americo had his doubts and so did I.

But, it was too late now. I had put my money down and bought my provisions. My leaving was certain. The date I had chosen for my departure was the day after my twenty-seventh birthday: a good way to start a new year of life.

Americo made little protest when he realized my decision was made. He was very supportive and his experience as a mountain guide was invaluable; without being patronizing, he showed me how to put my tent up and use my cooker.

'It will be better for you if you use petrol for the high altitudes, and kerosene in the valleys.'

'Why?' I asked, trying to memorize Americo's actions as he changed the cooker's fuel valve.

'The petrol will burn more powerfully at such heights,' he explained patiently.

I was worried that I would not remember how to change the valve.

'You will,' he said. 'Just stay calm, and remember, if things get too difficult or dangerous, you can always come back. The hiking is just as beautiful here.'

It was the closest Americo came to dissuading me from departure, and I thanked him in my heart for not making it more difficult than it already was for me.

Leaving was terrible. It was like the leaving of England a month earlier, but worse. I felt vulnerable and sad. Would we still care for each other when I returned six months from now? Was Callupe going to be at Chiquian? What would happen in the mountains? One thing only was certain: I was leaving and, although melodrama was dangerously close, once Americo had calmed my fears I was euphoric to be on my way at last.

The Mountains

My departure was, in the end, a frustrating anti-climax. In my mind I was already gone, but that day there was no truck for Chiquian. I pushed superstitious thoughts from my mind. It was a typical South American experience, I told myself: a decision that does not take South America into account is no decision at all. It *was* an omen, however, and if I had known what was to come, I would never have left Huaraz.

The truck was scheduled to leave for Chiquian the following day. Winding my way through the Indian market, a porter carrying my mountain of gear in his bicycle cart, I felt every bit the conspicuous *gringa* that I was, and my calm of the day before vanished, to be replaced by testy irritability.

The truck was a wobbly old Ford frame, with a wooden container welded on behind the driver's cabin. Inside at the front end was a plank for a lucky few to sit on. Everyone else would have to sit or stand on the bare floor boards, in between the cargo, their bodies bounced and bruised as the truck bounded over the inevitable pot-holes.

We waited around for about an hour, for fifty sacks of rice which were also to make the journey, and when they arrived we left.

Chiquian was only about 124 kilometres away, but it took us six hours to get there. The dirt road was in terrible shape, made worse by a steady downpour of rain throughout most of the drive, and often we all had to get out, for the truck to be gently manoeuvred round slippery hair-pin bends on the steep mountain sides. An old canvas tarpaulin was supposed to protect

43

passengers from the rain, but it was soon soaked, and we huddled where the least drips came through.

I was the only foreigner on board, the rest *campesinos* or traders; and I was the only woman, but no one stared at me unduly and, every now and then, I would even be included in a conversation. They discussed the failing economy, the crazy prices, politics, and religion; one man even read aloud from the Bible to make his point, although his audience seemed to lack conviction.

Religion in Peru seems little more than a social ritual: people cross themselves before a journey or when passing a church, and at festival times mass is attended. In the Andes, in particular, the idea of God seems remote: meaningless death and violence are never far away and survival in this ungenerous, if magnificent terrain is paramount. It is ironic, therefore, that the only people I met to whom God and faith are central are the peasants living in the most remote areas. And it is they, more than anyone, who appear to accept their fate completely. The poverty of their lives would seem to make them the perfect constituency for the *Senderos* and perhaps this will happen as their situation worsens and they become desperate. For the moment, religious fatalism keeps a lid on social change – if only in the mountains.

We arrived in Chiquian in the dark and it was still pouring with rain. As soon as the truck stopped, people began climbing over each other in search of their luggage; while outside, men in brown ponchos watched in silence as the rain splattered on to the road, and water dripped from their felt hats. I felt uneasy: all the baddies from every cowboy film I had ever seen seemed to be lurking under those hats.

Suddenly Callupe's face was close to mine in the darkness of the truck, and then he and two other men scurried off down the gloomy streets with my bags, leaving me to run behind.

In Huaraz I had arranged with Callupe to stay in the local hostel, but now we seemed to be going somewhere quite different, to a private house. I was filled with foreboding but, although the evening was a little strange, nothing sinister happened. The two other men turned out to be Callupe's brother Sergio and his friend. Sergio was an ugly giant of a man with a wart on the end of his nose and, as it soon became obvious that he was drunk, he endeared himself even less to me. My attention was irresistibly drawn to slimey bits of food, stuck around the edges of his mouth.

We had tea in a small *tienda*, a kind of bar, and the eerie feeling of before returned when the silent ponchos reappeared out of the rainy darkness. They sat, watching me. As there were only three tables in the place, quite close together, I felt self-conscious. A woman bustled about serving beers, but no one took any notice of her. All eyes were on me, the out-of-place *gringa*.

At the table next to ours sat a man on his own. He stood out from the rest with his silvery hair and his bright blue and white poncho. When he eventually spoke to me in perfect English I felt a sense of unreality and fear. Who was this man? What was he doing in this dead-end town? He gave very little away, remarking only that he had learned English in Lima, and had lived in Chiquian for the past thirteen years. No one sat at his table, but he was greeted with a silent nod by all who entered. Perhaps he was a moving force behind the local *Senderos*? I would have loved to find out more, but it was getting late, and I still had to discuss things with Callupe.

Where, for one thing, was my donkey? Callupe and I left the others in the bar, and went back to the house. He was quite nervous, and explained that he had not had time to finalize the purchase of the donkey, but that all was perfectly in order.

'I have borrowed another donkey for you. We will use him on our first day, and then I will get yours from its pasture. No problem,' he insisted.

I had to take his word for it. Sergio soon came lurching back but, before he could show me his mountain-guide credentials, I cut him short, and Callupe quickly got rid of him. I could see he was worried that Sergio might mess things up for him and, although the place was Sergio's, he was sent packing. Upstairs was one large room, filled with beds, like a dormitory. The two of us chose beds at opposite sides, and my opinion of Sergio continued to decline when I found soiled socks and underpants littering the floor, and a dirty old négligée and some crumpled-up tights on the end of my bed. Sleaze hung in the air, and I was relieved that only Callupe was to be sleeping here tonight. I slid fully-clothed under the dirt-stiffened blankets, and listened to Callupe creaking into his bed, on the other side of the room. The night went slowly, my mind full of Chiquian and its strangeness, and thoughts of the future. In the middle of the night someone came banging on the door, and Callupe disappeared into the darkness, leaving me without a word, only returning shortly after dawn.

'Where did you go?' I asked, my faith in my donkey driver dwindling rapidly.

'Ah, good morning señorita! I had to help my friend slaughter sheep for the Lima market. The truck leaves this morning.'

The temporary donkey took off at a fast trot. Callupe ran behind and I tried to keep up and maintain my dignity, as we careered past the staring eyes in doorways. The path leading out of Chiquian was downhill, but steep and rocky; Callupe had apparently forgotten his walking shoes and soon had to slow down.

The trail to the village of Llamac, our destination that day, began to wind up through a deep, beautiful canyon. The sides were layered with the varied greens of farming terraces, and along our path stood the tall flowering stems of the Andean cactus. The sun bore down and the walk was long.

I finally gave up when the track turned into little more than boulders to climb over, and admitted I could not possibly carry my rucksack another step. The poor donkey already had most of my gear on his back, and now we were adding another fifteen kilograms. After about five or six hours of walking, I began seriously to wonder what on earth it was I was doing here: my heels had both developed bloody blisters and the only thing that diverted my attention from the pain was the squawking of parakeets, feeding noisily off the cacti flowers.

We eventually made it to Llamac, 3300 metres up, and I sat in an exhausted daze, while Callupe went to get my new donkey from its highland pasture.

My doubts about Callupe were certainly not eased when he had not returned by the next morning. To make things worse, my gas stove decided to stop working, and even breakfast was unavailable. No cooker, no food, and no journey. My flashy little cooker, admired the night before by the villagers, was now the subject of critical examination by the local 'stove expert'; however, he could not solve the problem and, in the end, I had no choice but to pay an outrageous price for an ancient primus.

The hours passed and I reflected on my situation. Ascending to Llamac, we had met a group of Swiss tourists, who had come through the Huayhuash range. Had they had any trouble with *Senderos*? I had asked. The looks on their faces immediately betrayed that they had. Each nudged the other to tell me their tale and, finally, one explained that, yes, they'd been held up by twenty-five armed *Senderos*. As well as having been parted from their money, food and valuables, they had also been warned that anyone returning to the area would be shot, and that the next group of foreigners whom the *Senderos* encountered would be killed. They had been lucky to escape with their lives and, from the amazed expressions on their faces, as they watched me go on my way, it was clear that they thought I was mad to continue.

I was rattled. But according to the Swiss tourists, the terrorists were on the other side of the Cordillera Huayhuash and, from studying the maps, it looked as if I might be able to slip through, away from their camp over to the south near Laguna Viconga, and head off east, then north, putting a day's walk between me, the lake, and the *Senderos*.

Callupe turned up with my donkey late in the afternoon, limping conspicuously as soon as he saw me. He insisted that he had fallen the night before, while trying to catch the donkey. He had probably got drunk but I said nothing. He must have felt guilty, because he offered me two cigarettes, and then avoided me for the rest of the evening. I went over to say hallo to the donkey. I came close to stroke him, but he jerked his head away and gave me a mistrustful look. He seemed strong enough, though, and I hoped we would become friends. I was not doing very well so far. First Callupe, then the cooker, and the meeting with the Swiss; my spirits were low. My energy and faith had taken a battering – and that was only the first day. What was next, I wondered wearily.

During the night, I had an attack of diarrhoea and, by morning, I was weak, feverish, and blinded with headache. Feeling defeated and alone, I stayed in my bed, sleeping fitfully.

The nearest toilet was a patch of earth behind the pig-pen. It was reached by climbing over a crumbling mud wall, simple during the day, and if you were feeling well. Exhausted as I was, it was now a real effort to get over there and, to add insult to injury, I had to perform this frequent manoeuvre to an audience of assembled villagers. The whole thing made me cringe. That evening, a kind woman brought me a chamber-pot, for which I was very grateful. My guts were still in turmoil, and twice in the night I had to untangle myself from my sweaty sleeping-bag and stagger outside. The second time, my bowels beat me to it and I suffered a humiliation unknown since childhood. I dumped my knickers in the pot, and sat miserable and half-naked in the moonlight, unsavoury noises echoing out across the village.

In the morning I felt slightly better, and determined not to spend another day in Llamac, paying Callupe for doing nothing. We left by 7.30 a.m. I felt faint, Callupe was still limping, and only the donkey forged ahead, in spite of his forty-kilogram burden.

The day was a nightmare. The seven-hour walk from Chiquian was as nothing compared to climbing the 1000 metres up to the pass above Llamac. The path was full of rocks and stones, sometimes there was no path at all, and it took less than half an hour before I had to have the first of many rests. I was sweating almost as soon as we started, I felt weak and dizzy, and all I could think about was sleep. I tried to appreciate the beauty of the near-vertical strips of pasture tucked among the rich ochre of the rockface, but my attention was concentrated on keeping sight of Callupe and the donkey, both way ahead of me.

We reached the pass at an altitude of 4300 metres around noon. The path then took us along a level ridge above a canyon for three hours; and we made it to the Jahuacocha lakes, just in time to put our tents up before the rain came. I was so tired, I could not bear even to climb the small ridge that separated us from a view of the first of the two lakes. Our tents were pitched close to a small stone hut, and we cooked spaghetti with tuna and tomato paste, sheltered from the wind. I ate little, although hungry, and retired to my tent to listen to the wind and rain and the inquisitive squeaks of roving guinea-pigs, kept by shepherds and other mountain-dwellers, as people in the lowlands keep chickens.

While boiling our morning tea and porridge, we were greeted by a shepherd coming down the valley. His body was covered by a protective poncho, his legs wrapped in layers of sackcloth trousers, and on his feet he had nothing but rubber sandals, his toes like dirty lumps of smoked ham, rather than living flesh. His face also was tough and wind-beaten, but his expression was warm and friendly, and he gladly accepted the offer of some bread and an egg.

He wasted no time in telling us about the latest *Sendero* stories, gesticulating dramatically, sliding a finger across his throat, his eyes rolling, while muttering *muy peligroso, muy peligroso* (very dangerous). According to him, another group of foreigners, accompanied by two *arrieros*, had been attacked quite recently, made to lie face down on the ground, pistols shoved into their mouths. Callupe's bravura seeped visibly away.

'These men don't sound like the men I know,' he said. 'Maybe we should not continue?' he asked.

'We shall see,' I said grimly.

We broke camp by 8 a.m. and set off. I was feeling a little less racked and, thankfully, we were following a level, if soggy, trail alongside the Jahuacocha lakes, which lay in glistening splendour in the middle of the valley. The colour of the second lake was an arctic blue, almost unreal, like one of those 1950s technicolour postcards. For the first time, I really stood still and took in the beauty of my surroundings. Stronger within myself that day, I was also able to tell Callupe to wait for me, rather than silently and desperately trying to keep up with him.

Soon we began to wind our way up towards the next pass, slowly, as I still needed to rest every twenty minutes. Rain clouds hung low on the mountain tops, but I could see the crusted Yerupajá glacier and, although Yerupajá itself was not visible, Yerupajá Chico and quite a few of the surrounding peaks were. At 6634 metres, Yerupajá is the highest point of the vast Amazon basin, and my morale soared at the sight of it, a reminder of my goal. The base of the mountain rose almost vertically out of the valley, and the glacier was cracked by many crevasses, their deadly openings eerie in the silence. The final outcrops of ancient ice stood frozen, movement below the surface infinitesimal and invisible, the blue of the oldest layers clear against the white snow of the upper reaches.

The pass leading into the Rondoy valley was a much tougher prospect than the earlier ones. Instead of a path, there was just gravelled mountainside, sometimes almost as fine as sand, and the poor donkey sank deep under the weight on his back. The bags kept slipping from one side to the other, and often we would have to stop to unload and retie the awkward cargo of my assorted sacks, kerosene cans and water bottles. Each time the donkey nearly slipped or slid, I had visions of him bouncing down the mountainside. Worse still, he had an open wound on his hind thigh, and the strap supporting the cargo was slung round his rear and rubbed the raw injury, making it bleed and unable to heal. It was a deep, right-angled gash, and when I had pointed it out to Callupe, he had brushed it off as nothing, saying that it was the previous owner's mark, or brand. I realize now that it was a serious wound, and that the only reason I had obtained this excellent donkey, was because the owner had probably had doubts about the animal's chances of survival, it being possible that the infection would spread deep into the leg, a slow death the result.

It had been hard coming over the pass and down into the next valley, and for our own, as well as the donkey's sake, we decided to stop early that day. The sun came out as we reached level ground and my spirits blossomed. Other than some grazing cattle and horses, we were completely alone in the valley, and I relished the scenery, and the mountain silence, disturbed only by a river nearby. Callupe unloaded the donkey and I took the chance to be alone and went down to the water. My clothes shed, my stiff and sweaty body warmed by the sun, I washed after five days of illness and discomfort. It was bliss.

Curled in my sleeping-bag, rain again pelting down outside, I felt good for the first time since setting off, and even positive about the rest of the journey. Positive enough to be sensible too, and for the first time I allowed myself to admit that maybe I should change my route. I weighed up the significance of what the Swiss tourists and the shepherd had told me. A discovery crystallized in my mind: I wanted to live. Having used up most of my ready money for the primus stove in Llamac, I had very little to hand over to the *Senderos*, in case of a hold-up; furthermore, I had to admit that a hold-up was quite likely if I continued on my present course, as there was no reason to assume that the *Senderos* would stay in just one part of the mountains. My route depended on where one defined the source of the Marañon to be; I could reach the beginning of the river without going to Laguna Lauricocha, always cited as the fountainhead of the river but also uncomfortably close to the *Sendero* presence. On the maps, the Marañon begins where the small rivers Nupe and Lauricocha come together, and technically speaking, that point is therefore the source of the Marañon, and I could change my route accordingly. I held back from making my decision, but was glad that I had at least faced the facts about my situation.

Dawn. A grey sky, with rain pausing while we made breakfast and took down the tents, only to come down in a steady flow as we trudged off wearing our plastics, the donkey too, covered with a bright yellow sheet. The ground was marshy and wet grasses brushed against my legs. Soaked up to the waist, my feet squelching inside my boots at every step, and Callupe, as usual, way ahead of me; all this gave hopelessness – as well as the clammy chill – a new hold on me. The cold gets to me easily and I was still sick: I knew that if I walked all day in this kind of weather, I would risk being able to carry on at all.

We decided, therefore, to give up for that day, and found a conveniently abandoned hut in which to take shelter. I peeled off damp clothes and put on clean, dry ones, but the cold had already wormed its way into my bones, and my hands and feet had gone numb. Outside, the rain continued: there would be no opportunity to dry our clothes or gear. The thatched hut kept the rain off us, however, and dried Andean grass had been left for bedding by the shepherds. Come June, they would return to the Rondoy valley with their herds of sheep and cattle but, for the moment, the pastures were empty and we had the hut to ourselves.

Depression descended on me like a lead weight, and I sat in glum silence as Callupe tried to make a fire from some damp wood and pieces of grass. The resulting clouds of smoke filled our windowless hut and stung my eyes. We rolled logs as close to the smoking fire as was possible, and sat staring into the sputtering flames, taking it in turns to hold our soaked boots over the fire. It was without doubt one of the worst days I had had in a long, long time: it was the sixth day since we had set off and we were nowhere.

Once the fire had established itself, after an hour or so, Callupe set about making some soup, and I went off to empty my guts outside. The treeless valley spread out before me, as I squatted in the grasses, clutching my sodden toilet paper and feeling very sorry for myself. I returned to cry silently into my soup, hoping my face was hidden from Callupe in the gloom of the hut. Once

51

the tears had started I could not stop, frustration welling up, so I went outside to howl at the unhearing mountains. My dream was disappointed and I cried like a hurt child. Callupe pretended not to notice my tearful state and, by four that afternoon, we had crawled into our damp sleeping-bags in search of sleep.

The hours went by slowly. I knew I could not carry on like this. The effects of diarrhoea and the high altitude were rapidly dehydrating my body. I felt weak and tired, my leg and back muscles ached under the strain of daily eight-hour hikes, and my blistered feet would not heal. Heading for Laguna Lauricocha, at least another five days' walk away, was now out of the question; gambling on the risk of a hold-up with the *Senderos* and my deteriorating health was madness. I had to change my route. I had to see a doctor before I disintegrated completely. I decided that the only thing to do now was to get out of the Huayhuash, and on to the nearest road back to Huaraz. There I could rest, get better, and re-think my expedition.

The next morning Callupe and I studied the maps, and I decided that we would divert to the town of Baños, two days' walk away: from there we could get a truck home.

We set off early the next morning, smelling of smoked boots and cowdung. My boots were still very soggy inside, so I wore plastic bags over my still damp socks: with any luck it would not rain again today and, if it did, at least my feet would not get any wetter than they already were. We had yet another steep trail to follow up to the next pass and, as we steadily rose higher, I looked back down into the valley and marked out the hut where we had spent the night. The scene was tranquil, and I realized that it made no difference to this place, or any other for that matter, whether I lived or died, whether I succeeded in my venture or not. I was utterly insignificant, and this somehow seemed especially awful in such a beautiful place. I had a painful sense of how alone the individual really is, and it became clear to me that without a response from others, in which to set oneself in context, existence or achievement by itself means almost nothing.

Clouds engulfed us as we stood at the pass, and an atmosphere redolent of *Macbeth* blew across the barren heights. We must have been at least 4500 metres up and, as the clouds lifted, the view was spectacular. Miles and miles of jagged peaks stretched along the horizon, while in the valley below a rust-red lake glistened in the sun. We walked down into the highland valley, its sides a patchwork of greens and browns, and the only indication of human life in this silent world was the occasional stone hut. The landscape, by this stage, changed from deep rocky canyons and snow-capped peaks, to these wide open valleys, treeless and windswept. It looked very much like the Scottish highlands, on a much, much larger scale. Cattle and horses fed on the sodden slopes, but I could not help wondering what their owners fed on. No wood to make fires grew here, and the hills were too high even to grow potatoes, normally the staple crop and diet. At the same time, I began to have my own food fantasies, visions of hot redcurrant pie and fresh cream making my mouth water; my diet of porridge, packet soup, and pasta, was beginning to pall already.

Arriving at the base of the valley, we reached a lone homestead: a round stone hut, thatched with long grass, and a couple of animal pens staked out around it. As we approached a *campesino* with his small child came out to greet us. The two-year-old stared at me from behind her father's legs, while we chatted about the walking conditions ahead. Heavy rain had swelled the rivers coming from the glaciers, and the man warned us that we would not be able to cross them on foot, and there were no bridges. Quick to see an opportunity, he offered to rent us his horse to cross the two rivers in our path. The animal was way up on its pasture, so Callupe and I settled down to wait on the cold and windy hillside. I suggested making some tea, and Callupe shook his head at me in wonder; but I persuaded him to unload the donkey, and cups of tea soon warmed our hands. I enjoyed the feeling of being an eccentric explorer having tea in the middle of nowhere, while for a brief moment, an enormous condor soared past on the air currents above, its size and white neckband marking it out. They don't flap or flutter but glide majestically.

As we sat, the man's wife came out to meet us. She was very shy, and took my offer of tea with an embarrassed smile. I took the chance to ask her about what food they ate and how they cooked. She told me they made fires with the tough grass

53

growing here, and that their food was potatoes carried up from a day's walk away. I found it difficult to understand why they chose to live in such hardship, so far from a village and human companionship. The woman was heavily pregnant, and I shuddered at the thought of her giving birth up here, on the floor of their dark hut, with no one to help her but her husband. It also made me realize just how tough the human frame actually is; and, on the other hand, it brought home to me how trivial were so many of the things I thought necessary to my life. I do not want to go and live in a hut and eat nothing but potatoes. But a first-hand experience of life in the Third World shows our world for what it is: a world of dissatisfaction, the emphasis on material objects held up to satisfy emotional needs, rather than on human relationships.

We moved on and, as we crossed the second river and sent our friend with the horse home, we were met by a woman on horseback, accompanied by a new foal. She was a woman 'cowboy' and, wearing a bright pink shirt and a black *sombrero*, she was an unusual sight in Peru, where women almost never travel alone. I warmed to her immediately, and when she offered me her horse, I took the opportunity joyfully. I felt like a queen, riding along slowly and enjoying the fabulous views of clouds mirrored in lakes, framed in mountains. The sorrow of the day before melted away.

We reached the village of Queropalca in the late afternoon and, although tired, my spirits had lifted again, and I felt confident putting up my tent in front of the assembled villagers. We shared some tea and porridge, and joked about my fancy equipment: would I accept a bull in exchange for the tent, one man asked; or maybe some fresh trout in return for my jacket?

The next day was to be our last walk, and although it was going to be a long thirty kilometres, the knowledge that it was the last lap of this miserable episode gave me a new burst of energy. Rain pelted us for most of the day and, at one point, I slipped, falling flat on my back into the mud. Looking up at the sky, I laughed hysterically: it seemed the best thing to do at the time, and some nearby shepherds could not have agreed more. We arrived in Baños, tired and rain-soaked, but looking forward to real beds and the return to Huaraz.

A local shopkeeper agreed to take care of the donkey and my cargo, and the following morning we set off for Huaraz. The journey took three, gruelling days of truck and bus rides. At one point we got stuck for twenty-five hours at a miserable mine. Huansala was in a remote part of a mountain range lying on our way back to the Callejon de Huaylas, and because it was a Sunday no mining trucks were operating, and not a single private vehicle passed by that day. Callupe and I spent almost an entire afternoon chilled by the pouring rain, until we could persuade one of the shanty dwellers around the mine to give us shelter. Finally, we got a lift away the next afternoon, perched on the roof of a truck-driver's cabin. For six hours, we clung desperately to the spare wheel to avoid being flung into the silage below our feet; but the view from up there was astounding, the horizon an endless sea of snow-streaked mountains and, as we approached the main road to Huaraz, we passed the famous Puyas Raimondi – the world's largest bromeliad – that grow up to ten metres high. It almost made the nightmare journey worthwhile, although by the time I arrived in Huaraz my ribs were clearly visible through sickly skin, and I was as weak as a child.

No Surrender

If ever I seriously considered giving up, it was at this point. My body was weak and dehydrated, and my spirits were down to a faint flicker, depression threatening to snuff them out at any moment. To make things worse there was no one to encourage me; in fact, it was quite the other way, Americo telling me that I would be better off giving up the whole project, that it was a great idea, but simply impossible. Everyone else agreed with him.

I knew now how tough and unforgiving the mountains could be, and my heart sank at the idea of going back alone. There would be no Callupe this time. No one to make me tea in the morning or cook my supper; no one to load up the donkey or guard it during the night. Every last thing would be up to me and I did not relish the idea. In addition, Americo was about to leave for a skiing project on Huascaran and I would soon be alone in Huaraz, and facing these important decisions by myself. I tried half-heartedly to persuade him to come with me, but he declined, saying it was much too dangerous for him and, in any case, he had a living to earn. It was a perfectly reasonable response, but did not stop me from feeling abandoned. The responsibility was mine alone, and it was not lightened by the news, which was full of the latest battles between state and terrorist forces.

One of the worst was in the department of Junin, where sixty-two members of the guerrilla group MRTA, and six soldiers, were killed in a bloody shoot-out. The corpses of the revolutionaries were lined up on the ground and shown on national television for all to see in a display of gory propaganda. My conviction to go back into the mountains wavered.

There were, however, advantages to gaining an extra week. There were a number of things I had lacked during those first days, and now I had time to search them out in the market. One of the most important items missing was a tin opener. Walking from one stall to the next, I soon discovered that tin openers were in short supply, one trader after another saying that he did not stock them; when I found one eventually, it was hardly better than a knife, one of those ones that you stab into the lid and then work around the edge, usually ending up with a tiny jagged opening and half the contents stuck inside the tin.

Wandering around the markets, I could not help noticing the drastic price changes since I had arrived in Peru: the value of the Peruvian Inti against the American dollar had been around I/1,200 at the beginning of March; only two months later, it now stood at I/2,500, a situation which I could survive but the local people could not. The country was, in fact, careering into what is called hyper-inflation, only the tenth case in world economic history, and the experts are still arguing about a solution.

After three or four days, with penicillin to curb my diarrhoea, I regained my strength. I was eager to leave and forestall a complete loss of nerve; I did not want too much time to think about the future, and I decided to go after only a week of convalescence.

There was one more important thing to deal with, however, and I spent the last few days sorting it out. Having watched Callupe load up the donkey, I knew that I could not lift the heavy bags on to the animal's back, or figure out the complicated rope arrangements holding them in place. The solution seemed to be large saddle bags, which I could put on to the donkey empty, and then fill up, thus avoiding too much weight-lifting. Traditional leather saddle bags were too small, so I decided to make my own. For shopping bags, the *campesinos* use large, woven cloth ones which are very similar to saddle bags, but are usually slung over a shoulder, rather than an animal's back. I bought the largest ones I could find, made out of tough nylon thread, and set about adapting them for their special purpose. I added extra lengths of cloth at the sides and around the top, thereby doubling the capacity of the bags so they could easily hold my provisions, as well as most of the contents from my rucksack. I had learned that it was impossible for me to walk for eight hours with fifteen

57

kilograms on my back; in theory, you are supposed to be able to carry a third of your body weight, however, I could not comfortably manage more than five kilograms, especially when walking uphill at high altitudes. I enjoyed sewing the bags: it was a positive response to a specific problem, and I looked forward to trying them out.

By 30 April, I was all set to go, very apprehensive this time, but nevertheless determined. Stubborn I was, but I just could not have faced myself if I had given up: too many people were waiting to say 'I told you so'.

Siempre con dios, (May God be with you) Americo's mother said as I went on my way. It was good to know she had taken me to her heart, and comforting to think I had a home on this continent – a place where I was always welcome that was not the other side of the world.

The journey back to Baños could take three days and I steeled myself for the ordeal. This time, I succeeded in getting past Huansala in one day. I only had to wait two hours for a mining truck from the road outside the town of Catac, and at Huansala another truck left for Huallanca within an hour of my arrival.

I spent the night in Huallanca, staying in a tiny windowless cubicle. The walls on my cell were covered in the gross graffiti of schoolboy men. At the end of my bed an enormous cunt was etched into the plaster, fat legs spreading out on either side and a bloated prick pointing up between them. My eyes were drawn irresistibly to the horrible image, one which can be seen on walls all over the world and to which my usual response is nothing but passing disgust. But that night, alone in that dark little room, men filling every other cubicle around me, I felt uncomfortable and locked my door, not even opening the little air vent in the panel. I wrote in my diary by the light of my torch, trying not to feel scared and lonely, and admonishing myself yet again not to give up.

It was the beginning of May at this time, and springtime celebrations and processions were taking place all across the countryside, a mixture of pagan fertility rites and Catholic traditions. No hour of the day seemed to be too early or too late for *campesino* revellers. I was up at sunrise waiting for a truck out of

Huallanca, and already a ragged procession was inching its way along the streets, the inevitable brass band trumpeting the clammy dawn. Men and women staggered around in a drunken stupor, weariness and drink dulling their expressions and slowing their pace. Leading the way were people dressed in black, wearing negro masks with gaudy red lips. They danced in slow and jerky unison, like puppets, a macabre reminder of the African slaves who at one time worked the mines of the Andes in this land of *mestizos* and Indians.

My second night was spent at a dirt crossroads, about six hours' drive away from Baños. The people living in the surrounding hamlet recognized me from the week before, and I was grateful for their friendly welcome.

'Where's your husband?' they asked, referring to Callupe, and I quickly put them straight about our relationship.

'Fancy travelling all alone,' they marvelled, as I enjoyed their approval.

I spent the night on the floor of the local bar, braving curious groups of children as I unrolled my sleeping-bag and, later, the probing beams of drunk men's torches as I huddled under a table in the corner.

The following day, in the soft dawn light, I caught my first clear view of Yerupajá and the snow-capped summits of the Cordillera Huayhuash. After the misery of my first ten days out there, it was a gratifying comfort to see the peaks, and not least Yerupajá, so clearly now. Far away they were, yet bathed in the morning sun they appeared within walking distance. Yerupajá was indeed a splendid sight: the towering pinnacle of the Amazon basin, its prehistoric bulk jabbed the sky, a sight much more dramatic than the blunt contours of Huascaran, Peru's highest mountain (by only 134 metres).

Later that morning, a sheep had its throat cut. Two men held down its head as the blood spurted out into a bucket, death such an undramatic event here. In Huaraz I had seen Americo's mother cut the throats of a guinea pig and a rabbit; the knife sawed through their throats, and they were dead. Death is viewed as traumatic, emotional and frightening, by so many people; when in fact it is shockingly simple: a lack of life. I had imagined death differently, and it was chilling to realize just how much life depends on these mental constructs. I fear death or rather the process of dying; I have no orthodox faith. The drive behind my journey was, perhaps, this: an act of justification for my existence. Yet watching the sheep being reduced to heaps of gut and chunks of flesh, I thought what a waste it is to go through life alone. If all you're going to end up as is dead meat, achievement becomes almost irrelevant. The idea of having a family suddenly appeared very precious. My ambition remained undiminished, but I saw it in another light, that of the personal, familial sphere pitted against that of the material, and I promised myself that I would try and remember this when I went back to Europe, remember a way that I could be content and stop rushing around all the time forever dissatisfied.

I got a truck away from the crossroads late the next morning. It was only taking me as far as the nearest bridge, three hours away, but that was fine by me, as this was the exact spot where the rivers Lauricocha and Nupe joined to form the Marañon. I toyed with the idea of following the Lauricocha river to the lake, about three days' walk away; but I resisted the urge, reminding myself that I had escaped the Huayhuash once, and I should not tempt fate again. I stood in awe at the waters which formed the head of this great river, the Marañon, a river that was eventually to turn into the Amazon, the largest river in the world. It was going to grow up before my eyes, churning over mountain boulders and rocky rapids, ever larger and swifter, until it slid through into the jungle flatlands of the lower Amazon basin. It would have to pass through the tiny eye of a needle, the fearful rapids of the Pongo de Manseriche, and then it would spread out into a slow mass of brown water, ever wider, ever slower, until it reached the Atlantic. How long would it take me to get there, I wondered. The thrill of being at just this spot, the start of it all, was exquisite.

A truck crammed full of people picked me up within the hour. They were mostly *campesinos* heading for the May fiesta, which in Baños lasts a whole week, and I got chatting to some young blades with their girls. The guys turned out to be Colombian *toreros*, come to Baños to perform in the festival bullfights, and they soon invited me to join them as their guest. Their girls were not too keen, I could see, but with my shorn hair and travelling clothes I was hardly competition, and they accepted me as an odd addition to their crowd.

'You will be my guest of honour, Natascha!' said one of the *toreros* extravagantly.

'What a happy day for me, that you will join us,' said another, and I smiled, sneaking embarrassed glances at the girlfriends to reassure them.

How different to my last entry into Baños, when I was tired, sick and depressed. Now I was arriving with friends and in the happy atmosphere of fiesta. Although travelling alone, I knew where I was going and I had people to stay with: the family who had been looking after my donkey and equipment welcomed me with a cup of tea. This time there was nothing threatening about Baños and, where before it had seemed an ominous place with predatory men hanging around on street corners, the fiesta changed all that. Later I found out that there was another reason for the air of abandon: the *Senderos* had been here six months before and run the local police out of town, leaving the station a vandalized wreck, its walls riddled with bullet holes and daubed in red paint. The town had been left alone by all official bodies, and the people were just living by their own code, safe from terror as long as the police or army did not come back; but by the same token, without doctors, teachers, or other services.

I have always hated the idea of bull fighting. Fans tell me that it is an art, an exciting dance with death for both contestants; and besides, they say, in South America the bulls are not usually killed, so it is more humane. I do not think that quite follows, but being as big a hypocrite as the rest, I was not going to miss the climax of the fiesta.

The ring was about a kilometre outside town, on the small dirt road I had arrived on, earlier in the day. Now it was clogged with trucks and horse-riders, all coming towards the bull ring where brass bands blasted the air with riotous notes. Women sold freshly boiled cobs of corn and home-made cheese, roast meats and oranges and apples. There were *caramelos* (sweets) for the kids and fireworks for everyone. The horses were decked out in their finest tackle, halters and reins studded with silver, and the leather saddles embossed with intricate patterns. The horses themselves pranced about, nerves visibly twitching. Most people were already very drunk and some of those arriving on horseback galloped through the crowds with a jerky lack of control. The trucks, parked as close to the ring as possible, were festooned with the bodies of spectators. Occasionally one would fall off, probably bruising themselves quite badly; but nobody took any notice, not even the person who had fallen, and eventually he would either crawl back on to his perch, or just lie dribbling where he had fallen.

My Colombian friends and I climbed up the shaky ladders to the wooden spectators' stand, and sat on the planks bending under the strain of the heaving crowds. The stand was a few planks supported by large poles, at least five metres high, with nothing but a couple of nails to hold them in place. People had already been waiting over two hours for the fights to begin, and by now they were howling for action, while the two bands added to the din with two completely different tunes.

Finally, some men could be seen trying to coax a bull into the ring, but he steadfastly refused and the crowd jeered impatiently. The poor animal was eventually pulled out on a rope, and spectators threw fire crackers into the ring to make him crazy. They were the kind that crack the air with a sudden, loud bang, and they must have been terrifying for the bull. The bombs in Huaraz made me wary of every sudden noise and I could not help jumping every time I heard a bang.

Frightened though the bull must have been, instead of getting fighting mad, he ran around the ring instead, the *torero* made to look ridiculous as he chased the bull, trying to make him turn and face the red cloth. Briefly, the bull did turn to stab at the man's foil, and the *torero*, having skirmished for all of three seconds, proudly waved to the crowds as if he had just completed the most daring duel with death. The next two bulls were almost as disappointing as the first, and the crowd were twitchy for action. But thunder and black clouds hailed the end of play for that afternoon, and most people began to leave, the band trailing their doleful music behind.

I walked back to Baños quickly, thinking of the next day and wondering how it would all turn out. I decided to leave by dawn at the latest, to avoid too many curious eyes as I walked out of town. There were a lot of people here at the moment, and plenty of possible dangers for me, especially from men in festive mood.

As I climbed into my sleeping-bag that night, I must admit that I was not looking forward to the morning. I felt very vulnerable. What if someone followed me out of Baños? Would I do all right alone with the donkey? I still did not really know him, he had always been handled by Callupe and, although I had tried to watch carefully how he dealt with him, I wondered if I would be able to cope. How would people treat me along the way? My mind was full of questions and I had no answers to them.

3
Solita in the Marañon Valley

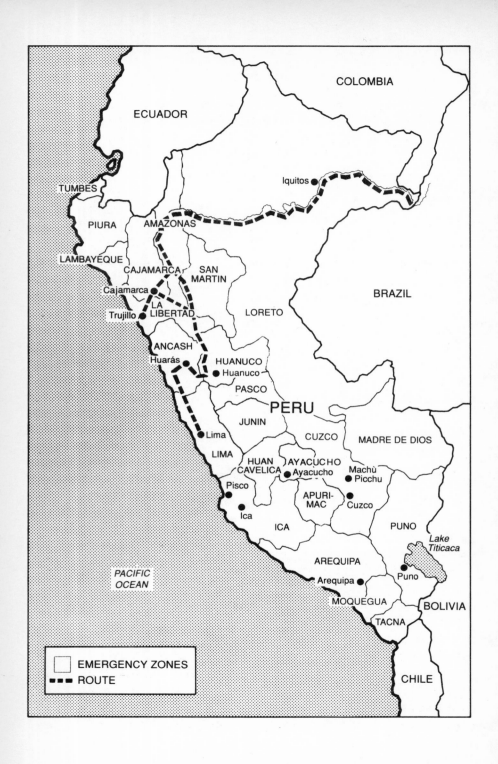

COLOMBIA

ECUADOR

Iquitos

TUMBES

PIURA

AMAZONAS

LAMBAYÉQUE

CAJAMARCA

SAN
MARTIN

BRAZIL

Cajamarca

LA
LIBERTAD

Trujillo

LORETO

ANCASH

Huarás

HUANUCO

Huanuco

PASCO

PERU

JUNIN

Lima

CUZCO

MADRE DE DIOS

LIMA

HUAN
CAVELICA

AYACUCHO

Ayacucho

Machù
Picchu

Pisco

APURI-
MAC

Cuzco

Ica

ICA

PUNO

Lake
Titicaca

AREQUIPA

Puno

PACIFIC
OCEAN

Arequipa

MOQUEGUA

BOLIVIA

TACNA

☐ EMERGENCY ZONES
▬▬▬ ROUTE

CHILE

Headlines

The Economy

Peru's GNP fell 23.9 per cent over the first quarter of 1989, while according to the National Statistics Institute, inflation for May was up by 28.6 per cent. The private consultancy Apoyo S.A. put the figure at 31.8 per cent. Over the period from mid May to mid June, the value of the Peruvian Inti to the US dollar went from I/ 3000 to I/3400.

The minister for the economy, Cesar Vasquez, cited capital flight as a major cause of the economic crisis. He said $3.8 billion, 32 per cent of the foreign debt at that time, had been transferred out of the country between 1974 and 1982. Meanwhile, the Central Bank of Peru began its programme of daily devaluations of the official base exchange rate by 1 per cent.

Death Toll due to Political Violence

The months of May and June saw some of the worst violence in 1989. The news was punctuated by regular reports of ambushes, battles and assassinations, with the state no closer to finding solutions to end the killing. Civilians were regularly among the dead, particularly municipal and government officials. Many local mayors resigned in fear of their lives, and potential candidates for the national municipal elections for the following December withdrew for the same reason.

During the period from mid May to mid June approximately thirty-two members of the police and army were killed in armed conflicts across the country. Seventy-three civilians died, either by assassination or in crossfire. Three of these were foreigners: a German couple and a British man. The murder of the naturalized Peruvian and prominent environmental reporter, Barbara d'Achille, caused particular outrage throughout Peru when she was shot by the *Senderos* for refusing to interview them. Fifty-two terrorists were shot during this time, either members of *Sendero*, *Tupac Amaru* (MRTA), or *Rodrigo Franco*. The minister for the interior, Augustin Mantilla, finally admitted the existence of the paramilitary death squad *Rodrigo Franco*, while opposition members claimed that the squad was, in fact, led by Mantilla's men.

The First Five Days

The sky was a mixture of angry pink and baby blue, a very unnatural dawn, as I walked out of Baños. I had rolled out of my sleeping-bag while it was still dark, hauling all my provisions and equipment out into the street and getting the donkey from his shed by torchlight. One of the family's sons and I set about fixing my home-made saddle-bags on to the donkey. I led him out myself, tugging tentatively at his rope. I tried not to let him sense my raw need of him, my nervousness and insecurity. I wanted to be loving and sweet, but there was no time for that at the moment. Making friends and getting to know each other would have to wait, and fortunately he trotted on quite willingly.

Protective darkness faded all too soon for my liking, and the first crumpled figures began to shuffle silently about the streets. In a moment of weakness I asked Fernando, my helper, to accompany me to the edge of town: I felt desperately self-conscious and wished that I could avoid walking through the main square, but that was the way out of town, so I just had to face it. I stared into the middle distance and tried to look confident as I walked through the square. A few drunks were sticking around like left-overs in doorways but, apart from them, almost no one was about, and I was grateful to be spared an audience. Out of sight of the last houses, we stopped to rearrange the bulging saddle-bags, clanging kerosene and petrol cans tied next to them, and an extra sackful of gear secured on top of everything else. I tried to balance the weight exactly on either side of the donkey's spine, but as soon as he started walking his movements loosened the ropes and everything sagged this way and that. Don't leave me, I thought as Fernando wished me luck, and then turned to leave.

'*Buena suerte, señorita,*' he said, and shook my hand gravely.

'*Muchas gracias*,' I said, and hurried off quickly, nervously tapping the donkey's buttocks with my stick.

By now the sun was up, and I headed along the same dirt road that the truck had brought me on the day before. I passed the bull ring, now empty and silent, and I began gradually to feel a little elated. I had studied the road carefully during the truck journey, so I knew where the turning-off point was, and I had time to enjoy watching and listening to the awakening land. Banks of milky mist sat on the damp pastures, thermal springs bubbling beneath them, and already there was a woman washing her clothes in the natural hot water. Layers and layers of differently coloured skirts were spread out on the stones and bushes to dry in the sun, while wet clothing was having the dirt beaten out of it with a wooden paddle. Beautifully patterned woven blankets were hung on the great cactus plants that lined the road, and I wondered how on earth the woman avoided ripping everything to shreds on their needling thorns. Great eucalyptus trees rustled dry leaves in the wind, and I passed houses of crumbling adobe with breakfast smoke already seeping through the thatch.

The eucalyptus was introduced to the Andes over a hundred years ago, and has proliferated ever since. Like a weed it grows fast, helping to prevent soil erosion, if planted densely enough. The trunks also make excellent construction timber, the branches good firewood, the leaves herbal remedies, and the blossom delicious honey.

I had to pass through one village before I could turn off the dirt road, and it was then that the donkey decided to go down every track, except the one straight ahead. I pranced about awkwardly, waving my arms at his face, to turn him away from field or house entrances, and we managed to proceed in an undignified zig-zag past the amused villagers.

'*Buenos dias*,' I said, already hot and red in the face from my efforts so far this morning. I did not stop to chat, though, answering over my shoulder that I was heading for Rondos, the nearest large village, not wanting people to know where I was really going, in case someone decided to follow me.

I was very nervous, and the sooner I got away from the main tracks and people the better. There was nothing adventurous about me at all this May morning. I just wanted to get through the day without getting lost or losing the donkey. As I found the

70

track turning off the road, an old man stopped me to ask about the donkey.

'*De quien es este burro?*' ('Whose is the donkey?') he enquired.

'*De mio,*' I said proudly, and started walking away but, by the next turning, he had caught up with me to say, '*Vende me tu burro.*' ('Sell me your donkey.') I laughed and told him I still needed him, and went on, determined not to be delayed any more. A young boy joined him, and together they followed me a while. I had dark thoughts about my donkey being stolen, and marched on as fast as I could, hissing at the donkey to go faster. They soon fell behind, and as I followed the winding trail up the valley's side I found that I was alone at last, to enjoy the day and the views of the valley.

After about three hours, I could see the confluence of the rios Lauricocha and Nupe, far below. I felt exhilarated for the first time that day. Resting, perched on the mountainside, I also felt a certain smugness. I had tried to leave Huaraz four times to get going on this journey: the first time, there was no truck leaving for Chiquian; the second, I was back within ten days; the third a supposed short-cut via Chavin frustrated me; and the fourth time, the day after that attempt, I had finally left for Huansala, and got going at last. Everyone had doubted my venture; no one had been prepared to encourage me, and if I were not so stubborn, I am sure I would have given up too. Americo's mother had said that, in Peru, people believe that if something does not work out three times in a row, it is bad luck to try again. Who but a crazy person would do this kind of thing?

Having passed through Rondos, the last large village for the next five days, I encountered my first serious problem. The path, leading down to one of the many rivers cutting the mountainside, suddenly became very steep, and the donkey's cargo slipped along his neck and almost on to his head. I was so concerned with getting ahead quickly that I tried to force him to carry on; but once the bags were actually around his ears, he steadfastly refused to move another inch. He stood, with his nose almost in the mud under the weight of the bags, while I frantically tried to think of a solution.

I knew I was being watched by some women knitting on the

71

hillside, and sweat streamed from my every pore in angry embarrassment. The path was deep in a narrow and muddy ravine, so it was impossible to manoeuvre the jittery donkey to rearrange the cargo. I pushed and shoved, slipping in the mud and losing my temper. The bags had got hopelessly tangled in the ropes, and I fumbled with knots I could not undo. One of the women nearby took pity on me and came down to help. I argued with her, trying to tell her that I did not want to unload everything, but she firmly told me there was no other way, and I let her take over, while I watched feeling stupid.

'Muchas gracias,' I said, once she had finished, and I stamped off with a crumpled ego.

Unfortunately, my problems were not yet over, because around the next bend the path dipped into another muddy ravine, and this time the bags slipped straight over the donkey's ears, anchoring his head firmly to the ground. And this time there was nobody to help. There was nothing for it but to lead the donkey to the bottom of the path, and then lug the canvas bags, the cans of fuel, and the other sack down to level ground. It took me about three or four trips to move my pile of gear and, although it was only noon, I was exhausted; on the other hand, I was so involved with the immediate situation that I did not have a moment to doubt my ability to handle things. Luck was also on my side: by the time I got everything ready to tie back on to my poor pack animal, two campesinos turned up and willingly stopped to help me, for which I gave them each the price of a beer.

The path continued to be difficult, but the cargo stayed on, and I was at ease until coming around one bend, a few hours later, when the path became wet and rocky, with pools of water separating islands of red mud. For some reason, the donkey absolutely refused to move past these pools, even though I tried to show him they were not at all deep by dipping my stick in them. Our choices were limited as we were hemmed in by a stone wall and a steep bank, but the donkey did not care to move. I wore out my stick beating his behind, and then gave up and retraced my steps to look for help. We had passed two homesteads a few minutes before, and I hoped there would be somebody there who knew how to make a donkey move when he did not want to.

*

Oscar and Antonio gave me delicious sweet corn stems to chew and I sucked them with relish. It was three in the afternoon, and I needed little persuasion to call it a day and accept their offer of shelter for the night. The setting was beautiful: two small adobe huts poised on an outcrop of hillside, with Yerupajá just peaking over the hills on the horizon towards Baños, and rich green farming country in the Marañon valley ahead. The altitude at this point was still around 3500 metres, but I felt as if I were out of the mountains, because the landscape was no longer encircled by snowy peaks, and I was walking not along barren highlands but the top of a deep and richly coloured river valley. The earth was a warm terracotta red, and crops of corn and cereals were just beginning to turn golden in the new summer sun. Lush grass grew in juicy green patches between the fields, and spanning all, the sky was a perfect blue, occasionally tufted with white cloud.

The two boys were trainee teachers home for the holidays, and they talked earnestly about Marx and socialism. They were eighteen and nineteen years old, with the familiar jet black hair and russet skin, but looking younger than their years. They had grown up here in this small hamlet but, unlike their family, they wore trainers instead of tyre sandals, and jeans and bomber jackets instead of woollen ponchos. They had whole-heartedly adopted the 'elevated' style of Huanuco, the town where they were studying, and they relished exchanging their new ideas with me. Meanwhile, the mother cooked potato soup in the cooking hut, and soon we were all sitting alongside the sleeping hut, spooning soup as dusk began to fall around half-past five. I made some tea on my gas stove and shared out some bread, while Oscar and Antonio went off to hobble my donkey in a nearby pasture.

I was exhausted from my first day's efforts, and gratefully accepted the family's one bed to sleep on. I told them I had a tent, but they would not hear of it, so I heaved my things into the dark, windowless hut, and unrolled my sleeping-bag on to the wooden bed. Only planks and blankets made up the bed, but that was still much more comfortable than the cold mud floor. The parents and two sons went off to carry on chatting by the warm fireside in the cooking hut.

It was an encouraging end to my first day alone: sleeping in a real bed, kind people looking after me and my donkey. A little later, Oscar and Antonio came to say goodbye before they left for their own house, an hour's walk away through the dark. I thanked them for their kindness and generosity. The parents were going to sleep with neighbours nearby, and I marvelled at their trust in letting a complete stranger, a foreigner even, stay in their home with all their possessions, while they went to stay elsewhere. It boded well for my journey, I thought, and fell asleep looking forward to the next day.

In the morning I was up at dawn and boiling tea by the time sunrays began to warm the chilled hillside. I brushed my teeth in the nearby stream, watched by some fascinated small children arguing about whether the *gringa* was a man or a woman. My disguise was working: before I had left England I had had my hair cropped to a quarter of an inch round the sides and not much longer on top; my clothes were masculine, trousers and long, baggy shirts; and, in Huaraz, I had bought myself a black *sombrero* against the powerful sun. If I did not speak I looked very much like a boy, and I hoped it would protect me from unwanted attention. *'Tu eres muy varonil'* – 'You're very boyish' – would soon become a familiar comment, and I took it as a compliment.

I made sweet porridge, happy to be able to save my generous hosts the usual hour's wait for their breakfast soup. Log fires might seem romantic to Westerners, but it takes a long time to bring water to the boil over a wood fire and, at high altitudes like these, it takes even longer. By eight o'clock I was all packed up and ready to go, and the boys' father helped me to rope on the cargo. One of the small boys was commandeered to lead the donkey around the offending puddles, and soon I was alone again and full of happy anticipation for the day ahead. The weather had definitely turned for the better; no more of the daily downpours of the Cordillera Huayhuash.

I aimed to walk about twenty to twenty-five kilometres daily, which the terrain did not always allow; but each day I walked for about seven to eight hours, with an hour's lunchbreak for me and the donkey. I could not unload him during this daytime break, but at least he had an hour to eat grass and have a rest. The only time he had a chance to eat anything else was during the night, so the lunchbreak was as important to him as it was to me. From the beginning, I talked to him as if he understood me, and his long ears often turned to listen as if he really did. He had a very expressive face and his large dark eyes could convey his moods as well as those of any human.

The first few days, he did his best to keep his distance, either ignoring me or staring at me with a blank gaze. Very soon, however, he got used to me and learned that I was not to be ignored. I had places to go and he was coming with me, whether he liked it or not. For the most part, though, he allowed himself to be directed without too much opposition, and I was surprised at how easy it was.

I soon got into a daily routine; up at dawn, away by 8.30 a.m., break around noon to half-past, and then a couple of hours more, before looking for a suitable place to spend the night. The most important consideration was always whether or not there was pasture for the donkey. If there was not anything for him to eat, we carried on, until pasture was found. I could go without food for a while if I had to, but the donkey had to be well fed every day; I could not otherwise expect him to carry such heavy loads continuously.

The reason I had such a mountain of cargo was that in addition to a tent and all my personal equipment, I was ready to be totally self-sufficient for the whole of the walk through the Andes. But I had no need for half the food I brought with me; wherever I went, the *campesinos* offered me hospitality and food. Often I had no need even of my tent; in fact, I was only to use it three times during the entire hike: once, when I got lost on the *puna* (tableland), and twice when villagers felt they had nowhere suitable for me to sleep. A sleeping-bag and staple goods – like sugar, salt, bread, and rice – to give away in exchange for meals would have sufficed but, of course, it was good to have much more and be able to be generous. I could offer the families not only kilograms of spaghetti, or packet soups, but luxuries like dried fruit, tea, chocolate, porridge, kerosene, tomato paste, and useful items like large sewing needles and medicines.

Many people on the way complained to me about headaches and toothaches, and I gave them paracetamols, taking care to explain that the pills were not a cure, but only alleviated the pain for a short while. But they were grateful even for this, and often I wished I had been a nurse or doctor, and could have helped more. I felt cruelly inadequate when people came to me with their medical problems, assuming that a *gringa* must know how

75

to deal with them. They were sure I would have pills to cure their pains or the chronic bronchitis, goitre, and diarrhoea their children suffered from and I hated having to admit that I could not help them.

Those first five days of walking were wonderful. I enjoyed studying my maps, and working out how far I would get each day; inevitably, it was not the place I had marked on the map, but my sense of achievement was none the less for all that. I felt at ease with the land, instead of threatened, as I had been in the Huay-huash; and the *campesinos* that passed me on the lonely paths greeted me with friendly curiosity. '*Mira la gringa con su burro!*' ('Look at the *gringa* with her donkey!') they would exclaim, asking '*Que cosas para vender?*' ('What have you for sale?') with an eye to my bulky cargo. I suppose I must have looked like a wandering salesman to them: a stranger with a loaded donkey – what other reason could I possibly have for walking through these remote areas? There were many other questions too: '*De donde vienes?*' ('Where are you from?') '*Solita te vas?*' ('Are you alone?') '*De que familia?*' ('Of which family?') '*De que pais?*' ('From which country?') They were to become familiar questions, and I soon found out which answers were the most plausible. If I had no time for a long conversation, I would fib a little and say I was a tourist from Huaraz, exploring the countryside. '*Estoy viajando para conocer,*' I would say, and they accepted my answer without a challenge.

Why I was travelling alone was a question more difficult to explain. Women in Peru almost never travel alone, and certainly not long distances in remote areas. I explained that where I came from women travelled alone all the time, that it was common. I showed them my maps, and sometimes I said I was a student researching the geography of the Marañon valley, which usually satisfied them, although they still wondered at the strangeness and bravura of my venture, and took care to warn me of villages where the inhabitants were *mala gente*, bad people.

My hosts during this first week were all very different. There was the school teacher in Carhuac, with his over-worked wife and seven sons. There were the villagers of Vilcabamba, who brought me delicious hot soup, boiled cobs, and fried corn kernels, called *gancha*. There was the bereaved blacksmith of

76

Quipas, who worked a smelting machine made of stone, wood and leather, that looked like something out of the Middle Ages. And on the fifth day, I found refuge with Señora Virginia de Mena, in the small town of Quivilla. She had a lovely, large adobe house on the banks of the Marañon. All of them welcomed me into their homes for no better reason than that I asked for pasture for the donkey and somewhere to sleep. Only the blacksmith asked for money in return, and he had two small children to care for on his own.

Where, in the so-called civilized world, could I just turn up at someone's house and ask them for petrol for my car and a place to stay the night? Most people would probably think I was mad, and either ignore me or tell me to push off; yet the poor farmers of the Peruvian Andes shared all they had with me, giving freely not just what I asked for but much more: warm meals, advice, help, and friendship. Often, they would invite me to stay a few days, and it was difficult to tear myself away. I realize that I was a novelty: everyone wanted to be the *gringa's* friend and sometimes they got quite competitive with each other, especially when it came to food offerings, which I felt I had to eat whether I could manage more or not. Arguments flared over which was the best rope formation for tying on the saddle-bags and, on a few occasions, I found myself having to be very diplomatic. In spite of my novelty value, there was genuine kindness and generosity: I was a traveller passing by, and they offered me help and shelter, as they would to any other who asked for it.

Sometimes I could do something really useful in return. In particular, I remember the morning with Señor Aquino Lopez and his seven sons. The donkey was all loaded up and I was just about to set off, when I noticed the father had seated one of the young ones down on the roadside, and was about to cut his hair. He had a pair of proper barber's scissors, but he obviously did not have a clue how to use them, and I could not bear to see him hacking away at the poor boy's locks. I led the donkey back to the house, and offered to do the job.

I have always enjoyed hair-cutting, and there was a time when I would have fancied becoming a hairdresser. The boy was about seven or eight years old, and his hair was filthy and matted. I made him wet it, so I could comb and cut better, and he sat on the grassy bank with a scrunched-up face. I admired his trust in me. The other boys, ranging from two to seventeen years old, watched in fascinated silence. My small customer soon had short, neat hair: I was pleased with the result. He patted his head in search of the hair left to him and, once he had had a look in a piece of cracked mirror, he agreed with me. The mother was very pleased, and I found myself cutting everyone's hair, my fingers aching by the time I got to number three.

Vilcabamba was a remote little place, a day's walk away from the nearest dirt road, and it was one of the very few places I used my tent, the villagers watching closely the spectacle of me putting it up. Everyone wanted to see inside, and when I got my sleeping-bag out of its sack, they were even more intrigued, and oohed and aahed in wonder. I explained that it was my bed, whereupon they were even more amazed and immediately wanted to buy it. *'Cuanto seria este bolsa?'* ('How much is the bag?') they asked wistfully, just like the villagers of Queropalca, two weeks earlier. When I got out my tiny Coleman stove, they could not believe their eyes: this little thing was going to boil water and cook my supper? They were very impressed, and I could see the women giving it covetous glances. I wished I could have given them all a stove of their own, but without money for kerosene they would not have been able to use it. It is a serious problem throughout the Andes: hardly anyone can afford to buy kerosene, therefore trees are chopped down for firewood, the erosion of the steep valleys continues without the protective network of trees and roots, wind and constant rain wash the precious and limited soil into the rivers below, and many areas of once arable land are becoming dusty expanses of brown.

I can admit now that the reason my brand-new stove had not worked in the Huayhuash was because I had not turned the air pump to the 'open' position, before I tried to use it. There had been nothing wrong with it at all: I was just too ignorant to use it. Did Americo laugh when he found out what I had done? He certainly did, and I am glad to say that I did too, although I hated being known to be such an idiot. Now I was in command of all my equipment and I enjoyed demonstrating it to my hosts.

In Quipas I cooked rich tomato soup for the blacksmith and his two young children, and we ate it sitting on the ground, ranged around the warmth of the kitchen fire, while the guinea-pigs dared each other to explore my bags. The guinea-pigs of the Peruvian *campesinos* live in dark corners of the kitchen area, and feed off scraps of potato peel and other vegetable waste. On special occasions one of them finds itself chosen for the pot, a quick hand grabs a squeaking bundle from the crowd and, within minutes, its throat is cut, its body dipped in boiling water to remove the fur, and into the pot it goes.

A small town straddling both sides of the Marañon, Quivilla even had a road connection with the outside world, and was therefore quite cosmopolitan compared with the other places in which I had stayed that week. There were shops with lemonade and beer, and a large college for the children from the surrounding area. I could hear them chanting their teacher's instructions by rote as I arrived in the early afternoon. A one-legged drunk attached himself to me as I reached the main square, and curious eyes followed our entourage.

It did not take long to find Señora Virginia – everyone knows each other in these places – and she spirited the donkey and I away, into the protective courtyard of her enormous, two-storey house. She was an aunt of Señor Tarazona in Carhauc and, in return for bringing her a letter from him, she willingly let me stay the night. I was glad to rest my blistered feet, which horrified Virginia when she saw the bloody sores all over them, and soon she was dabbing precious iodine on my wounds.

Later, her husband came home from the fields, and we all talked long into the night about what I was doing and where I came from. Did I believe in God? the husband wanted to know. I made the mistake of saying that I did not, and I only realized later what a blow to my reputation that was. What kind of agriculture was there in England, what kind of plants? he asked. I told him that we eat a lot of potatoes, just like them, and that reassured him a little. However, when the time came to sleep, I was put not in the main house, as suggested earlier, but on the other side of the courtyard. I heard the husband telling Virginia you could never be sure with people who did not believe in God, and I made a note to myself that I wouldn't say I was an unbeliever again.

Getting to Know the Donkey

Donkeys fart. It must be all that grass they eat. Farting is all very well, but as I always walked behind the donkey, his behind was exactly level with my face whenever we went uphill, and I was a prime target. Sometimes the farts would be harmless puffy ones but, at other times, there would be a sudden explosive noise, and a fart would spatter me with speckles of pungent green. It took me a while to learn to keep my distance, but over the weeks grassy donkey farts become a comfortingly familiar smell. At times, of course, I would forget and come too close, but by that time I was hardened enough not to mind, and to laugh at him, telling him his manners were disgusting. I never did give him a name. I had wanted to at first, but then it did not seem appropriate: he was a working animal, not a pet, and just as he would not let me cuddle him, I could not give him a name.

In spite of our first day's zig-zagging, driving him was not difficult, as Andean donkeys are all trained to respond to the same commands. To make him go, it was usually enough to smack my lips in loud kissing sounds; or, if that did not work, a mock angry growl and hand-clapping did the trick; and a last resort was to shout 'Burro!' at him, while giving him a good whack or a kick up the bum. I did not kick him very often, but I am ashamed to say I whacked him quite regularly. Everyone did it; I tried to excuse it to myself. Making him stop was easy: all it needed was a shushing sound, and he would stop instantly, but I have to admit that on occasion my lip muscles were worn out with the constant smacking and shushing.

One afternoon, he pricked up his ears suddenly and started rushing ahead. I shushed at him but he took no notice, grunting excited donkey honks as he began to gallop full-tilt with my cargo bouncing about all over the place. I was amazed how fast he could go when he wanted to, and promised myself not to let him feign the need for a slow walk again. The reason for all this excitement was a female donkey on the other side of the valley, which I found rather surprising, as my donkey was castrated. I had to run fast to keep up with him, but luckily the track was a steep one, criss-crossing down the mountainside, and I managed to catch him by cutting straight down instead of following the path.

My relationship with the donkey threw up some disturbing traits in my character. It is not that I mistreated him: his lot with me was very hard, but not much worse than that of any other Andean donkey. What made me uncomfortable was the discovery of how bossy a little dictator I could be. I was in a hurry to get ahead, perhaps over-compensating for all the time lost in Huaraz, or perhaps because I wanted to reach Cajamarca by early June. Whatever the reason, I walked at a very brisk pace and insisted that the donkey keep up with me. I had been told that he could carry up to sixty kilograms and felt that my load of thirty was a comparatively easy one for him, and that he could easily walk as fast as me. My stick, protection against vicious Peruvian guard dogs, therefore became the weapon of my will. I was appalled to find how tyrannical I became with a stick in my hand. It was automatic. We would set off in the morning and I would give him a whack to wake him up; if he slowed down or stopped to nibble grass, I would shout at him and down came the stick on his behind; if he took the wrong path, downhill instead of up, I would come rushing round to shriek in his face and wave my stick at him. This was not, of course, the whole picture: often, I would let him stop for a graze if I felt we were making good time; or I would steal some juicy corn stems – his favourite food – for him. Over all I think I probably have to admit that I was very strict. The truth is, whether I like it or not, that it came naturally to me to beat the donkey. It was more often a smack than a whack, but equally often it was as big a whack as I could muster, dust puffing up from the donkey's fur under its force. I tried hard not to use the stick once I realized my abuse of its power, but it was a real battle. I needed a stick against the dogs, I could not abolish its existence, and therefore held on to it, constantly having to will my arm to stay down.

A donkey does not cry or shout back, and the lack of protest makes thoughtlessness and even brutality easy. He did get his own back occasionally, however, by just sitting down; getting a full-grown donkey off the ground, without his co-operation, is absolutely impossible even with any amount of kicking and tugging.

I seemed naturally to slip into German, my first language, when it came to shouting at the donkey. *'Vamos jetzt!'* was my most common bark. *'Stell Dich nicht so an!'* I would insist, when I thought he was walking too slowly, picking his way through dangerous rocks or coming up or down one of the many mountain passes. If I got really angry I switched back to English with a 'What the fuck d'you think you're doing?' And then there was always the simple favourite, *'Burro! Andale carajo!'* which means something like, 'Move it, damn you!' I think the odd passer-by was sometimes a bit confused, but I tried to keep most of my outbursts private, and there were only the occasional embarrassing moments, when I found that a shepherd was watching my antics from some treacherously concealed post on the hillside above.

I left Quivilla somewhat refreshed after my half a day's rest, but my left heel hurt like hell if I stepped on it the wrong way. I was relieved that the path following the river was level. It was the first time that I had walked alongside the Marañon, and it felt good. The Marañon was now a wide, fast-flowing river, and its valley an agricultural paradise. All kinds of plants grew here, from giant cacti with flower stems the size of young tree trunks to a kaleidoscope of flowering bushes, hung with blooms in shades of purple, blue, pink, white and yellow. I was only six walking days away from the towering heights of the Huayhuash and yet the scenery was already very different. It was much warmer, almost tropical, the land buzzing with the hum of insects, and the pathways dusty dry. Sometimes I would catch a glimpse of a minute humming-bird, dipping its needling beak into wayside flowers; green, raucous parakeets would screech past overhead. It was strange knowing that I was high up in the Andes while seeing cactus plants and tropical birds. Towering cliffs of red and brown rock reminded me that we were, in fact, still in the mountains and, as the day progressed, the path climbed agonisingly up and up the Culquish canyon in which we now were. We walked over and around huge boulders, fallen from the rock faces above, and the river was suddenly far below, no longer a large river, but channelled thin and churned up by the Culquish rock. Its boiling white water gushed over deadly rapids, and I remembered reading about some Americans who had run the river in the 1970s. They had chosen to portage around this part of it, and I'm not surprised.

Then, for the first time so far, I got lost. The track climbing up the canyon's side suddenly seemed to disappear into a crease of rock, and there seemed to be no way directly ahead. I thought I could see a path below but, when I had fought my way down a steep, brambled incline, I found it was a cleverly constructed water canal, built into the rock. Retracing my steps, I could not find the path, and a thousand pebbles crumbled away under the donkey's hooves as we scrambled about among the thorny bushes. The wide canvas saddle-bags ripped on the sharp plants, and a trail of salt, or sugar, followed the donkey and I.

By the time I found the trail again, I was totally exhausted. It was around three in the afternoon, and I decided to stop for the day at the first opportunity. The trail led through a tight gap in the canyon's side, and into a small green side valley, whence came the water for the canal I had just seen. A small homestead stood perched on a rock, surrounded by pasture for the donkey, and I hoped that I would find a willing host.

It nearly seemed that I was out of luck, because the only people home, so early in the day, were two young girls. They were desperately shy, so much so that they were almost too timid to speak to me. I must have been a very strange sight to them, admittedly, and it was to their credit that they offered me shelter and pasture once I had chatted to them for a short while. I explained that I was on my way to Singa, a small town one and a half days' walk away. I mentioned Señora Virginia from Quivilla, to show I was known to respectable people nearby, and soon they relaxed their guard.

They stood and stared in silence as I unloaded the donkey, and carted everything down steep, stone steps leading from the path to their dirt courtyard. They waited for me to take the initiative, paralysed by not knowing how to treat me; when I had caught my breath, I set up the stove to boil some tea, and soon I was handing out hot, sweet drinks and bread smeared with delicious honey. The girls shared theirs in the protective obscurity of the kitchen hut, while I had mine outside. I knew, though, that they

83

were beginning to feel at ease, and I smiled at them whenever they peeped out at me from the adobe darkness.

It felt a bit like getting to know a wild animal. There was tremendous tension in the air. A false move could scare them witless. I sat quietly in the sun and the daylight hours remaining. There was an enormous turkey stalking the yard, very territorial, snapping his fan of black feathers up, and poking his ugly face at me. The red scrotumish flesh hanging off his beak shook grotesquely as he pecked at me and, although I was intimidated, I tried to shoo him off. He kept coming at me, however, gurgling a turkey scream, and the eldest girl came to my rescue. She grabbed him deftly by the throat and hauled him flapping to a field nearby. He kept coming back for more, though, and soon the game became just what I needed to get the children's confidence. They protected me from their stroppy old turkey, and when the goat dared to nose in my bags they both came at him, shouting and laughing. We were friends by the time their father came back from the potato fields and they introduced me to him and he accepted me without question.

In the morning the father was up and away to his *chacra*, or patch of land, before I had a chance to load up the donkey. For the first time I was faced with the prospect of trying to fix the cargo on by myself, and it was not a prospect I looked forward to. I went to get him from his field and noticed a deep, bloody wound on his spine near the neck. I could not think how he could have got such a wound until the girls told me it must have been a bat. My poor *burrito*! The blood had dried into a thick crust around the wound and a red stain ran all the way down to his left front hoof. I washed his fur and cleaned the wound with disinfectant, hoping that the bat had not given him rabies.

Loading him up was a fiasco. I had watched the cargo being tied on at least five times by now, but I still could not remember the knotting of the rope. The formation decided upon as best, was called *Jamashowa*, and involved S-bend loops around each saddle-bag. Fiddling around with the rope made me wish that I knew at least one good knot. The two girls watched me in respectful silence. I tried to relieve my own tension by making fun of my obvious ineptitude. Funnier by half was the donkey, who decided to deposit a watery pile on my rucksack which I had stupidly put down behind him. The girls giggled with barely-concealed delight. I stared blankly at the ground. It was only 8.30

a.m. and my nerves were already in shreds. Somehow I managed to make the bags stay on the donkey's back and we got going, local farmers staring in amazement: here she came, a *gringa* on her own, accompanied by a donkey with the strangest contraption of ropes ever seen.

The Culquish canyon was almost vertical on my side of the Marañon and I therefore had to divert up and along the top. It was an exhausting day, walking back up to an altitude of 3600 metres, and each time I passed a crew of likely-looking men I felt uneasy about asking them for help with my cargo. I was unwilling to admit my lack of skill to whole groups of people: one to one I could take, but six or ten laughing *campesinos* at a time was too much for my pride.

I planned to stop in a village called Punchao that day but, as luck would have it, this was the most godforsaken settlement I had come to yet. The two people I asked about pasture for my *burro* seemed to have little idea where to find it, and therefore I decided to press on.

Just above the village, I tried my chances at a large, hacienda-style homestead. I need not have bothered, however, because the only person home was an ancient, one-eyed woman, who spoke only Quechua, the language of the Indians. I tried to explain myself. She muttered at me in Quechua, and we stared at each other, silenced by the language barrier.

It was already 3 p.m. and I needed to hurry because nightfall came swiftly in these parts, and shortly after six o'clock only the stars and the moon gave any light. I decided to use the local shortcut, instead of the track marked on my map, and thus I found myself climbing steeply up to a pass and then along a narrow trail clinging to the cliffside of the valley ahead. It was soon dusk and a cold shadow spread over us from the neighbouring mountain. The path began descending steeply and the cargo decided to slip dangerously close to the donkey's neck. I tried again to fix the rope, looking anxiously at my watch: it was gone 5 p.m. The thought of spending the night on this narrow ledge of a path filled me with dread, and I wondered if the donkey could stand remaining loaded all night, because there was surely not going to be anyone to help me here the next morning.

Fortunately, I made the bags stay on long enough to sidle around the mountain and down to Viscas, where I stopped at the very first house I came to.

There too the woman spoke only Quechua, and I began to wonder whether the region was so remote that Spanish was no longer spoken. However, her husband spoke Spanish and, after the usual conversation in which I requested a place to stay for me and my *burro*, they agreed. It was nearly six o'clock, my bedtime, and I still had not eaten. Wearily I started up the cooker, to begin my ritual of soup and tea-making. Just then the wife brought me the most delicious soup I had encountered so far: it was a broth of potatoes with fresh green herbs, and even had an egg in it. I gulped it down straight away, barely able to tear myself away long enough to check the progress of my paltry packet soup. I greedily peeled extra boiled potatoes into my bowl and, when a cooked worm squelched out under my fingernail, I just flicked it to the guinea-pigs without a thought. *Buen accostumbrado* was the expression for that, and well accustomed I was: in England I would have felt sick with disgust; here, I just carried on eating.

As I sat, eating my soup, a young boy of about six came to chat with me.

'Have you heard about the troubles?' he wanted to know.

'What troubles are those?' I asked.

'*Los Senderistas*,' he said, widening his eyes as he spoke.

'They were here just a few months ago. In this village, in Viscas. The police came to get them, to kill the terrorists. Boom! Bam! Through the eye went the bullet, and the man was dead,' he said, getting breathless with excitement.

'Another bullet went through the neck – just here,' he showed me, pointing to his own neck.

'And his horse died too, behind that tree, along the track.' The tree stood not more than fifty metres from where we sat; it had a delicate little trunk that showed no sign of the deaths it had witnessed.

'Later the police came on their horses, and gave everybody sweets and bread!'

It was clearly the most exciting thing that he had ever seen, and he told me his brother was going to be a policeman, just like the ones who had shot the terrorists. I did not speak to his parents about this, as I had no desire to get the boy into any trouble for telling me these things.

It made me realize, though, that I was far from safe; until now, there had always been a couple of months between the visits of the *Senderos* and myself to any one place. It was a situation, though, that could change at any time, a matter of luck. I never expressed any opinions about the *Senderos* to anyone; you could never be sure who you were talking to. The most unexpected people had turned out to be policemen and, by the same token, someone could just as easily turn out to be a *Sendero*. In conversation, I would always ask what my hosts thought about the issue, and then agree with their opinion, or else plead ignorance: a trick I had learned from the *campesinos* in their dealings with strangers.

I was grateful to be offered the floor in the family's hut that night. This particular family were so poor that they only had a single-roomed hut, where the family and all the guinea-pigs lived together, the humans sleeping in the one wooden bed, the animals underneath it. The adobe walls were pasted with old newspaper cuttings and magazine pictures, and clothes hung piled over a wire that ran all around the top of the room. I spread my ground sheet, mat and sleeping-bag out on the floor, and climbed quickly inside, my body tired and my feet aching. The guinea-pigs munched leaves at my head, or scuttled noisily around the floor, warbling quietly to each other. The next morning my plastic sheet was covered in droppings and piss, but I had slept well, and that was all that mattered. I cooked porridge for everyone, as was my custom and, grateful for the expert help in fixing the cargo, I set off once more.

The trail from Viscas was a wide dirt road, a relief after the tough mountain trails of the days before. It wound its way round river gorges which cut into the mountainside, and led eventually to the regional centre of Singa. I was glad, for the sake of the donkey and my sore feet, that we had an easy time of it for a while. The sun shone warmly, birds sang in the eucalyptus trees, and I felt happy and at peace. The looping road followed a circuitous route, but I did not mind. The day was beautiful and, although I was high up and away from the river, the views of the grey peaks and the green valleys beneath them gave me a tremendous lift. I could look back into the distance to where I had come from, and ahead to the unknown horizon, and my sense of satisfaction was complete. My legs were beginning to get used to the daily pain of long walks, the sores on my feet were beginning to crust up into numb patches, my diarrhoea was under control, and my mind was free to wander, unfettered by my body.

Just below Singa the road crossed yet another river, turning into a series of rock and mud slides. A truck coming down from the village was stuck, and the passengers stood around disconsolately, splashing water at each other and throwing rocks into the river. Coming up with my donkey, I by-passed them and the bad road, feeling, I confess, a little superior.

Singa was a large village with a grassy meadow for a main square, and a neglected church with twin towers leaned at one end. The paint had come off the adobe walls and enormous cracks gaped everywhere, as on parched earth. Along the sides large, white lettering announced *'Esta prohibido orinar en esta pared'* – 'It is forbidden to urinate against this wall.' It was also forbidden to let your animals defecate near the wall, according to another sign, but I could see evidence that the notices went unheeded.

I found a shop and treated myself to a lemonade. School had just finished for the afternoon siesta and, at one stage, it seemed like the entire school population of Singa was in the shop with me. They stared at me and whispered little jokes to each other while I chatted with the shop-keeper. After a while, I went to sit in the sun outside, and the crowd got bigger and bigger. What an audience for drinking a lemonade! The eavesdroppers from inside the shop relayed all they had heard from my conversation to the newcomers: *'La gringa es de Inglaterra . . .'*. One eager girl came rushing round the corner in her excitement to join the throng, and slipped and fell, causing wild laughter. I felt sorry for her, knowing how humiliating it must have been to fall at just that moment, in front of all her peers and in front of a stranger too. I imagined my eight-year-old self in such circumstances, and tried to cheer her up by giving her the only smile I had shown so far. Having finished my drink, I crossed the square to buy some bread, pretending not to notice the horde of children tip-toeing behind me. The bread shop was tiny, but everyone crowded in with me and, as I was by now beginning to feel distinctly claustrophobic, I decided to play my own joke, and turned suddenly, roaring like a lion. The children scattered out of the shop with excited screams, and after a second's fright they laughed but kept a little more distance from me. I walked out of Singa with a hundred eyes on my back, but I did not look round: Clint Eastwood could not have done it better.

I was aiming for a small hamlet called Higin and, although it was already five that evening when I reached the penultimate settlement, I decided to push on, undaunted by my fears of the day before. I should have known better: what looked like a short distance on the map turned out to be yet another winding path clinging to a steep cliffside. In places it was nothing but rocks and gravel, descending at frightening angles and wreaking havoc with the donkey's cargo. I was again making him walk late and on a tough path. Each time we turned a corner I thought we must have made it, but no, there was another bend round the mountain and no village in sight. Thankfully, I reached Higin just in time, and the first person I came to welcomed me enthusiastically. Within less than half an hour my donkey was unloaded and grazing, and I was sitting by a warm fire, waiting for my supper.

My host was a young woman with a newborn baby wrapped on to her back, and I asked where its father was.

'Oh, he was killed in the *selva*, working on the coca plantations.' Her apparent acceptance of his fate was without sentiment, but she was not unfeeling. This was Andean fatalism, the people's way of dealing with their brutal lives, where life is lived without help against disease or cold or hunger. Many young men from the Andes leave home for the jungle to make money. They return about once a year, bringing precious gifts, radios with batteries, car tyre sandals, sugar, rice, and medicines. From Higin, it was only about a three-day walk to the jungle in the east, and the pull to go was therefore very strong. Many never return: some are killed, others hitch up with another woman, or are unable to return because their wages have gone on drink to alleviate the loneliness. The peasants of the *sierra* swap a hard life in the mountains for a lonely wooden shack in the jungle, racked by disease, and at the mercy of the coca barons, who have them caught in a trap from which they rarely escape. The peasants are given a patch of land to cultivate coca; if they leave it, even for a few weeks, it is given to someone else and they lose the right to return and earn money from it. Sometimes they get permission to visit their families, often many days' walk away, but it is always with a threat hanging over them: if they return late they lose all or, much worse, henchmen come looking for them with a punishment. Sometimes it is death. They have no rights and fear keeps them away from the police who search out the plantations in areas like the Huallaga valley.

Dreadful revenge awaits people who renege. I heard of two young women who decided to inform but, before they got the chance, they were tied to a tree and repeatedly speared in a torture to the death. Villagers were forced to watch, ensuring that other aspirant informers would think twice about going to the police.

The women in the mountains, meanwhile, are left to cope alone with their brood of annually conceived children, their lives even harder than they were before their husbands left.

I did not enjoy my next day's walk. The Marañon was again being forced through a rocky, uninhabited, and pathless canyon. Again, I had to climb high on to the *puna* above, and scramble across the barren wasteland of the Andean rooftops. It was a climb from 3500 metres up to around 4100 metres, and we made our way slowly and with difficulty. Once over the pass and on to the highland plateau, we were in a silent, treeless landscape, and the wind blew cold. I was uneasy up here alone. Memories of the cold and unforgiving Huayhuash were still fresh in my mind. I tried to hurry, but walking was tough at this height and, later, as we were crossing the watery grasslands, the ground gave way at every step, making progress slow and exhausting. At times the trail disappeared into the wetlands, and it was impossible to tell the tracks of animals from the human path.

My map said one thing, but I decided that a lone shepherd I met must know better, so I followed his directions and found myself lost among rocks and ponds in the strange moonscape of the plateau. The utter silence was oppressive, and I began to panic, my thoughts whizzing around inside my head like electricity gone mad. I had to try hard not to get scared, but it was difficult to control my fear: I could die up here and no one would know or care; I could scream and no one would hear me.

At last I found a path big enough to warrant following, but I lost my temper with the donkey, kicking him and shouting insults when he strayed from the path or stopped for a snippet of grass. I felt guilty at taking my fear out on him; especially as, by this stage, we had become quite good friends. I could tell he was upset when he did not buck against my stick – usually he would respond in some way – but today he just walked on. I explained to him how worried I was and apologized for hitting him, hoping he could detect the remorse in my tone of voice.

We descended finally into a valley with the promise of a settlement. The path was steep, however, and the bags slipped down on to the donkey's neck. I was so frantic to find a place for the night that I refused to stop, and the poor animal walked with heavy weights hanging off his neck. I tried to push them back on to his spine, but it was impossible, and so we continued.

The next morning, loading up, I saw that the ropes had rubbed open wounds behind both of his front legs. I was full of regret; I had been so aggressive. *Pobresito!* I decided that day – a Sunday – we would only walk until lunchtime, and then I would look for some medication for the donkey's wounds, and give him a well-deserved rest.

Vilma, Maximo and the Pushca Canyon

Huacchis was a large village overlooking the Marañon valley, a thousand metres above the river itself. It was a particularly attractive settlement, with picturesque wooden balconies fronting two-storey adobe houses. The place was almost reminiscent of a sleepy Swiss mountain village and, although there were no geraniums on the balconies, the wood carving on some of them was very elegant in its simplicity. There were dirt roads threading around the mud houses, and the inhabitants, with their traditional felt hats and colourful clothing, had the classic features of the Quechua Indians. In the distance, across the deep chasm of the Marañon, you could see smoke rising from other villages and, above them, stood the lonely Chavin ruins from the era before the reign of the Incas. They seemed quite close, being at the same level as Huacchis itself; but overland the distance was at least a day's walk because of the deep cut in the landscape.

The valley was ribbed with green and golden farming terraces that clung to the slopes, making them look like pyramids. Every patch of arable land was being utilized, no matter how steep the incline. High up, underneath the ruins, the potato and cereal fields were almost vertical in places, and their owners had to till the earth with foot ploughs instead of the usual wooden plough and oxen. It was tough work: I had stopped to watch them in many places, the gangs of men and women coming together to work one field, the men ploughing, the women sowing, a tradition that goes back centuries. It is such a vital part of Andean life that when young Quechua couples want to get married they often demand certain rituals of each other, one of which is that a man must be able to plough a field of perfectly straight lines; if not, he will not do as a husband and the girl will spurn him. She, in turn, must make him a poncho; spinning and dyeing her own wool, and then weaving it to form the warm and almost water-proof fabric that will last her husband a lifetime.

It was 14 May and Mother's Day when we arrived in this beautiful place, and all the mothers sported red roses on their chests. It was a Sunday, and unusually busy for eleven in the morning; the inhabitants of Huacchis were not in the fields, but out and about in their best suits and dresses, ready to watch the local school presentation in honour of their women.

I was in search of medication for donkey sores, and when I asked about it, I was directed to Maximo Castro's house. He was the one to see, they told me, and off I went. I knocked on the door, which was answered to my surprise by a woman with short, cropped hair, wearing trousers. I explained that I needed something for the donkey's wounds, and with one professional glance she advised Sulfanil, shouting into the house for Maximo to get a move on and serve the customer.

Out shuffled Maximo, dressed in a crumpled felt hat, thread-bare jumper and old trousers.

'Que tal señorita?' ('How are you?') he said, and shook my hand. He patted the donkey, mumbling calming words and examining the wounds in his own good time, while his wife and I looked on impatiently.

'It's nothing to worry about, you know. The sores are not deep. All he needs is a few days' rest, to let the skin heal,' was the verdict. My conscience was glad, and I dug out some money for the medicine.

'So, you come from Huaraz? That's a long way, my girl. What are you thinking of, travelling around all by yourself?' Vilma came straight to the point.

'I like travelling like this,' I said, feeling shy in the presence of this forthright woman. She soon extracted a more detailed expla-nation from me and was so excited by what I was doing, that I could not help liking her. Maximo ambled back to daub pink fluid on to the donkey's sores, the animal twitching at the sting.

'What he needs is a rest,' they agreed.

'Why don't you stay here with us?' asked Vilma and, before I knew it, she was untying my ropes and sending Maximo off to lead the donkey to their pasture.

*

93

From the road their house appeared to be a two-storey one like the others I had seen in Huacchis. Once inside, however, I found myself looking out into a lovely private courtyard, three storeys below. Towards the back the ground was much lower, and the house was built into the hillside. The kitchen and animal sheds were in separate buildings opposite the main house, and the whole was enclosed by high walls. The sun shone directly in all day long, and a pink-blossomed vine grew up the balconies and over parts of the yard. It was idyllic, and I was overwhelmed by such surroundings and by the friendship of this unusual couple. They were in their late forties and I quickly assumed the role of their surrogate daughter, Vilma fussing over my filthy clothes and making me bolt down a bowl of soup, before we hurried off to catch the school show. I was very lucky that they had been in when I called.

Vilma introduced me as her friend, and no one questioned her further, the men shaking my hand and the women giving me a kiss on the cheek. I felt self-conscious at first, but the villagers did not stare at me unduly, and it was easy to relax and enjoy the children's songs and dances. Parents beamed at individual efforts as well as group ones, even when patently out of tune or when lines were forgotten. Everyone laughed benignly when something went wrong, while the head teacher scurried about with a red face, trying to keep the children in order. We all clapped enthusiastically at the end of each rendition, and when a few mothers were invited to join a dance with the teachers, we all shouted encouragement as the embarrassed women hid their faces in their hands. They giggled shyly, reluctant to go, but the crowd insisted, and their husbands dragged them up to join the other dancers. The dances were a mixture of slow and dignified waltzes and traditional peasant dances. The men would move only slightly, jigging from one foot to the other, while the women would twirl their skirts in front of them or circle their dancing partners gracefully, their faces terribly stiff and serious.

I noticed during the school show that everyone seemed to know and look up to Vilma and Maximo. They were greeted with special deference and affection, and Vilma, especially, seemed to know everyone intimately. I almost felt as if I were included in an audience with the queen. She listened patiently to everyone who came to greet her, and enquired about all their children by name, making each person feel her warmth and concern. Later, as the three of us went for a stroll to their favourite viewing point, she explained that she was the local *promadora de salud*, the official health-care representative. Many of these remote villages never get the benefit of a doctor, but in some there are health promoters, who are not formally trained but have a wealth of experience and contacts with travelling salesmen who bring medicines and surgical tools.

This was a perfect opportunity to ask questions that I had been thinking about for some time. What did women do when they had their periods, for instance? They use cloth rags, which they have to wash every day; or, if they are rich, they can buy a packet of very expensive sanitary towels. Vilma had never heard of tampons and, when I explained how they worked, she was fascinated. Could she see one, she asked, and I promised to show her some when we got back to the house. Maximo was quite undaunted by this turn in the conversation, and we returned to the house sooner than planned, so that Vilma could examine a tampon. I took one out of its wrapper and explained how it worked, and we spent at least ten minutes pushing the tampon out and sticking it back into its tube. I made her a present of it, at which she was delighted, placing it on the shelf in her surgery to show to her women customers at the earliest opportunity. She also determined to speak to the travelling salesman the next time he came, to see if these items could be brought up for sale from the coast.

In return for my demonstration, Maximo showed me their surgery. It was a bare room with only a wooden table and chair, and a couple of shelves filled with large bottles of pills and fluids. On the table was a large white metal bowl, which Maximo used when extracting teeth, his job. One needs to be quite strong to pull out a tooth, he said. I cringed at the idea of coming under his pliers without an anaesthetic, and he laughed at my squeamishness; without electricity for drills, the only answer to a rotten tooth is extraction and, as Peruvians love sugar above all else, very many of them have few teeth left by the time they reach adulthood.

I was only going to stay one night but, in the event, I stayed for three. Vilma and Maximo took me to their hearts with an affection

I have rarely encountered in strangers. Fortune had turned in my favour and I was grateful. It was good to rest for a while, and it was good for the donkey too. He could eat solidly for three days and, with daily daubings, his sores healed up quickly. I visited him every day, and for the first time he let me pat and stroke him, on one flattering occasion even trying to follow me out of his pasture.

When Vilma heard how far I planned on going, she shook her head in amazement and insisted on feeding me up with the delicious potato and egg soups, home-made bread and cheese, and wonderful fire-roasted cobs of corn, which she conjured.

Her kitchen was dark and windowless, like all the others I had seen; but it had one difference and that a real luxury: one whole side of the room was elevated into a waist-high cooking area, the fires built so that she could cook standing up, instead of having to crouch on the ground. Maximo's job was to chop the firewood, and to keep it coming fast enough to forestall a sharp comment from Vilma, although that never seemed to make him rush.

His other duty was to make the cheese in the wooden cheese press. It looked like a giant nutcracker to me: there was a small box on the ground, with a pole above it that could be twisted down on to the lid of the box, squeezing all the water out of the cheese in the process. It only took two or three days for the cow's milk to be turned into cheese, and Maximo proudly showed me a collection drying on a long shelf in the courtyard.

In the evenings Vilma's blackened pots bubbled with her excellent soups, and the three of us would sit on home-made wooden chairs, eating at a table also made by Maximo. Once darkness fell, we sat by candlelight and chatted about our respective lives.

'*Que tal señorita*,' came Maximo's familiar phrase, as if to say 'Well, well.'

He had something of Americo's tranquillity about him, never saying much, unlike his ebullient wife, but when he did speak, you knew he had taken in every word said. Our evenings were short, however, as it was the time of the potato harvest, and Vilma and Maximo had to get up early to go and work their fields. The house had at least ten rooms in it, but instead of putting me in one of these I was taken to their bedroom, and offered the floor at the end of their bed: we were a family for

96

those few days, and I felt honoured to be included in the private sphere of their bedroom.

I decided to accompany them and their donkey to the fields for the potato harvesting. By seven that morning, we were off and, as we walked through the village, others joined us until there was quite a procession of people and donkeys winding their way up the mountain. It was a cold and drizzly morning but we were all sweating as we walked uphill, I more than others. Vilma and Maximo marched on ahead without a single rest. They were twice my age but they took this steep climb in their stride, laughing and chatting with the other villagers without getting out of breath, while I wheezed on a long way behind them.

After about an hour, we came to a wind-sheltered bowl of a valley, with a small lake in the middle of it and tilled fields all around, ranging up the sides of the bowl. Each family had their own pattern of territory in this patchwork, with a small pole-and-thatch shelter where someone would stand guard day and night, protecting the crop against thieves.

The villagers were most of them bent over the ground, hacking the earth up with something that looked like a pickaxe. In the old days it would have been made of wood, but now the traders supply metal and tools are much stronger. Some of the women were sorting the vegetables into large canvas sacks, which the donkeys would have to carry back home. Each one of these sacks weighed around fifty to sixty kilograms and the animals had to carry two each, one roped to either side of their spine. Most people were harvesting potatoes, but there was another crop called *oca*, an orangey-pink colour, shaped like a short, fat carrot with very lumpy contours. It was delicious, raw or cooked, with a subtle, sweet flavour of which I got very fond.

I left the others to work the fields and climbed up above the valley to explore some of the ancient Chavin towers. There were three, each in a state of severe decay, but there was still enough brickwork left to see that there were excellent masons in Peru, long before the Romans were building in Europe. The stone was slate grey, hewn into regular oblong shapes and fitted tightly together even without cement of any kind. The wind blew hard and cold up here, at almost 4000 metres, and I could imagine the vigilant Chavin warriors looking out over the Marañon valley to the mountains beyond. They would have been able to see people coming for at least three days before they reached the vicinity of Huacchis, and would then have been well prepared for an assault in the tight valley below. The architectural style of the Chavin towers is very similar to that of early medieval keeps in Europe: a tiny entrance at the base, and then no openings or windows until high up, at a point where they are no longer accessible. From here, I could see everyone far below, working and laughing. Every now and then, donkeys would honk across the valley, and dogs chased each other round the lake. This fertile patch must have been growing potatoes as far back as the Chavin era and little has changed in all those centuries. Now there are donkeys where before there would have been only people and perhaps a few alpacas and llamas, although they were never really strong enough to carry heavy weights, the men heaving their crops on their backs, with a band around their foreheads, just as many Third World workers still do today.

I could have stayed in Huacchis for a very long time. Vilma and Maximo were very good to me. But after three days, I was impatient to get moving again. The longer I stayed, the harder it would be to leave, and I could see that I was being treated like a daughter which, although flattering, was also a little restricting.

They had a daughter about my age, but she had been sent to school in Lima and was now living on the coast, enjoying the comforts of life there, such as electricity, running water, commercial goods, and easy travelling connections with Lima. Vilma, especially, seemed to miss her terribly and spent many hours telling me about her, and how they loved visiting her on the coast.

They planned soon to give up their life in Huacchis and move down to the coast. Who would look after the villagers when they were gone, I asked? There would be no one, Vilma shrugged. They would have to walk a day or two, to Aczo, which had a road connection with the outside world.

We promised to write to each other and, with all my clothes freshly washed, my donkey healed, and home-made bread and cheese in my pockets, I left Huacchis. My last view of Vilma and

Maximo was of them waving goodbye. I could see their home for a long time to come, until I rounded the next bend in the valley.

I took it easy that first day out of Huacchis. We were getting close to the massive Pushca canyon, which cuts a great gash into the mountains as the river which forms it comes to join the Maranon. To reach its rim I would have to cross high *puna* once more, and I chose to spend the night beneath the entrance pass, lessening the danger of getting lost up there close to nightfall.

Luckily for me, the woman I asked to put me up was a relative of the Castro family, so confidence was rapidly established. She lived alone in a derelict mud house and was obviously poor; not only was the house crumbling and rain-washed, but she had only two chickens, five guinea-pigs and one sheep, which is little by Andean standards. She told me that she had a husband and four sons, but that they had left to work in the jungle and never returned. Now she was an old, forgotten woman, with nobody to chop her wood or help harvest her potatoes. As I arrived she was haggling with someone to put new thatch on her leaky roof, but I got the impression the young blood she was speaking to did not feel like working for her: what could she pay him with?

It was a shock to come across such a neglected woman after meeting so many close-knit families. She laughed toothlessly to herself as she told me her story, and there was something slightly mad about her. She had retreated into her own little world of memories, talking to herself while she peeled her potatoes with an ancient rusty knife. The two mangy chickens came scratching into the cooking area and she did not seem to mind them pecking at her vegetables. Dragging a black pot out of a corner, she groped around in it and pulled out a putrid-looking piece of fish, and placed it in the soup. Trout from the lakes are a luxurious addition to an Andean meal, but this one looked distinctly unsavoury. I said nothing, of course, and took my bowl with thanks. In return I gave her some sugar, rice, and some of Vilma's fabulous bread. She was pleased with this, telling me that she had not had sugar for months.

In the morning loading up was easy because Maximo had made a wooden, triangular bridge to place on the donkey's back and, once this was strapped firmly down, I could just throw the bags on without tying them up and there they stayed without slipping. I enjoyed loading up in front of an admiring audience of Andean housewives; it is normally a man's job to load up the donkeys, and they thought I was very clever to do it all by myself, especially as I was a *gringa*.

I left feeling good and promised myself that I would not let the *puna* frighten me this time. It was a grey, rainy morning, with thick clouds low in the air, but walking was easier in such cool weather and I felt invigorated. We climbed up and up through the rocks, enshrouded in a milky mist in which visibility was very restricted.

After an hour or so, I began to head down towards a valley, pleased to have got through so quickly. Then some shepherds warned me that I would not be able to get through that way with the donkey, and my fast-blooming confidence shrivelled away at the thought of having to retrace my steps and cross more *puna* to reach a more accessible path. This time I did get lost among the mists and bogs, and I swore at the surrounding silence. It was early afternoon before I found the way, and I had lost a good two hours tramping around in the sky.

My original plan for that day had been to cross the Pushca canyon in one go but, as I came out into the sunlight, I was confronted with a journey of proportions quite insurmountable in the hours left to me. The depth of the canyon was about a kilometre, but its width at this point was about fifteen; instead of a neat cut into the mountains, it yawned wide, lined with an interminable series of ledges and hillsides. The trail leading downhill was perilous: small rocks and pebbles sent me tripping and sliding down the mountain, feet sinking deep with every step, toes squashed against my boots. The momentum gathered during the downhill pace often made me lose my footing, and the donkey slipped too, his hooves catching among the rocks. We sweated through this for about four hours, but still were far from the bottom, and the deeper we got into the canyon, the drier and hotter it became. It was like descending into an oven, and even the landscape changed – from green to sandy-brown. Prickly bushes and cacti were soon the only vegetation, and there was no water or pasture to be seen. Rounding yet another ledge, a green patch at last came into view below, an oasis of shady trees and pasture. There were no houses in sight, but I could see

100

a field with a protective tree in its centre, perfect for making camp.

Some *campesino* travellers passed me then on the trail, and I hung back, walking slowly so that I could sneak off the track without being seen. Spending the night alone here, in the middle of nowhere, was a potentially dangerous thing to do. There was no one to help me guard the donkey, and there were quite a few men coming through the canyon, bringing large sacks of coca leaves from the Huallga valley, six days to the east.

These men were not *narcos*; they represented the cottage industry of the drug trade, bringing as much as they could carry on their backs to sell to the Andean farmers. Chewing the leaves, the farmers could work all day without feeling the pangs of hunger, and each man had his own stash of coca and home-made calabash bottle containing the white phosphate, known locally as *cal*. With the extractive help of a little powder in their mouths, they masticate coca leaves all day, their teeth and lips stained green from the invigorating juices. I tried some myself, but the only effect I could detect was a complete numbing of the mouth and throat; it is tame stuff compared to the powdery drug sold on Western streets. In its natural state, it is no more powerful a stimulant than coffee, but I suppose the constant chewing at least gives the farmers the illusory sensation of eating something, although it does nothing to assuage their very real hunger.

I left the trail unseen and picked my way through thorny shrubland to reach my chosen field. It was enclosed by a stone wall and prickly branches lay along the top. What had looked like pasture from a distance turned out to be rich clover, obviously meant for harvest and not for grazing. Although I felt guilty abusing someone's crop like this, I had no choice: the donkey had to eat, and I untangled a stretch of branches and dismantled the wall enough for him to jump into the field. I headed for the camouflage of the lone central tree. Its branches hung wide and low, and I was confident that we could not easily be spotted from paths higher up the canyon. This was, of course, the one day I had neglected to fill my water bottle, and now I found myself with no water for cooking supper and not a stream in sight. We had passed one earlier, about a kilometre back and, in spite of the risks of leaving all my possessions unattended, I decided to head back and fetch water. The risk was serious: if I lost my provisions and my donkey, the journey was over; not to mention the possible predicament of losing my money, passport and maps to find my way out of the mountains. We had had a very tough day, however, and I could not bear to go without supper or even a cup of tea.

I tied the donkey to the tree and headed back up the canyon, half expecting everything to be gone when I returned. It was late afternoon and it seemed as if I were alone. One could never be sure of that, though; many times I had discovered that I was being watched by silent witnesses sitting on hillsides above. On one embarrassing occasion, I was just stripping off to wash in the river when I noticed a grinning *campesino* watching me from the other side of the water.

I reached the stream we had passed earlier and found it to be an opaque, rust colour. It tasted very strange with a sweet flavour, but each gulp left my mouth feeling dry and furred by a foul aftertaste. No matter, I thought, hot tea in my mind as I filled up my bottle and hurried back downhill. Rounding the final ledge, I could see the donkey grazing by the tree and all seemed well. But after taking such risks to get the water, I decided that perhaps I should not use it; maybe it was poisonous and, being so far from help, even severe diarrhoea would be a serious problem. No tea or supper for me. At least the donkey was happy: clover all night. I hoped he would not find it too rich after his frugal diet. I feared a sick donkey even more than a sick me.

Night came swiftly, and I unpacked my tent. The ground was rock-hard and sun-cracked, though, and not a single pin would sink into the ground. It was warm down in the canyon and, as long as it did not rain, I would sleep out in the open. It was a tranquil, balmy evening. I lay in my sleeping-bag, watching a giant, full moon rise up over the canyon's dark edge. I was now about nine degrees south of the equator, and the black sky, so much bigger and higher than in Europe, was sprinkled with a million stars. It was a wonderful feeling to lie on the earth and look up into the galaxy. I lay awake for hours, dreaming about food, home, Americo, and the future. The moon shone in my face so brightly and the contented munching sounds were so loud nearby, that it was difficult to sleep. But my sense of contentment was complete. Uncertainties did not matter. I set my alarm for 5 a.m. I would be gone before daylight could expose my trespassing for all to see.

Me, a Terrorist?

I rebuilt the hole I had made in the wall as best I could, and we left, stumbling down the same wretched path towards the pit of the canyon. Happily, the climb up the other side was on a dirt road, and we progressed slowly but with ease. Rain began to pour down by mid morning and I thanked the stars for sparing me during the night. The change in the weather was to be expected; when there is a new moon, the weather in the Andes turns for the worse. Local mountaineers in Huaraz even plan their trips according to the celestial cycle and, if the dates do not fit in with the moon's phases, you can be sure they will postpone their departure.

Today I would reach, for the first time in days, a *pueblo*, or town, that was connected to the outside world by road. From what I had heard it even had shops and a hostel, and I promised myself that if the hostel had a shower I would splash out on a room. The rain evaporated under a hot and sweaty sun as the day wore on but, even taking it easy, I managed to arrive in Chingas by two that afternoon, thoughts of fried meat and chips having hurried me up the canyon.

The place was indeed touched by civilization. Trucks were revving up their filthy engines on the main square, and street vendors sold fruit and vegetables. I gorged myself on two bananas and five oranges, hoping my guts wouldn't revenge themselves too cruelly later on.

I asked for the local hostel and was told that Chingas had a hotel, no less. I walked on eagerly, ignoring the curious looks that followed me all the way up the main street. It was in small towns like these that I felt most vulnerable. In the remote mountain villages, people were kind and generous; here there were drunks, locked doors, occasionally the police or the army, and other man-made dangers.

103

The 'hotel' turned out to be an extremely dirty house, its floors ankle-deep in sheep droppings, and a shifty-looking *dueño* sitting lazily in the doorway. He was handsome, in a spaghetti western sort of a way, with piercing blue eyes drawing the attention away from his stubbled chin and bulging gut. I asked if there was a shower in the hotel and was shown a pipe sticking out of the ceiling in the toilet cubicle; but even this was something after a week without a wash, and I decided to stay. The *dueño* turned out to be quite friendly, in spite of his roguish looks, and while I went off to have a shower he led my donkey off to pasture. He assured me there were men guarding his fields and I trusted him with my most precious possession.

Meanwhile, I found the shower end of the toilet had not been used for some time, the tap was rusted solid with neglect and, judging from the sludge on the concrete floor, I was not entirely convinced that the shower had not been used as an extended toilet facility. Luckily, freezing cold water jetted out of the ceiling pipe in force, I rinsed the floor as best I could, and blasted away the sweat and dirt of previous days. The wall separating the shower cubicle was about head high and, only a few footsteps away, there were a number of local men, the *dueño*'s field-hands, sitting at a late lunch. I could hear them discussing who I might be, and hoped none of them would be rude enough to come looking over the wall.

On the other hand, my experiences so far had shown me that the notorious *machismo* was less of a threat than I had been led to presume. I had not suffered sexual harassment even on the streets of Lima. I found most men very respectful, their attentions always friendly and good-natured, and never offensively lecherous as in Europe. Perhaps my androgyny had something to do with it; or perhaps I was seen in terms of the virgin-whore dichotomy, reputed to be a common motif in the culture of South America, where images of women are polarized into two categories: either idolized as virgins and mothers, or denigrated as temptresses and whores. Men stake their lives and honour – if only figuratively – on the former, while the latter are fair game as sex objects.

I prefer to believe that it was because Peruvian men and women retain a wonder at each other, a sense of difference which infuses their relationships with a mutual respect, as well as love.

After my shower I ate the dreamed-of lamb steak and chips and, later, I smoked my first cigarette in two weeks. I did not smoke while I was in the mountains and missed it not at all, but as soon as I got to a shop that sold cigarettes, I craved the relaxation of a smoke. To make sure all was well, after supper I went to see where the donkey was being kept. He was in a field of freshly harvested wheat which, during the day, the field-hands were stooking into bundles, tied with string. The wheat was cut down with a sickle, and to me it seemed like trying to cut a lawn with a pair of scissors: I was not surprised when they told me each field took them at least a week to harvest. The donkey was happy there and I returned to the hotel. Chingas had a generator to give electricity for a few hours each night, and my host and I talked for much longer than mountain people usually did.

'So, do you have a boyfriend?' the *dueño* asked, with a twinkle in his eye.

'I do, actually,' I replied, feeling strange as I said it: might it be tempting fate to talk about Americo before we saw each other again?

'Ah, he is lucky, I have no one to care for me,' he sighed; which I knew was untrue, the cook having told me all about his wife in Lima.

He got out his radio in my honour, and we listened to some salsa music from the coast. He enjoyed the attention of the townspeople who came to inspect his unusual guest, and adopted quite a proprietorial attitude for the rest of the evening. In the morning, a whole group of them accompanied me out of town, and when I made to pay for my room, the *dueño* refused to accept a single Inti. (I was very pleased, especially as the price he had quoted me the day before had been outrageous, considering the state of his so-called hotel.)

From Chingas onwards the mountains creased up like a giant accordion, and a twenty-kilometre stretch as the crow flies took me five hard days of walking up and down hot folds of rock. The Marañon valley was changing from a green, agricultural paradise into a hard, sunbaked landscape of barren sand and rock. My maps showed spaghetti circles of tight brown contours – the *cerro* – which soon materialized into the lifeless mountainside I began to traverse. In the distance below, the Marañon wound its way

105

north in serpentine bends, large sand banks filling in the curves. I wished I was on the water and cursed the endless ledges, and the lack of shade and pasture which made travelling tough on both the donkey and I. Wherever possible I tried to obtain sugary maize stems for him to chew; but he needed more to eat than that and, for the first time, I had to buy precious pasture to supplement his food.

I found my mind wandering during this time and mainly to food; I barely noticed the landscapes I was passing. There was life in this region which, had I been less tired, I would have enjoyed with greater attention. There were the flocks of noisy parakeets, for example, who fed off the tree-trunk-like flowers of the giant cacti; there were lizards, beetles and tiny, sparrowish birds, that lived among the rocks; and there were, of course, the ancient geological patterns of the Andes themselves, the lines of erosion in the rocks possessing a strange kind of beauty.

My mind, however, was concentrated on the familiar routine of journeying: 'four more hours to go, two more hours to go, lunch, a few hours more.' Food apart, I recalled moments of my life, or places I knew well, often insignificant, their only virtue their familiarity. The walking was becoming very hard, the environment hostile, and I myself, for the first time, lonely, these memories of familiar things giving small comfort.

All this was not apparent to an observer. Each evening I went through the ritual of introducing myself to potential hosts, talking about where I came from and what I was doing. Loading and unloading the donkey, cooking, demonstrating my sleeping-bag and gas stove, all this carried on.

'*Que cosas para vender?*' had now been answered a hundred times; as had '*De que pais?*' and '*Cuanto es la pasaje de Inglaterra?*' I always had difficulty with these last two. Very few people had heard of England, so I often explained that I was from Europe. Even this was not very helpful, though, as most of the people I talked to had never been further than the next valley, and could not conceive where Lima or Colombia were, let alone England or Europe. They would say things like, 'I suppose it's a very long bus ride from your home?' Or they would ask me if England was in North America. I tried to couch my answers in concepts they could relate to, saying that to get to England you had to travel right to the other side of South America, and then it was a two-month journey by boat across the Atlantic ocean. To say that England was on the other side of the world was of little help. I could only tell them that I came from far away and that I was here to learn about Peru and their way of life. They liked that. They enjoyed the idea of me coming especially to see them, and we laughed at each other's ignorance and each taught the other something new.

The question of how much it cost to come to Peru was a tricky one, though, and I tried to avoid answering it: there was no point mentioning some astronomical figure in Intis or dollars but, if pressed, I would say that it cost the equivalent of a labourer's annual wages, or the price of a full-grown bull – the most valuable thing they could own. It was a question their practical minds were interested in, but it was never because they were trying to sound out my worth, or to ask me for anything. It was therefore all the more enjoyable to be generous with my food and medicines. Occasionally, I might pay for someone to have a tooth extracted, but an exchange of money was rare; they had little use for it: a kilogram of rice was much more valuable because it could be traded or used for the family.

And so it went on. I confess at this time I was abstracted, and therefore what happened when I reached a small place called Pumpa came as a *complete* surprise . . .

It had been another hard day of scuttling up and down rocky paths, and it was nearing 5 p.m. when I made the descent into Pumpa, about 1700 metres above the Marañon. On the way down I was joined by shepherds herding their goats, cows, and donkeys home for the night and, as we jostled each other along the slippery sandstone, they asked if I were not scared to travel alone. I assured them that all the people I met were very good to me, and that so far I had had no reason to worry.

In the village I asked a young woman if she could recommend anyone who had pasture. Pumpa was situated on a green ledge above the dry *cerro*, there seemed to be plenty of grazing available, and no doubt I would easily find someone to put both me and the donkey up – but the woman surprised me by saying she thought not. I might have trouble finding someone who would accept me, was her opinion. 'There's always someone who will take me in,' I said breezily, and walked on.

The village was made up of at least thirty adobe homesteads, built close to each other in shelter from the wind. Already smoke ascended through some of the thatched roofs, and I looked forward to the possibility of fresh potato soup. The women sat hidden in their smoky kitchens, the men were securing their animals, and barefoot children sat peeling sweetcorn stems with their teeth. All were winding down after another tiring day in the highland fields and pastures, and an air of peaceful relaxation pervaded the place.

I set about making my enquiries, and was surprised to find that one house after another claimed it had no pasture. After half an hour of this, I began to feel quite anxious. It was getting close to nightfall, black rain clouds thickened the dusk, and it was rapidly getting cold. The atmosphere suddenly seemed ominously quiet. I was ignored or brushed off with feeble excuses, and soon became so self-conscious that I was too embarrassed to ask anyone else for shelter. I would have to spend the night in a field; this time it was not going to be a dry one. I gave up and steered the donkey to a patch of grass in between corn fields. As I unloaded the donkey and set up my cooker, some villagers watched me from a distance. I felt unwelcome. The ground was again too hard to put up the tent, and the prospect of sitting through twelve hours of the wet dark filled me with dread.

What the hell was going on? I pretended not to notice the spying eyes beyond my patch and, trying to look unconcerned, I cooked myself a delicious tomato and spaghetti soup. Necks craned to see how I was cooking without a fire, but they were too far off, and for a moment I felt like a wicked witch and enjoyed it; but I was still very worried. What was going to happen when it was dark? I felt isolated and vulnerable and every bit the outsider that I was. In those mud houses with their warming fires there were people who were safe and secure, but I was outside and soon to be alone in the cold, starless night.

As I settled down to eat my soup, a young man approached, watching me in silence. There were only about two metres between us, but he said nothing, and I decided to ignore him.

After an oppressive silence, he spoke; quietly, almost in a whisper, he asked me, '*Una preguntita: es verdad que tu eres compañera?*'

It took me a couple of seconds to realize what he was asking; was I a *compañera*, a *Senderista*? It was incredible: the villagers thought I was a terrorist. I let out a tirade of demotic Spanish: it was the most ridiculous suggestion I had ever heard! Was it not obvious from my dress and appearance that I was a foreigner? And, in any case, how often had he heard of female *Senderos* travelling alone? '*Estoy tourista, no terrorista!*'

The first wave of anger abated and I am ashamed to say that tears welled up, while the young *campesino* looked on in embarrassment. Soon there were two young men watching me, and the nervous tension was just too much. The two of them whispered to each other, trying to decide what to make of me. I like to think that my tears were the result of five hard days; of tiredness most of all, and shock at the first cold reception I had received. If I am honest, though, there might have been just a touch of artifice in my display of helplessness. What true Peruvian would let a young woman in tears spend the night alone in a field, without protection and without cover from the oncoming rain? It was not long before the first young man asked if I would like to stay at his house; but by this time I was feeling very sorry for myself and I sulkily said no. It was almost completely dark now, large raindrops began pounding the earth, and they tried to persuade me more urgently, even offering to reload the donkey. I stayed sitting on the ground and insisted that I would eat my soup before I went anywhere, but soon the sky had fallen and I gave in. We packed up my things, and I let myself be led away, soaked and sniffing loudly as I stumbled through the rainy darkness.

My gallant rescuer was about nineteen, dressed in the usual raggedy trousers and brown, woollen poncho, but worn with brand-new trainers rather than tyre sandals. There was an air of gravity about him, and he seemed to command deferential respect from his friend, even though the latter was obviously older. Meanwhile, I found myself escorted into a small courtyard, empty except for two donkeys, who lazily munched their feed in the rain. Pablo, he finally told me his name, was alone this week. The rest of the family was harvesting potatoes far away, sleeping in cane and thatch huts, like the ones I had seen near Vilma and Maximo's.

'Horrible time to be sleeping out,' I said, trying to make conversation. Pablo was not very talkative, however, and it soon transpired that I was not going to be sleeping inside the house. Instead my things were stacked neatly on the porch, and it was suggested I could sleep there. Was he still wary of me? Or was he just an unpractised host? He knew as well as I did that this was not the way you treated someone who was staying at your house; and, as if to explain, he said he had no key for the lock on the front door. Grateful not to have to sleep in the rain, I was not bothered as to the truth; but I could not help being intrigued by the enigmatic Pablo, and I continued to try and draw him into a conversation.

What on earth had made them think that I was a *compañera*? I asked. He shrugged his shoulders awkwardly, until finally he said that the week before three *Senderistas* had passed by, and he, Pablo, had put them up. (So that was why he had been the one to approach me: everyone else had been too scared.) They had given him the new shoes, and he was seriously considering joining up the next time they came. They were good people, he told me.

'They only kill rich people, landowners, and corrupt people in power, who abuse the poor. Those people on the coast who rule Peru, they don't care anything about what happens to the *campesinos*. The government has abandoned the people of the mountains, the *sierra*, and instead they lead a life of luxury in Lima. They have everything on the coast and we have nothing. There is no help for us when we are sick or hungry. The *Sendero Luminoso* will destroy the corrupt elite and we will have Communism. Everybody will have equal rights to everything.'

What was Communism? I asked. He did not know. All he knew was that he was a poor peasant with a bleak future, and that the *Senderos* he had met had been good people, giving him proper shoes, for nothing in return. They said they were going to get rid of corruption and poverty, and if that meant having to shoot a few bad men, that was all right with him. Good, honest people had nothing to fear. But what about the rest of the village? Why were they scared?

'They are just stupid,' Pablo told me with a grim face. 'They don't understand. They haven't talked with them like I have.'

He was as serious and humourless as any recent convert, and it made me sad. The attraction of *Sendero* was, however, obvious.

Most of their guerrillas are boys and young men between the ages of fifteen and twenty-five; poor and mostly unschooled, they come from lonely mountain regions, where their lives are mapped out for them in the same way as for generations: a basic subsistence living from the land, with no reference to the state's money economy. Peru is now in a state of economic collapse, though; nobody will pay the *campesinos* for their produce in the markets. The pittance they are paid hardly covers the cost of the walk and truck journey to the nearest town, let alone the purchase of goods like sugar, salt and other basics. It is no surprise that the boys are running away to the coca plantations or to join *Sendero*. The former option brings money, and the second option something even more important – self-esteem. They can command respect in the villages and they have the ultimate power: to take life. The possession of such power is intoxicating; just as the consequences are vicious and sad.

In the morning, the community's *presidente* came to apologize for the day before. He explained that if I had approached him in the first place this would never have happened, and he hoped I would not think badly of his village for the *mal attencion*.

What he said was true: of course I should have gone to him first, as I should have been doing everywhere I went. But to tell the truth, I had thought that I was going to be camping for the whole trek, and had never contemplated the proper procedures for seeking shelter in villages and, so far, had never had occasion to worry about it.

This was new territory, though, close to the coca-producing Huallaga valley, and to scenes of heavy fighting between the state forces and the guerrillas. Only three days before I reached Pumpa, there had been a massacre in Huacaybamba, the other side of the Marañon valley, and it was for that reason I was walking along the left side of the river.

Speaking with the community president reminded me of these facts, and I promised myself to be more aware of official etiquette from now on; some villagers might not stop to ask questions if they suspected me of being a *compañera*. I would have to pay more attention.

111

Donkey Trouble and Don Angel

Studying the maps, I realized that from now on there would be virtually nothing for the donkey to eat. If I continued on the left bank of the Marañon, there would be dry *cerro* and very little else; much the same could be said for the other side; except for the fact that about three days' walk away from the nearest bridge there was a road leading down to the Marañon, crossing the river at Chagual, about 100 kilometres north of my present position. If I followed this road I would at least be passing small towns and settlements where I could buy pasture brought in for local animals, and most of the road did not follow the Marañon but wended its way 1600 metres higher up, along parallel valleys that were therefore fertile and green.

I had also heard that from Chagual onwards the Marañon is easily navigable; perhaps I would be able to continue by boat or raft. There are many mines in that area, which were reputed to have motorized boats, used by employees for prospecting areas along the river, and perhaps I could persuade someone to give me a lift.

The idea of continuing my journey on the river filled me with excitement. I had not planned to get on to the river until I reached Bagua, on the edge of the Amazon jungle itself, and now it seemed I might get there sooner than I thought possible. It would be sad to sell the donkey, but I could not take him with me. My idea originally had been to walk as far as Balsas, where a road cuts the river on its way to the coast; to sell the donkey and rest in Cajamarca for a while, and then get a truck to Bagua to continue by whatever waterborne craft I could find. This idea was now adapted, and I decided to head for Chagual along the road that began in the remote and notorious town of Huacrachuco.

The place was notorious as the setting for severe clashes

between *Sendero Luminoso* and the army the year before, and was said now to be heavy with army and definitely to be avoided.

'The one place you should not go is Huacrachuco,' Americo and others had told me. It seemed to me now, though, that I had no choice, although I was uneasy at the prospect of coming face to face with the army.

I was almost more scared of the army than anyone else: they could arrest me, lock me up, force me to abandon my journey, or to do anything else they wanted. Other than my passport, I had nothing to say who I was or what I was doing, and this was in the emergency zone of Huanuco, where no foreigners were supposed to be travelling without special reason and permission. (After going to all that trouble to get official recommendations in Lima, I had decided that I would be safer without them. Few people I had spoken to made a distinction between writers and journalists and, as the *Sendero* had a habit of killing anyone they suspected of being a journalist, I did not want to run the risk of carrying compromising papers during this part of the journey. All official documents were waiting for me in Trujillo, to be collected during my rest period in Cajamarca, eight hours' drive from the coast.)

Huacrachuco it was then, in spite of misgivings, and the donkey and I left Pumpa heading for Socos bridge. For a while the trail followed the mountainside on a more or less level ridge, but by midday we were heading over a shoulder of suncracked mud and rock and sliding down into yet another infernal canyon. The pebbly path twisted back and forth in tight zig-zags, clouds of white dust swirling up to coat our bodies and parch our throats. The descent took three, long hours under the glaring sun and I was relieved that we were at least going downhill. Sweat trickled down my chest in rivulets, soaked up by the waistband of my trousers. At one stage, almost at the bottom, I passed a group of coca traders coming the other way, and I pitied them their climb ahead. Each man was loaded down with a heavy sack on his back, the bands around their foreheads plastered down with sticky sweat. The profits, even for them, must be immense, to compensate for all that tough walking: from the bridge to the jungle plantations alone was a six-day walk.

Socos bridge hardly deserves to call itself so. It must have been one once, but what I found was half a bridge coming from the far side of the river bank, continued at the halfway mark with sticks laid horizontally over two wires, and a plank walkway leading across. The whole contraption sloped dangerously to the right, and I knew as soon as I saw it that the donkey would refuse to cross. It was bad enough trying to get him on to an ordinary bridge. He seemed to have a phobia against running water and bridges, and even steel and concrete was not safe enough for his liking. Back in Quivilla he had needed some serious cajoling to get over a perfectly good bridge, and my heart sank at the thought of having to retrace my steps up the canyon, to the next bridge, which was at least three days' walk away, and unlikely to be any better than this one. I could also see from my map that the other crossing had no settlements near it and little chance therefore of anyone passing by to help me. Here there seemed to be people passing through, and the orange and banana plantations along the river were some assurance that *campesinos* would be coming to tend the crops. (It was the one advantage these canyon heat traps had: all kinds of fruit grew wherever the river banks were wide enough. In the north of the Peruvian Andes, climate and vegetation change completely according to altitude: in one day's walk you can go from treeless, grazing *puna* at around 4000 metres, to potato and cereal farming between 3500 and 2500 metres, and tropical agriculture at 1800 metres.)

Stubborn as usual, I decided to try my luck. I walked the donkey down to the bridge and, sure enough, he refused to set foot on it. I knew it was going to happen but the alternatives were so disheartening that I insisted on trying the impossible.

I am ashamed to say that I proceeded to beat the poor animal's behind as hard as I could. It had no effect. I kicked him up the bum, I tugged at him with a rope, I screamed, I shouted, but he would not move. I made everything worse by being so brutal and we glared at each other in silent outrage.

Finally, I led him away, down a path leading to a small homestead nearby. It was all locked up, and had been for some time. I unloaded the poor donkey, tied him to the courtyard tree, and began to make supper, feeling guilty and mean: there was nothing for him to eat other than a few dried-up banana tree leaves.

The homestead comprised two small adobe buildings standing opposite each other. The roofs on both overhung by at least a metre, creating shady verandahs to sit under. I arranged all my gear in their protective shade and sank on to a wooden bench to

above: Yerupajá and the Huayhuash range, where I spent ten miserable days sick, wet and dangerously close to a terrorist camp.

right: Jahuacocha Lake in the Huayhuash.

below: Huascarán mountain, overlooking Huaraz and the Callejon de Huaylas – my morning view.

Above: The Senderos would paint slogans during the night and then disappear, leaving fear.

Below left: Easter Sunday in Huaraz.
Below right: Taking the pig to market in Huaraz.

ove: The pink rider in the
uayhuash.

ove right: Oscar and family –
y first hosts on the Andean
ɛk.

ht: Three generations at the
ɔssroads bar before Baños:
here's your husband?' they
ınted to know.

ow right: The schoolteacher of
rhuac and his seven sons.

Above left: Birthplace of the Marañon, at the confluence of th rivers Nupe and Lauricocha.

Above: My girl hosts who enjoyed watching me struggle with my donkey cargo.

Left: I resisted the temptation to head back into the Huayhuash mountains and comforted myself with this picture at the birthplace of the Marañon.

Below left: The Marañon just after Quivilla.

Below: Wherever I went, the children were always the first to explore my things.

bove: Harvest at Chingas.

bove right: Traditional local ploughing
ith oxen.

ght: Vilma and Maximo.

low right: Lolita.

ttom right: Vertical farming in the
ndes.

low: Socos bridge – our Waterloo!

Above left: Rubbish piled high at Iquitos market.

Above: The mad old German on his raft in Saramarisa.

Left: The *Juliana*, the boat Werner Herzog used for 'Fitzcarraldo'.

Below left: Hammocks next to you, under you, over you – all in a suspended sardine can.

Below: Amazon travel can be very boring!

bove left: Brillo Nuevo: washing yucca in preparation for the big party on 28 July,
dependence Day.

bove right: The curaca's mother in the *maloca*. In the background the *manguare*, the talking
rums.

low left: Hernan, who helped to open the 'wall of hospitality'.

low right: Leonidas' house, where I stayed.

Above: The oxbow lake outside Brillo Nuevo.

Below: Leonidas let me use his dugout canoe to go exploring.

Above: Five year-old Bora children parading with wooden guns on Independence Day.

Below: The curaca's house next to the *maloca*. The only doubledecker one in the village!

calm down and accustom my mind to the possibility of having to return up the canyon the following morning.

By nightfall the temperature had dropped to a balmy warmth, and a gentle breeze swayed the nearby banana trees. Moon and starlight did not penetrate the depth of this canyon, and soon complete blackness surrounded me. I was sipping my tea when a man popped his head round the corner. The owner, I thought, and jumped up from the verandah on which I had made myself so at home.

He was not the owner, however, but a relative who was harvesting oranges and bananas across the river. I told him about my problems with the donkey and he promised to help me the next morning. It was late by now and we each bedded down under the two separate verandahs and went to sleep, not without a little suspicion on my part. I woke in the morning to find him already gone to take advantage of the cool dawn hour before the full heat of the morning sun, and my suspicions unfounded.

After breakfast I went to see the donkey, and my guilt from the day before returned anew when I saw that he had been leeched again by a bat. A crusty trail of blood led from his neck down his front leg, and, when I washed the wound, I found a neat, nasty hole on his spine. I scraped the blood clots from his fur and hoped the ordeal had not weakened him too much. Whatever happened that day, I would be easy on him and not walk for too long in the afternoon.

By 8 a.m., my friend had still not returned from across the river, and I decided to try the bridge one more time. I tried the bag-over-the-head trick, like at the horse races when an animal does not want to enter the starting box. I tied my shirt around the donkey's eyes in a blindfold and led him down to the bridge. He had obviously never been blindfolded before and swayed uncertainly from leg to leg. The path leading down to the river was quite steep and pebbly, and I had to let him see where he was going until we reached level ground. My heart sank when we approached the site of yesterday's confrontation: predictably the trick did not work. This time he would not even come within stepping distance of the first plank, and I knew it was a lost cause. I tugged at him for a short while, but it was no use, so I tied him to a nearby tree and left him there. I wanted him to know that I had not yet given up.

At last the fruitman returned from the plantations and we went down to the river with two of his donkeys, the idea being that if his would cross, then mine would follow. His donkeys, however, decided that they did not want to cross the bridge that morning. I tried hard not to lose hope and persuaded my friend to try one more time, this time with him pulling and me pushing. He tied a rope halter around my donkey's head and coaxed him up to the first plank, while I got ready behind him, hoping that he would not kick me. As soon as we began to move the donkey went into reverse mode, jamming his feet rigidly into the ground, his head lowered and neck stretched out in front, straining against the rope. I pushed myself up against his behind as hard as I could, our combined efforts tipped him off balance and he jerked ahead, propelled on to the swaying planks despite himself. Once on the bridge, it was not too difficult to make him cross, and we hurried him on quickly, praying that he would not rear up or panic, as disaster would be sure to follow. The fast-flowing Marañon below would have swept us all away if we had fallen off the bridge; and perhaps even worse was the possibility of one of the donkey's feet slipping off the planks and getting caught among the branches underneath: it did not bear thinking about, but fortunately we made it across without a hitch.

We laughed, exhausted from the nervous tension, while the donkey looked on, bemused. All that remained was to haul all the cargo across the bridge, and we were ready for another day. I bought some fresh bananas from my friend, and we headed off uphill through the plantation.

In spite of my earlier remorse, I found myself getting impatient with our slow progress and, before I knew it, I was flicking my stick again. As we turned a sharp bend, my stick caught the donkey's eye by mistake, and immediately he squeezed it shut, tears trickling silently down his furry face. How could I be such a bitch? I had not done it on purpose, but I should not have been swinging out with the stick in the first place. I patted and stroked him, cringing at the pain I knew I had caused.

'Please forgive me,' I pleaded softly and hugged his neck. The eye had not been damaged; but it was weeping and swollen shut and I put anti-biotic eye-drops in, in case of infection.

A little further on, a passing woman told me that I would not be able to get through on the path I was heading for, but I went on regardless. I should have listened because we soon came to a tight corner in the sandy rock, where the trail had almost completely fallen away into the gulley below. There was no way the donkey was going to get round there loaded; on the other hand, there was a chance he would get by without the bags, so I unloaded everything and then encouraged him to try the path. He hesitated briefly, sniffing the treacherous ground as if to see if it would hold his weight, but then he went for it. Stones and sand fell away under his hooves as he scrambled along the rockface, but he made it to the opposite ledge, and all that remained was for me to carry the bags over. It was a dangerous procedure, and every time I looked down I got a rush of nerves that felt like a claw clenching inside my chest. What was I doing? The easy day I had planned had turned into a gruelling circus of events: not only had I hit the donkey, but I had risked his life too. My ruthlessness amazed me, as did my undeserved luck.

The trail we continued on had obviously not been used for quite some time. Ancient cowpats lay along the way. There were no more dangerous ledges to sidle by, and, as we rounded yet another bend, we came across a waterfall pouring out from a ridge above. The water was falling from a ridge at least ten metres high, and it came down in a straight drop, forming a shallow, sandy pool before tailing off in a little stream. Lush grass grew thickly around this lovely spot and, without a second thought, I unloaded the donkey and let him graze. Given the state of the track, I was almost certain that no one was going to be passing this way, and I stripped off and stepped into the fabulously cold water. A passer-by would, in any case, have seen a very skinny, small woman, covered in scratched flea bites from the neck down, her face and arms burned black, in unfavourable contrast to the rest of her body, which was pallid white. We stayed for hours, both of us enjoying the rest, and I was relieved to see that the swelling on the donkey's eye was already subsiding.

That night I got lost further along the Marañon valley. After the waterfall the track disappeared altogether under prickly bushes and banana plantations. We fought our way through, though the saddle-bags were almost shredded in the process, but by the time we were back on dry *cerro*, my way was completely lost.

Far below, near the river, I could see a few houses in among the plantations, and I decided to head down to ask advice and stay the night there. On arrival, I found that all the dwellings were locked up and uninhabited. Rusty old tuna tins and fireplaces indicated that people did spend time here, but the houses were very small and plain and did not feel like homes. I made my way through a lime and orange grove and came upon a small set of buildings almost totally obscured by a couple of enormous trees. There was even a patch of grass and a pond, so I decided to stay and wait for someone to turn up. I secured the donkey to a tree and went off to explore the surrounding fields.

There were all kinds of strange fruit growing here, only some of which I recognized. There were lemon, lime and orange trees in full fruit, banana trees with their bulbous purple flowers arching out from the crowns, some spindly root plants that turned out to be peanuts, and a delicate creeping vine hung with wrinkly yellow fruit the size of tennis balls. I cut one open to see what it could be, and recognized it as a passion-fruit. Unfortunately, they were not yet ripe, and I went in search of a juicy orange. All the ripe ones were far too high for me to reach and I had to make do with ones already on the ground. I found one that seemed undamaged and peeled it eagerly; it tasted odd though, bitter, and, on closer inspection, I could see little white worms wriggling around at the centre. All these wonderful fruits and I couldn't get at any of them. Back at the house, I realized that the enormous trees that shaded the courtyard were festooned with giant avocados. I tugged at the branches to make one drop, but alas, the avocados were not yet ripe either, and I had to content myself with a few refreshing limes.

As night came on, I could hear whistles and shouts from the trail above. A large group of people seemed to be approaching, and I disposed of the evidence of my fruit picking. Ten curious boys, between the ages of eight and fifteen, made me the object of their scrutiny and explained that these plantations were the property of the villagers of San Buenaventura, high up on the facing mountain. Each weekend the men and boys came down to tend the plantations, pick selected fruit to ripen in the houses, and gather up stores to be sold in the mountains above. I was lucky to be here at this particular time; if it had been the middle of the week, no one would have come, and I would have had to find my own way out. The boys' fathers arrived soon after, each one heading for his own sheds. The man who came to find me his unexpected guest was high on distilled alcohol and his mouth dribbled green with coca. He accepted my presence without much concern, offering me a swig from his hip flask.

'What you need is a bed fellow,' he slurred, to the delight of the listening boys. 'You European women are very free about sex aren't you? You do all kinds of things don't you?'

He was only talking to himself, though, and soon staggered off with his machete, mumbling something about getting to work. All through the night, he went back and forth, hauling in bananas and getting drunker and drunker. His three sons huddled together under one blanket on a ledge under the porch, while I slept on the ground opposite. When I awoke in the morning, the father was snoring loudly on the ledge, and the boys had all gone.

The father woke and farted, accepted some tea I offered and promised to get one of the boys to show me the trail up to the village. He even made me a present of a large, ripe avocado, which I looked forward to eating for lunch. That was a long time coming: the climb up from the river bed took four exhausting hours; the higher we got, the steeper the trail. We walked into San Buenaventura at a snail's pace, my legs aching from hip to foot, my joints jellied, all feeling numbed. The avocado made luxurious eating after that: I savoured every mouthful, the soft green ripeness made perfect with a light dusting of salt.

The donkey and I were again at peace with each other, and I was happy to find our trail on the map. One more day of walking, and we would reach Huacrachuco and a well-deserved rest, after almost a month of walking.

Huacrachuco lay in a cusp at the top of a beautiful, fecund valley, buzzing with the work of harvest time. Golden wheat fields swayed in the wind, and the paths in the villages were alive with contented animals sunning themselves on the warm earth. In the fields where the cereals had already been cut down, were neat circles on the ground, where pairs of mules or oxen were made to walk in endless rounds, freeing seeds from the chaff as their hooves pounded the dry crop underfoot. Great sheets were laid out in front of almost every home, covered in drying corn kernels or other seed, and freshly slaughtered meat hung on wire washing lines drying to jerky for the winter months.

It was hard to imagine any violence or bloodshed taking place in this lovely spot, but I was nevertheless tense as I descended into Huacrachuco itself. As we wound our way down steep dirt tracks past the first houses, I was pushed off the path by a stampede of galloping horsemen. They were Indian *campesinos* dressed in their best Sunday suits and they were completely drunk, swinging in their saddles uncertainly and tugging their horses this way and that. The animals knew their way home, even if their riders did not, and they came thundering up the track heading to the villages in the valley beyond. Their wives came shuffling along behind, only marginally less drunk, but we all tut-tutted at the trail of dust their husbands had raised, which was just settling on our clothes.

I made enquiries for a place to stay and got chatting to a young woman who led me to the town's hostel. The house was locked up, however, and she explained that the owner was probably at the fiesta. She was going herself, and invited me to leave my things and the donkey at her house, and join her for the party. This I did, and was soon sitting around a long wooden table with a beer in one hand and a freshly roasted kebab in the other.

The afternoon progressed and the townspeople fell into loud discussions about where the *gringa* should stay. Not the hostel, they all agreed, a dirty hovel, full of men and military, and no place for a woman alone.

It was at this point that Don Angel came into the conversation. He was a middle-aged man with a sad, red face and receding hairline, seeming out of place among the others – he was older and more serious for one thing – but there was something else about him that was unusual. He was dressed in a neat woollen cardigan and pressed grey flannel trousers that made him look more like a European businessman than a Peruvian farmer. He was very light-skinned too, and his manner was quiet, almost shy; there was definitely something of the retired bank manager about him, and an urbanity that implied a city education and worldly knowledge rather than remote mountain life.

He suggested that I should be his guest and I was very pleased

120

to accept. I said goodbye to the friendly girl who had brought me here, and Don Angel commissioned a young man to help fetch my cargo and the donkey.

His house was very grand; a mansion even. A small wooden door led through a wall bordering the street and into a large paved courtyard. The main house was built in traditional colonial style, with three large columns supporting a spacious verandah, while smaller buildings making up the kitchen and stable area opposite closed off the open space.

It transpired that Don Angel lived here alone, but there were a number of dependants and destitutes under his protection who lived in the out-buildings around the main house. There was a *campesino* couple who were mainly responsible for the daily chores of the house and fields, helped by their children; and there was also a mother and her deaf-and-dumb teenage son, who had been abandoned by the father to starve when they sought Don Angel's help. They had been there for a couple of months, doing odd jobs in return for food and shelter.

Inside was a tiled bathroom with a ceramic flush-toilet and a working shower, which Don Angel took particular pride in showing me. In my room a bed had been freshly made up and a battery-operated radio stood by its side. Don Angel was the perfect host, his name describing him exactly, and, without engaging me in long questioning conversation, he left me to myself to have a shower and a rest. He would return to the fiesta and be back in time for supper when we could talk at leisure. In the freedom of the enclosed courtyard, I rested without the fear of prying eyes; and, even better, I had slipped into town without meeting a single soldier, and, should any appear, I was the personal guest of a highly respected member of the community, and beyond suspicion.

At dinner, Don Angel brought out a bottle of home-made wine to go with our meal, candles flickered between the dishes, and there was a distinctly festive atmosphere to the evening. Don Angel was an avid listener to long-wave radio, and was thrilled to be able to talk about subjects few of his aquaintances had an opinion on. What did I think of the Salman Rushdie affair? he wanted to know. He knew about the latest international news, but was also bursting to share his literary and musical interests. He had been living by himself for some years now and was clearly very lonely. He had never married, and his mother, brothers and sisters had all left Huacrachuco to live in other valleys or on the coast. His mother had not been up for at least two years; she was old now, and the journey from Lima was an expensive, four-day marathon by bus and truck along dreadful dirt roads. Don Angel had not been able to face the journey for the past year either, and felt starved both of his mother's company and the cosmopolitan delights of Lima. No postal service reached as far as here, and the radio was his only solace. He did not dwell on the sad facts of his life, however, being much too keen to talk about world events, and it was a pleasure to join him in this.

I spent the following day resting and washing my filthy clothes, and more dinner-table conversations with Don Angel followed. Why didn't I stay a couple of days? he asked. I was tempted but June approached, and I felt that if I stayed longer, my departure would be harder. It was better to leave now.

Promising to write to his mother's address in Lima, and clutching a precious present of tinned peaches, I set off down the valley, accompanied by Don Angel, past the army base busy with morning parades, to the edge of town. Huacrachuco had long been free of terrorist trouble and the army had settled back into the peaceful routine of a resident unit.

As I looked back from time to time, I could still see the lonely figure of Don Angel waving me goodbye. If only the post reached this far; I would have loved to send him some books and long letters. Instead I would have to write to his mother and one day, perhaps, he would make the journey to Lima and find his post awaiting him.

Don't Cry *Gringita*!

From Huacrachuco, it was a steady walk downhill to where towering dry *cerros* cut the valley dead and the rio Huacrachuco squeezed through a tight crease, heading for the Marañon, three kilometres due west. The valley sloped at a gentle angle, so walking was comfortable, and for most of the way we were able to use the dirt road, for which our feet were grateful. Before turning west, the river is joined by another, and at the bridge crossing this confluence, there is a roadside bar and the homestead of Señora Lolita.

Don Angel had recommended that I stay with her, and I had permission to use his name to vouch for me when asking for her hospitality. He had given me a letter of recommendation for a homestead further down the road as well, so for the next few days my shelter was assured. In the larger towns and villages it was always better to have a contact rather than to arouse too much attention by asking around in public, something I wanted to avoid on this side of the Marañon.

By the time I reached *el puente* (the bridge) in the late afternoon, we had walked about twenty-five kilometres and my legs had that rubbery feeling again. For the last hour, the valley had become tighter and tighter, with nothing but grey sand and flaky mud banks, the baked dirt road hard against the bones of my tired feet. It seemed impossible that there could be any living beings resident down here, and I had begun to doubt my path. There was no other to be seen, but it just did not feel right.

Eventually, though, coarse-leafed sugar-cane and bamboo announced cultivated land and the probability of people. The two rivers coming together at this point had created a triangular corner in the valley where fruit plantations and even grazing fields thrived. Walling it in, the barren *cerro* soared up towards the sky, at its base this oasis of water and greenery, home to

123

Señora Lolita, her daughter, and the few others who tended their fruit in the dry recesses of the triangle.

It was as remote a place as any mountain village I had visited. An eerie wind blew dust into eye-burning spirals around the few adobe houses which lay spread out before the bridge, and a large herd of goats sat on the earth, ears twitching at the flies. A young girl was seated on a wooden bench, a baby at her feet. She seemed to be the only person about, so I explained where I had come from and asked for Señora Lolita.

She wasn't here at the moment, the girl explained, but she was her daughter, and accepted me on her behalf. The girl was about eighteen, with large brown eyes that sparkled with intelligence. She went indoors to warm up some soup for me, and I joined her in the cool darkness of the kitchen hut. There was a long wooden table, where truckers and their passengers came to eat and rest before continuing on the road that loops up into the next mountain valley. Piles of old tin plates were stacked at one end of the table, and flies were busy on them, fighting for the dregs of soup and gristle.

'Don't you get lonely here?' I asked the girl.

To me it seemed a frightening and empty place – a dead end, a trap. In the mountains you still had a view, but down here there was nothing to see beyond the immediate vicinity. Strangers in trucks came by quite regularly, it was true; but they were just passing and once the sound of their engines had gone, nothing but lonely silence, the noise of the wind and the animals remained again, serving only to highlight the lack of people and companionship.

'Oh yes,' she said, 'it gets very lonely. No one to talk to except the occasional trucker, and lots of hours sitting on the bench doing nothing.'

Her father had left a few years before, gone to work in the jungle. He was not coming back. They were sure of that.

There was no grass for the donkey near the house, so Nellie gave me directions for the nearest field, where she said I would probably find her mother too, watching over their two bulls and gathering kitchen herbs. The grass that grew down here was tough and chewy, barely covering the ground; but it was precious nevertheless, and was walled in to protect it from the greedy goats. Tangles of cactus bushes blocked the entrance and, as I

124

began tugging it away, I spotted a barefoot woman, sitting cross-legged on the ground, winding fresh wool on to her wooden spool. She looked like a young girl herself, with thick, shiny black hair. As soon as she saw me, she stood up and came strolling gracefully over. She smiled, although she was obviously a little surprised, and I answered her questioning look with my explanation, which she accepted without further demur.

'Don Angel is a good man,' she said, and we agreed that he was.

She gathered up her wool and suggested that, while she herded the bulls back home, I go and cut down some sugar-cane. I had no idea how to tell which cane was ready for cutting, but was too embarrassed to admit this and went off with the machete she had given me.

It felt good to be in this female household, among strong women living their lives independently. They had had no choice, of course, after Lolita's husband abandoned her. She had turned her hand to business, making money from the travellers, as well as getting her produce to distant markets by making special deals with the truck drivers. Mother and daughter had an unusual self-assurance about them, exuding the strength of the self-reliant, and, when some male field hands came along for supper, it was clear who was boss: and it was not the men.

I was too tired to stay awake long, and gratefully accepted a wooden bed to sleep on. Just before I bedded down, Nellie came in and asked me if I would like a stick to protect me in the darkness, thinking I might be scared alone in the dark.

In the morning Lolita helped me rope up the cargo; like so many men before her, she laughed at me for still not being able to remember the knots. For me, her name clashed ridiculously with her person and age, but she was one of the most beautiful women I met in Peru. She must have been at least forty years old, but she had the face and body of a younger woman – fit and strong – and in spite of her bare feet and worn-out clothes, it was this youthful air and her warm smile that made the most memorable impression.

A few days later I found out from another host that Nellie's child was the result of a rape by bandits. Lolita had been away, selling fruit, and her daughter had been alone when the men turned up one night. They took her in turn and left her for dead, to be found by her mother days later. My sense of fear down there had not been unreasonable after all, my dark visions had already been realized. Instead of bitterness, however, there was strength, and when I had asked Nellie how she coped with the baby, she had told me she loved her very much and shrugged her shoulders at the difficulties of being a single mother. I remembered the warmth of the two women's smiles, their kindness and openness, and my admiration for their strength grew greater still.

The climb from the bridge took four, long hours. Each step uphill was a battle but I now knew how to pace myself and the donkey and I took hourly rests. Nellie had stuffed my rucksack with ripe passion fruit, and at each stop I cut open a couple, sucking cool juice out of their sun-toughened skins. The very first taste always refreshed me, keeping me going for the next hour. The fruit was sweet, but it seemed there was a shot of lemon in each one, enough to wake up tired senses and quench my never-ending thirst.

By the time I reached a level path at 3300 metres, I had eaten ten of these lovely fruit, and my stomach was awash with acid and I knew it would dog me later. No matter! I was used to that too by now. The functioning, or lack of it, of various parts of my body no longer impinged on my experience. Every week that passed I felt more and more free of physical needs and material comforts such as beds or washing.

What mattered to me was the time with my many hosts, eating fresh fruit, and relishing the flavours, sights, sounds, and smells of the mountains. I was experiencing a sense of peace, of contentment I had never felt before. How to describe the happiness of fulfilment? Even the familiarity of daily chores was a pleasure I valued, the routine bolstering my confidence that I was in control.

But, above all else, my dream was coming true. I had not known how the journey was going to turn out, or really pictured how my days were going to be, but, as the story unfurled, I found I loved it. I was not nearly good enough at coping with the difficult moments yet, still losing my temper much too easily, but I did detect some change in myself; slowly, I was beginning to be able to accept defeat without taking it as a personal affront:

126

whether it was a bridge we could not cross, a supper we could not have, or simply a change of plan. To some, these changes might seem trivial, but for me it was important, a way of learning how to conserve and direct my nervous energies to things that mattered.

Huancaspata was much smaller than Huacrachuco, a village rather than a town, even though it did have a paved main square and a large church. On the way in, I passed a cemetery crowded with elaborate marble headstones and remembered Don Angel mentioning that there was an order of missionary sisters here. The *campesinos* keep their graveyards quite a distance from their homes, and this was the first cemetery I had seen in a rural area. Coming up to the main square I passed the mission building, which was built of bricks and mortar, with iron-grilled glass windows and a metal door. Adjoining buildings, and even the church itself, were made of adobe.

I have always wondered why most missionaries live in so much more comfort than their flock. I was to meet various missionaries on my journey, all of whom, without exception, lived in far greater comfort than their congregation. Having said that, the mothers of Huancaspata were in very close contact with the local people, more so than any other order I saw. They are a Peruvian order and, although most of the women came from the coastal cities, they had all grown up with a knowledge of the land and the people, and found it easier.

I had a letter from Don Angel addressed to Señora Sarah. Enquiries revealed that her house was on the main square. As I approached, I saw the woman I thought I was looking for was knitting in the doorway. We engaged in a lengthy conversation, during which she did not open the letter. I thought that was strange, but even stranger, she was not at all keen on having me to stay, which seemed very odd indeed considering my recommendation from Don Angel and his standing. She avoided my eyes and made excuses, and I began to wonder where else I could stay. But there was no need to rush, so I sat in silence, letting her size me up and pretending to be unconcerned. A little girl came over to see the stranger, and, while I affected not to notice, she read Don Angel's letter out aloud. So that was it, the poor woman had been too embarrassed to admit she could not read. The girl was sent over to tell me to bring the donkey into their yard, and over a cup of tea I finally found out the real reason for the problem.

This lady was not Señora Sarah, but her middle-aged daughter. The mother had been bed-ridden for years and was now senile. She had been a great friend of Don Angel's mother in her youth, but now she could not even recognize her own daughter, let alone act as host to strangers. Unaware, Don Angel had quite unintentionally caused considerable distress by sending me here. In the light of this, it was a great act of trust as well as kindness, for Señora Sarah's daughter to invite me into her home. I tried to lighten her sense of embarrassment and awkwardness by telling her about my grandmother, who had also gone senile. We shared sad tales about the disintegration of family relationships when the mind is destroyed, and the strain of caring for someone like her mother.

I was taken to meet Señora Sarah, who was kept in another house, at the other end of town. The sight of her was pitiful. Her skin hung limply on her, long wisps of grey hair dangled to her slumped shoulders, framing a wizened face that seemed to collapse in where the flesh had shrivelled over her toothless gums. She sat hunched in bed, chewing her gums and staring into space. A dead chicken lay on the floorboards, next to the bed, and her daughter tried to get an explanation. *Que passa con este pollito?* (What happened to the chicken?) she shouted to her mother. The old woman shook her head, agitated by the shouting. Her daughter insisted on an answer, but all she could find out was that it had died in the morning. *Este señorita es una amiga de Don Angel!* (The young lady is a friend of Don Angel) the daughter boomed, and for the first time the old lady focused on me. *Buenos dias muchacho* (Good morning young man), she said, kneading her boney hands. I smiled at her and we left the room. Outside, her daughter explained to me that her mother could walk perfectly well when she wanted to, and that she had a dreadful habit of strangling the chickens when no one was looking. The old crone always pretended she had no idea how it happened. Her daughter was worn out by it, engaged in an on-going battle rather than just caring for an invalid. She found solace in religion, and when I expressed interest in seeing the

128

interior of the church, she was delighted to take me to her friend, the Mother Superior.

I felt a bit of a fraud. My interest was purely architectural, and I dreaded being asked about my faith. My upbringing had made me adept at evading commitment both to outright truth and lies, and I skirted the issue diplomatically. Mother Frederica was a stocky, no-nonsense woman with a big smile and sharp eyes. She took my hand in a firm handshake when we met, and soon I was being marched around her church. The interior was very plain and empty. There were no pews – removed to make room for dancing, Mother Frederica explained; a very good reason, I thought. The only colour came from the main altar, which was made of wood and painted in garishly bright blue and white, with a kitschy, rosy-cheeked madonna and child at its centre.

We did not stay long, but Mother Frederica invited me for tea at the convent. She was intrigued to find out more about me, and I was happy to exchange stories for the treat of home-made cake and biscuits. The convent had been here about twelve years, and there were eight resident *madres*. They lived off the land, digging their fields and slaughtering their animals, just like everyone else. It so happened that their annual pig had just been slaughtered and, to my squeamish dismay, the Mother Superior proudly presented me with a fresh black pudding. This was not how I had imagined a religious order, and I could not help but be impressed with the down-to-earth style of these women. We enjoyed each other's company in spite of our differences, and, as I left, the Mother Superior handed me an enormous bag of freshly baked bread, apples, and bananas.

'Perhaps we will see each other soon,' she said. 'I am driving an injured man to the nearest hospital on the coast in a few days' time, so I will probably pass you on the road.'

She was going to spend one night in Tayabamba, in the regional episcopal residence, and no sooner had she said this than she suggested she radio ahead, to ask her friend the bishop to put me up. Could this good luck last me the rest of my journey?

Perhaps at this point I should make a confession: while I was in Lima I neglected to buy all the maps I needed for the journey. It seems an impossible thing for me to have done, but I simply did not get round to it, and once I was in Huaraz I could not countenance the idea of returning to Lima just to buy maps.

129

Those I had took me as far as the Huacrachuco area, but from there on – other than a general map of Peru – I was mapless and completely dependent on local advice. I had persuaded myself that somehow I would get by when the time came; I was, after all, following a very large river.

I discussed my options with the practical Mother Frederica. If I were to travel onwards by rivercraft from Chagual, I needed to sell the donkey before I got there as no one was likely to want a donkey where pasture was sparse. The places to sell him would be in the green highland valleys, before I descended to the dusty canyon of the Marañon itself. On the other hand, what if there were no boats? Mother Frederica knew nothing of the boats belonging to the mines, and doubted their existence. I wanted time to think, but in the meantime, I needed to walk from Huancaspata to Tayabamba without a map. Mother Frederica had walked the route once herself, and said it could be done in a day. She gave me directions as well as her memory allowed, but she was worried, and so was I, because the path led across empty *puna* and there was a considerable risk of getting lost. More *puna*. How I hated the idea of being alone up there again. The road made so many loops around the mountainsides, though, that it would have doubled the distance: it was foolish not to take the shortcut . . .

'Go left where the paths cross and then follow the road for a while, until you reach a small stream and *quebrada* (anything from a gulley to a large valley), then follow that across the mountains.' That's what Mother Frederica had said, but after walking around in circles on the *puna*, I found that I had walked along the road in the wrong direction and was nearly back in Huancaspata.

It was now early afternoon, and there was no chance of making it to Tayabamba today. I decided to head on rather than return, and tried once more to find the blasted *quebrada* I was supposed to follow. I found it in the late afternoon, exhausted and fed up, after having walked up and down every little side stream I had passed along the road, each little track giving me the wrong clue, until finally I had found a well-worn path leading off along a sizeable river, and knew that this must be it. Two shepherds, taking their sheep home for the night, confirmed that I had found

130

the right path. It was too late to carry on now, though, and I prepared to camp out for the night.

The temperature dropped quickly as the sun disappeared behind the mountains, and I set some packet asparagus soup cooking and put the tent up, deciding not to bother with the groundsheet and inner tent as it looked unlikely to rain. I settled to my hot soup and looked forward to Don Angel's tinned peaches for afters. The side valley I had turned into was narrow, with high rockfaces jutting up on either side and sheltering it from the cold winds of the *puna* beyond and the mountaintops above. Because of the river, the grass here grew high and the ground was soft with porous moss. I sat among the soft-tailed grass, and listened to the sound of the donkey eating and the river's movement, my irritation dissipating. I slept.

I was woken at 5 a.m. by rain hammering the nylon. Although I was not yet wet myself, the bottom of my sleeping-bag was already soaked and everything else was wet on the sides facing the opening between the ground and the tent. That would teach me: next time I would put the whole tent up. I peered out to see if the donkey was still there, and then retreated into the sanctuary of my warm sleeping-bag for another hour.

The hour slipped by very quickly and I could no longer postpone getting up and putting on my cold, clammy clothes. The rain eased off a bit. I finished off the peaches, and loaded up the cargo. The donkey was soaked to his skin, his fur parted into streaky clumps by the water running down his body, and his ears bedraggled. I knew he was reared to withstand this weather, but I still could not help worrying that he might catch cold, and we got moving as soon as possible.

As we headed uphill, picking our way through boulders, the gulley panned out into a wider expanse, rimmed at the top by grey slabs of granite sticking out from beneath a thin layer of snow. We proceeded slowly, away from the river, the air still and silent. I had come from the deadening heat of Lolita's canyon, to the rain and greenery of Huancaspata and, now only forty-eight hours later, to snow settling on the *puna* I traversed. I walked through the falling snow in nothing but a shirt, my body steaming with the heat of exertion, and my senses captivated by the cold air on my face, the sounds of our feet scrunching in the silence of our mountain world, and the thin altitude cutting into my lungs. It was a brief moment of complete solitude that will always stay with me.

Beyond the pass, we skirted a few small lakes and some round shepherds' huts along the way. There were a number of dips and ledges to traverse before the final pass into the next valley, but nothing too strenuous and I encouraged the donkey to walk at a brisk pace. Occasionally he tripped on the small rocks in our path, but he always caught himself well enough, and I let him pick his own way, for once controlling my tyrannical stick. We rounded the last ledge, and the view opened up on to a wide patchwork of farmland and villages far below. Once more the horizon stretched far into the distance, and I could see that in the lower reaches of the Tayabamba valley it was a sunny day. My goal was in sight, when the donkey suddenly refused to walk any further. We were on the level ground of the road by now, and had only been walking for about three hours, so there seemed no reason at all for this sudden strike. It soon became obvious, though, that he had hurt his right foreleg, perhaps during one of the stumbles earlier on. He was clearly limping, and after a few forced paces he absolutely refused to move. No amount of shouting, hitting, or tugging made an impression, and then it began to rain again. If only I could persuade him to walk, even if only slowly. We were so close to our destination, no more than two hours away, and all downhill too.

I decided to take a gentle approach, and let him rest for an hour. I had no wish to make him walk if it was painful for him, but, on the other hand, we could not stay here all day. The nearest village was only about 500 metres away: surely he could make it that far. After an hour of standing in the rain the donkey was immovable still, only swaying on his feet as if his hooves were glued to the ground when I tried to lead him on a halter. I inspected his leg again: there was no visible swelling and I decided that the damage to his leg, even if painful, was certainly not serious. How to explain to a donkey that if he would only walk a few steps, he could then rest for the whole day? The frustration of the day before lost me my temper, and I began to shout abuse loudly at my poor friend.

A battle of wills was on: I knew by now that I could not match the donkey's strength, but I realized that if I tied a rope around one foot, I had enough body weight to make him lift his hoof and shift one step. The first few steps on level ground were easy to accomplish, but then the path went steeply downhill, and here the donkey really threw his whole weight against me, somehow managing to angle his body in such a way that even standing on three legs he did not move forward. The leg attached to my rope stuck out like that of a Prussian soldier, and we heaved and grunted at each other. I knew all this was probably causing much more pain than the donkey had been feeling in the first place, but I just could not bear to spend the rest of the day there. I wanted to get him the few hundred metres to the nearest village, leave him with someone, and return for him the following day. It was only a matter of a few minutes. But the donkey knew nothing about all this: he was not moving, and he groaned miserably. He must have been in pain to make a noise at all, and my anger and frustration was mixed with a great deal of fear and panic that something was badly wrong with him.

It took me an hour to make him move twenty metres and I wondered if this dreadful day would ever end. I cried with exhaustion and nerves, heaving at the rope, and coaxing him further.

In the middle of all this, an old man came shuffling by in the rain, and, seeing the tears on my face he shook his head and said, 'No llora gringita!' – 'don't cry little foreigner' – and carried on his way, never looking back at a spectacle he had surely never seen before, nor would again. I hated him for not offering to help me. I promised myself that this was the last time I would fight with the donkey.

Trucking with Mother Frederica

I returned to collect the donkey from the man who had agreed to keep him for the night and all was well. The foreleg seemed to be back to normal and it was almost as if nothing had ever happened; I could hardly believe the trouble we had been through the day before. I gave Señor Izquierda a kilogram of rice and some fruit juice for his favour, and set off to retrace my steps to Tayabamba and my latest refuge – the regional episcopal residence.

Tayabamba lay on an incline, huddled around the main square and its large church, with narrow streets leading steeply to the houses and local stores. The square itself was lined with hardware and grocery shops, the local police station, and the municipal offices. At its centre was a flagpole surrounded by small lawns intersected by concrete paths fanning in the points of a star from the pole. There were a couple of bushes too, pruned into giant ducks and even helicopters (a peculiar design favoured all over Peru).

As the donkey and I arrived, we passed staring storeholders and housewives: this small town had seen *gringos* before, mainly visiting missionaries and geographic researchers, but I was still an odd sight, leading my donkey unaided by an *arriero*.

I led the donkey into the bishop's concrete yard, and secured him outside a large, domed baking oven. The place was teeming with about a hundred catechists who were attending a weekend training session, and some local women were busily preparing bread rolls for everyone, bustling past me in a proprietorial swirl of skirts and screwing up their noses at the sight of a donkey in the hallowed heart of the residence. Later, to my embarrassment, he fouled the yard with a number of droppings, and I swept them away in front of a disdainful audience.

Mother Frederica had told me that the bishop was *un negrito*;

but I thought he looked more Malaysian or even Polynesian. He was young for his job, not more than thirty-five, and he had welcomed me the day before with a warm meal and comforting words when I told him about my troubles with the donkey. He had expected me a day earlier, of course, and when I told him about my night in the *quebrada* he shook his head in sympathy: it had happened to him recently, as he had only been here a couple of months and still knew little of the surrounding area.

In spite of the catechists, I was given a whole room to myself and told I could stay as long as I liked. Once more I had a real bed to sleep in and the use of a shower and toilet. I was very grateful, although, as before in Huancaspata, I felt a little awkward accepting the hospitality of people whose faith I had no part in; but the bishop was a very practical and open-minded man, and I am sure that my faith – or the lack of it – made no difference to him. An American missionary called Father Thomas was also staying at the residence. He lived on the coast in the city of Chimbote, but had come up to help with the instruction of the catechists. He was a lean and lanky man, with ginger hair and an exuberant beard. The first time I set eyes on him he was wearing a local woollen poncho and a large stetson, the picture of an American *gringo*; but, in spite of his looks, he was a quiet, shy man, and I enjoyed speaking English for the first time since I had left Huaraz.

The following day was a Sunday, and I went to listen to him give the sermon in place of the bishop. The church was filled with *campesino* Indians and townspeople. Father Thomas began, his shyness transformed: he spoke firmly to the congregation about the country's economic hardship and the terrible suffering of the people. I wondered how the people viewed the foreign priest and his sermon, and whether there was any resentment, either of him or his message. I could not detect any.

Outside an army marching band was playing so loudly over the speakers in the square, that the sermon could hardly be heard at times; Sunday is the day for every Peruvian town, however small or insignificant, to hold a parade on the main square. Local dignitaries hoist the national flag to the sound of brass music and clapping, and people like the mayor or the police chief make political speeches to the assembled crowd. Up here, in the remote and embattled Andes, attending these functions was an important way of showing public support for the government and state forces, the attendance at mass – or the concentration during the sermon – suffering as a consequence, especially in this valley, where there was a resident army unit.

I had, meanwhile, decided that the recent battle with the donkey had been the last, and that Tayabamba was as good a place as any to sell him. I was worried that his gammy leg might prejudice a future chance to sell him and, as he was by now extremely fit and well-fed, his various wounds healed up, now was the time. I would be sorry to let him go, but I knew that his life from now on would be easier: the daily long distances replaced by trips carrying loads from surrounding fields, or an occasional person.

I let it be known around the shops and the crowds on the main square that I was looking to sell my donkey, and went to await the offers on the steps of the residence. I was sure there would be plenty because the donkey had been admired so often during the journey, and I knew that he was a prize animal. Many a time a *campesino* had opened the donkey's mouth to check his age by the teeth (when the hollow dips on the tops of his incisors are worn flat, you know the animal is old), and confidently judged him to be about six years old – the ideal age for a working donkey.

One man came to have a look and examined the donkey from head to foot.

'He's got a tumour on his neck,' he said, shaking his head ponderously.

'That's ridiculous!' I cried, shocked at the suggestion. Obviously the man was trying to rubbish the animal so that I would drop my price, but I could not help taking it personally, when it was just business.

Two more men came to view, one a *campesino* and the other rather grand, dressed in a leather coat. His face and manner, however, showed him to be a hard-nosed trader, his air professional and his expression sharp as knives. I felt sorry for the *campesino*, who seemed to lose his nerve in the company of the other man. He hovered around the donkey, nodding to every comment the trader made as he ran his hands along the animal's back and hind legs.

'He's a good strong donkey,' I chipped in cheerily, and the

men nodded and carried on examining the animal without talking to me.

'How much do you want then?' said Señor Salazar, the trader. I explained all the virtues of the donkey, that he was *tierno*, young; that he was bred for high altitudes and had shown incredible strength in walking all the way from the department of Ancash from where, everyone knows, the best donkeys come; and, of course, there were also the fine ropes, saddle-bags and wooden bridge to be bought. Taking all this into consideration, I felt 400,000 Intis was a fair price. The two men shook their heads in mock horror, and Señor Salazar told me, straight up, there was no way I would get that kind of money.

'Fine,' I said, 'for you I'll make it 300,000 Intis, which is an enormous reduction but, as you know, I'm in a hurry to sell.'

'No,' he said, he could not see how he could pay more than 200,000 Intis.

He was doing me down outrageously. I had asked many people from Huacrachuco onwards, how much donkeys went for in this region, and 300,000 Intis was a good price. What Señor Salazar did not realize, was that Ancash prices were much cheaper, so, although he thought he was doing me over, he was actually offering me almost three times the amount I had paid. What a game! I feigned disappointment and we did the deal. Inflation considered, I was probably not making a profit at all, but the haggling was more than enough compensation.

Now, though, came the time to say goodbye to the donkey and I was sorry to see a stranger leading him off down the road.

'You will treat the donkey well, won't you?' I asked hopefully.

'Yes, yes, he'll be all right with me,' said Salazar. 'You can come and visit him any time you like,' he continued, and I felt embarrassed to be so girly.

But the donkey had been my best friend and I had come to love him dearly. He had stood up heroically to my bullying and shouting, and I hoped he had forgiven me. Our relationship had a strange night-and-day duality: in the day it was a battle of wills which ensued as the challenges of that day emerged; but at night, once camp had been set up, I would sit on the ground drinking my tea, and the donkey's nose would come nuzzling over my shoulder, and I felt then that we were friends. As we reached

Señor Salazar's house, I patted the donkey on the neck one last time and walked away without looking back. I hate goodbyes.

By now I had given away almost all my supplies of food along the way. The donkey, saddle-bags, and the rest of the paraphernalia were gone, and all that remained was the gear in my rucksack. Chagual, on the banks of the Marañon, was about three days' walk away; but with the donkey gone, carrying on alone seemed a dismal prospect. I knew that Mother Frederica would be arriving in Tayabamba on Sunday night to continue the four-day drive to the coast the following morning, and I decided to hitch a lift with her, if she had no objections, thus making it only a six-hour drive as far as the river.

Mother Frederica duly arrived, and when I enquired about a lift she generously agreed. I would have to share the boot with her injured patient and all the supplies, but that hardly mattered to me.

My journey had suddenly and subtly changed and I felt a little disorientated. I had been walking alone for almost two months. I had, of course, met people along the way, and even stayed a while in places; but in principle I was alone and made my own way. Now I was suddenly back in 'civilization', surrounded by people at all times, and my movements and mealtimes linked inextricably to the needs and habits of others.

My vision of the next phase of my journey was blurred both by this development and by not knowing what I would find in Chagual. If there were no boats, what then? I had planned on getting as far as Balsas before I ended the trek and went to rest in Cajamarca; alternatively, though, I could head straight on to Cajamarca from Chagual, and then continue on from Balsas. It would mean having to walk for at least another week before reaching trucks setting out for Bagua and the Amazon jungle, but perhaps it would make for a more interesting journey: instead of enduring the 100-kilometre stretch of barren canyon between Chagual and Balsas, I would witness the gradual change of landscape as the Marañon enters the humid jungle. I would just have to wait and see.

We set off at five in the morning while it was still dark. Father Thomas had managed to cadge a lift as well, and we were now five people squeezed into a Toyota station wagon: Mother Frederica, another nun, Father Thomas, the injured *campesino* and myself. We also shared the car with two large petrol cannisters, piles of bags and rucksacks, provisions, and spare parts for the van; the *campesino* and I were therefore packed in the back, just under the roof, almost horizontal on a mattress.

The poor man had been shot in the face by bandits, who had held him up on the way back from working in the coca plantations. He had been away from his village a full year, and was bringing back all his savings, and luxuries like a cassette recorder, batteries, and expensive perfume for his wife and daughters. He told me the story of the hold-up and how he had been the only one injured in the group of five who had been with him. He had the air of an unlucky man about him. Why did he go? I asked. He explained that as an agricultural labourer in the mountains he could earn 3000 Intis a day; the *narcos* paid 7000 Intis.

The injury had happened almost two months ago, and the right side of his face was still distorted by the swelling where countless pieces of shrapnel had produced infected wounds. His right eye was covered in a makeshift bandage, which would have to be removed once he was in the hospital. The poor man had been waiting all this time for a free lift to the nearest hospital, four days' drive away if nothing went wrong. The fare for the journey would have been about 300,000 Intis, an astronomical sum for this man, and it was therefore his good fortune that Mother Frederica was making her annual journey for medical supplies to Trujillo. He would lose his eye from the long infection, but at least his wounds were going to get treated and would heal eventually. His only worry was that the other eye might pack up under the strain. His stoicism was remarkable. It needed to be: he had no choice but to leave for the coca fields, and running the gauntlet of an encounter with bandits, who haunt all paths leading back home, was also inevitable. He would go again, he told me. There was nothing else for him to do.

Up in front, Mother Frederica was manoeuvring us along the dirt road, swerving expertly around countless hairpin bends and driving at speeds that made me quite breathless. Her black habit fluttered out of the open window, her sturdy arms spinning the steering wheel effortlessly, and all the while she laughed and talked with the other two on the front seat. *'Todo bien?'* (Every-thing okay?) she would turn to ask us occasionally, looking away from the road for just a fraction longer than made me happy.

Now we were out of the green of the higher altitudes, and were winding our way into the brown creases that hid the Marañon. Out of the back, I got the odd, brief glimpse of the river, a glittering lead snake in the depths below, and I wondered if soon I would be on the water.

Chagual was a few adobe houses, lying dusty and silent on the parched roadside, amid even dustier banana trees. Most of the residents were hiding in the cooler space inside the *cantina*, and we parked outside it to stop for lunch. It was 1 p.m. and we had been travelling for eight hours. Mother Frederica knew the proprietress, and we were arranged round the best table and served hot potato soup.

I was to stay the night here with the Señora, and then see what I could find out about the mining boats. I had seen nothing on the river as we had come up to Chagual, and when we asked the Señora about it, she was certain that the mines did not have boats, and even if they did, they certainly would not travel long distances, like from here to Balsas. Well, that was that. The river was clearly navigable; I had read of several expeditions that had used this location as their starting point for a river journey. But mine was not to be one of them. I put my rucksack back in the van. Mother Frederica's route would pass through Huamachuco, where I could get a truck in the direction of Cajamarca. We set off once more, with a very long drive ahead of us. According to Mother Frederica, we should reach Huamachuco, about 120 kilometres away, by the early evening. She was worried, as the road crossed high wastes of *puna*, and, without any road signs, it was easy to mistake one dirt road for another, especially in the dark.

The station wagon crawled up sandy walls beyond the Mara-ñon. We were headed for another layer of mountain chain which hides a fertile plateau lying between the last ridges of the Andes, before the landscape crumbles towards Peru's desert coast. Huamachuco lies at the southern end of this last haven of agriculture, and Cajamarca is also to be found there, about 130 kilometres further north. We climbed around and up countless creases, towards Aricapampa, 2604 metres high, and other places like it before reaching the open *puna* and the last descent. Hour followed hour, and my neighbour and I settled into a silent stupor as we stared out of the window, dropping off to sleep now and then, only to be jerked awake by some particularly violent bump over yet another crater in the road.

At last, the road uncurled on to the barren heights of sodden grassland and rock; a cold wind buffeted the wagon. It was close to dusk now, and my hungry stomach and my stiff bones began to protest. No food until Huamachuco, I thought wistfully, but at that moment the van lurched to a halt, and Mother Frederica came bounding to the back to let us out.

'You didn't think we'd travel without food and drink did you?' she asked cheerfully, as she passed round the delicious cold guinea-pig meat, home-made biscuits and sweet thermos tea. We huddled together against the wind and ate with gusto, all except the injured *campesino*. His mouth was numb and whatever he put in just fell out again. All his food had to be broken up into tiny, soft pieces, and tea poured in very slowly to enable him to swallow.

Supper over, we all piled back in, and the bouncing and jerking began anew. Almost the only vehicles that use these roads are large trucks, loaded to breaking point with passengers and cargo. Their wide wheels and enormous weight leave deep furrows in the mud, and our wheels rarely matched their contours; even with four-wheel drive it was a very tough business getting out of some of the sludgy dips in the road. At other times the wheels sank so low in the furrows that the spare tyre under the floor got wedged into the mud and had to be dug out with a spade. Each time we approached a specially deep track we all held our breath to see if we would make it, and most times Mother Frederica's excellent driving ensured that we did, even when it looked to be impossible. Once darkness had fallen, however, it was a different matter, and we finally came to a thudding halt on an island of mud. Father Thomas had previously stood by and watched the two nuns dig away in the sludge, but this time he offered to dig. Torches were shone under the van, and the Father got down on his knees. He meant well, but he was not a practical man, and Mother Frederica soon lost patience with him.

'No, Father Thomas, you must dig here!' she cried, with barely-contained exasperation, and finally, 'Please give me the shovel,' as she swept her habit over her shoulder, hoiked up her black skirts, and got shovelling.

I wished I could have been useful, but not only was I too weedy, I did not know where was the most effective place to dig. The two nuns took it in turns to shovel and try to get the wagon going, and I watched in silent admiration as they sweated away, their crisp gowns getting muddier and muddier. But it was no good: we were stuck, and worse, we were lost. Mother Frederica had taken the wrong turning some hours back and now admitted that she had no idea where we were. There was nothing for it but to wait in the dark and hope a truck would come by. To our great relief one did, and soon the men in it were tying ropes around the wagon, and the engine pulled the Toyota off its mud perch as if it were a weightless toy. One of the men offered to drive the wagon until the road became less difficult, and the exhausted Mother Superior accepted gratefully.

Now there were three of us in the back as the other nun, a giggly little woman with a squeaky voice, joined us. We entertained each other by swapping travelling stories, sleep being impossible, and the tension about our journey's progress too great.

The truckers were leading us through the blackness and on to the right track towards Huamachuco, but we were now about to run out of petrol. The large cannisters in the back were empty, ready to be filled with cheap fuel on the coast. Midnight approached as we made it to a village on the last drop of petrol. The truckers assured us that the place sold fuel, and left us to wait out the night to buy some in the morning. It was a great relief to all of us to be out of the *puna* and no longer lost. We were also near other people now and could sleep easy. I took my groundmat and rolled it out underneath the van, while the others contorted their bodies into sleep inside. It was a crisp, cold night and I had nothing but a thin blanket, but exhaustion sent me off to sleep and I did not wake until the clammy dawn and the first cockerel's call.

Mother Frederica had some difficulty persuading anyone to sell their valuable fuel, but her position as Mother Superior stood her in good stead, and she eventually found someone who gave in to her charming but insistent request.

At last, in the late morning, we reached the market town of Huamachuco, and I found myself in a new world. This was no longer the remote Andes: here there were paved roads, cars, concrete buildings, electricity, and running water. The main square was alive with market stalls and vending carts selling everything from fresh sugared rolls, to plastic hairgrips and tyre sandals. Men and women wore outsized, creamy-coloured grass fibre hats, quite unlike those of the *campesinos* of the Central Andes. These were the distinctive woven hats of the north, in particular of the vale of Cajamarca: the central part of the hat was woven in the shape of a wide top hat, a neat edge around the crown instead of the rounded contours of the felt hats I had seen so far. The brim was very exaggerated, the overall effect rather comical, heads and faces almost invisible underneath them.

This was where Mother Frederica and I parted company, and I thanked her for her generous help and hospitality. We wished each other luck for the rest of our respective journeys, and then I left to find a truck leaving in the direction of Cajamarca. I was likely never to see her again, but the vision of her digging away under the Toyota will always be with me.

I got a truck away from Huamachuco in the early afternoon. It was the same as that I had travelled in all that time ago, from Huaraz to Chiquian. My rucksack was squeezed in amongst a lumpy layer of bags, boxes and sacks of potatoes, and I found a perch near the front of the wooden box that was the combined cargo and passenger compartment. This was, I had learned by now, the best place, as the truck bounced less at the front, and was also furthest away from the clouds of dust that came through the loose doors at the back. A wooden pole was positioned along the length of the open-top truck, so that a tarpaulin could be spread over in case of rain. For the moment, it made a good balancing handle, and a few of the male passengers sat on top of the side-planks, their feet resting on the central pole. I preferred to stand, my feet wedged among the cargo and my hands holding on to the tops of the planks; that way I could not be thrown off balance, and could just see over the edge and watch the countryside roll by. The distance from Huamachuco to Cajabamba was only about fifty kilometres, but the road was so bad that the journey took six hours.

Cajabamba's lights winked like stars in the distance as the truck creaked through the night. Another hour later, we reached the first houses with electricity on the road into town. I had made

143

friends with a young woman, also travelling alone, and we decided to share a hotel room. She was collecting banking documents from all the regional towns of the department of Cajamarca, and was on her way back to the coastal town of Trujillo. It was an unusual job for a Peruvian woman, I thought, but then, we were very close to the coast, where society is Westernized and women more independent. We found a beautiful old hotel, with a leafy inner courtyard and a wooden balcony running around the second floor, where most of the rooms were. There was just time to catch a meal in one of the restaurants that lined the streets, and I enjoyed my first *Lomo Saltado* (a traditional Peruvian dish of fried pieces of lamb, mixed in with onions, rice and chips) for a long time.

During the night, I was woken by the sudden noise of a large explosion. In the morning I wondered if I had not imagined it, but my friend had heard it too, and as I waited for the dawn bus to Cajamarca, I heard other passengers talk of the bomb that had ripped through a local bank during the night. Apparently, it was the first bomb to go off in these parts. The *Senderos* had been advancing north at roughly the same pace as myself, and it was only in Cajamarca that I was to find out how much worse things had become since I had set off from Huaraz. Two months had made an enormous difference to Peru's state of emergency, and when I phoned my mother, she was immensely relieved to hear from me, the deaths of foreign tourists in Peru having made the news in Europe.

Woman Trouble in Cajamarca

The whole time that I had been walking through the Andes, I had thought I was pregnant. Americo and I had been very desultory about contraception, and my periods had stopped as soon as I left Huaraz. It was a strange feeling. I had fallen very much in love with Americo, and the thought of our child was enticing. On the other hand, I was not here to get involved with a man or, for that matter, to get pregnant. I liked both ideas, but the timing was wrong, and I knew in my heart of hearts that I was not prepared to give up my journey or my independence.

I spent hours, though, with endless thoughts about what to do if . . . I thought sometimes that I could continue, pregnant, on the journey; however, visions of my pregnant self in the jungle, with no medical help were not attractive. I also knew that the anti-malarial pills I would be taking were very dangerous for pregnant women and their unborn children. The advice on the packet went on to say that women planning to get pregnant should wait at least three months after the last dose before conception. What would I do? End my journey now, and return to Huaraz, perhaps never to see the Amazon jungle? I could not reconcile myself to that. On the other hand, if I did not want to continue with the pregnancy, I would have to fly back to England immediately; there are no legal abortions available in Peru and, if I were to face that particular trauma, I would rather do it at home. Oh, but the possibilities were many, and they had gone round and round in my mind, as my legs carried me through the mountains.

Worse still, I felt a tremendous urge to have a child, and that, coupled with my recent thoughts about the value of sharing life, made it impossible for me to come to a conclusion.

As with everything else on this journey I would just have to wait and see; and I therefore decided to have a pregnancy test in Cajamarca. The traveller in me was feeling very cross about the whole thing: to set off on this great journey and then get pregnant: how like a woman!

I was lucky to have an introduction in Cajamarca, to stay with Rosa who taught at the local university. She had a small flat, in a side street just above the main square, which she shared with her friend Paula, also a teacher. The two of them were the first independent women I had met in Peru, other than Naomi: they were both in their late twenties, from the coast and middle-class, urban backgrounds, but they had chosen to live away from their families and have a career. They were still in very close contact with their parents, both of them phoning their mothers every weekend, not only to catch up on family news, but also to assure them that they were all right. The bonds were very strong, and as long as they remained unmarried, this would continue. They laughed at the absurdity of their mothers checking up on them at their age, but explained that this was the way it was in Peru. They gasped at the idea of my journey, and when I confided in them about my pregnancy worries, they positively shrieked, unsure whether to be shocked or impressed at my apparent sangfroid. For them, such a problem would be unspeakable, redeemed only by immediate marriage to avoid disgrace. Their response to the danger was simple: to completely avoid relationships with men. The pill was expensive, contraception in any form terribly embarrassing, while condoms were still a male preserve. The idea of a woman buying one was quite impossible: in Huaraz I had bought one once, the chemist's eyes nearly popping out of his head in amazement.

The freedom of my new friends was still on very limited terms, in spite of their independent lives. Money did afford them a certain degree of independence, if only the ability to choose whether and when they would get married. Paula seemed to be looking forward to getting married and having a family; Rosa, however, treasured the freedom of coming home and having nobody's supper to cook and nobody's clothes to wash and iron, except her own, and nobody to check up on her if she felt like going out with friends. To her, the price for having a husband and family seemed too high, Peruvian husbands being an old-fashioned lot, however liberal and educated. Woman as wife and mother is the reigning ideal; and the only way to avoid it is to avoid marriage.

Just outside the town, in Baños, were the old Inca baths, fed by thermal springs, where the king used to bathe with his women servants and concubines. Today they are open to the public and I went to bathe my battered body at the earliest opportunity. There were large communal pools for entire families, and also individual pools, each in a private tiled room, where you could stay as long as you liked. It was bliss to have my first hot bath in over three months, and I decided to make a habit of it and catch a bus to Baños every morning while I stayed here.

Back in town, I visited the *Cuarto del Rescate*, where the last Inca king, Atahualpa, is said to have been held by the Spanish. It was here, in Cajamarca, that Pizarro's handful of men overcame the great Inca warriors and kidnapped their leader. The year was 1532, and after various voyages as far as the north Peruvian coast, Pizarro had decided to head inland with just sixty-two horsemen and 166 foot-soldiers. They met Atahualpa and his army, estimated from 40,000 to 80,000 soldiers, in the valley of Cajamarca. Atahualpa had allowed them to advance unhindered, thinking this small group could do him no harm, and he was even persuaded to meet Pizarro on the main square, attended only by unarmed men. It was a terrible misjudgement which led to the ambush and massacre of at least 6000 unarmed Indians, and the capture of Atahualpa himself. Thus, in the space of a few hours, the Spanish sealed the defeat of an empire that encompassed the entire region between Quito in the north and central Chile in the south. Atahualpa tried to save himself by offering the famous ransom of a roomful of gold. Once he had collected as much gold as the Spanish had patience to wait for he too was killed, sentenced to be burned at the stake, but was garotted instead, when he agreed to be baptized into the Christian faith.

The conquest of the Inca Empire is a sad story, full of tragic mistakes and betrayals. The Incas were the most powerful South American nation, who had built up their enormous territory in less than one hundred years, and whose armies vastly outnumbered their opponents. The Spanish took only a few decades to destroy it, largely because circumstance and the Incas themselves

147

played into their hands. Atahualpa had just fought a successful civil war with his brother, when Pizarro's men penetrated Peru, and the empire was still divided between the loyalties of the two warring factions. There were also many tribes and regions that had only been recently subjugated by the Incas, and who were more than ready to support the Spanish invasion. The capture of Atahualpa enabled them to proceed with an effective divide-and-rule policy, and by the turn of the sixteenth century, Peru was the heart of the Spanish colonial empire, the Indians their slaves and servants. Most of the Inca gold was melted down and shipped back to Europe, although a few excellent collections of artefacts remain, most notably those of the Gold Museum in Lima.

Cajamarca today shows few signs of the old Inca settlement, characterized instead by the Spanish colonial architecture of the seventeenth and eighteenth century, and possessing some of Peru's most beautiful churches. The main legacy of the Incas is the population of Quechua Indians, who throng in the busy market, selling their rugs, hats, and agricultural produce. The land around the town is very fertile, and the vale of Cajamarca is famous for its dairy produce and local honey.

For all its beauty, its history ensures a certain melancholy. Walking about the spacious main square, with its manicured bushes and park benches, I thought of the thousands that had fallen in Pizarro's massacre. There is nothing in the square to commemorate that dreadful day, but the sense of Cajamarca's bloody history haunted me.

When I had visited Trujillo and Huanchaco with Abby, I had taken the opportunity to deposit all my jungle gear with the local FOPTUR office, to be collected once I reached Cajamarca, thus cutting down on the amount of equipment I would carry on the Andean trek. The journey down to the coast was about eight hours by bus, and, after a few days in Cajamarca, I decided to head down to Trujillo and collect the gear. My mountain equipment and clothes would be sent back to Huaraz, dispensing with bulky or heavy items, such as my tent, sleeping-bag and walking boots, and replacing them with a lightweight hammock, mosquito net and canvas boots. I would also collect my papers, which

I would need to help me reach Lonya Grande, over one hundred kilometres downriver, and the point where my walking would finally come to an end.

It was strange to return to a place I had visited when I first arrived in Peru. So much had happened since then, but the world had not changed because I had, and Trujillo was the same as before; although now it was winter on the coast, and rainy skies had replaced the burning sun of my previous visit.

The seasons are opposed on Peru's coast and in the Andes: while the mountains follow a seasonal pattern almost equivalent to the European timescale, the coast follows the opposite pattern, their winter our summer. The jungle follows its own pattern of rainy and dry seasons that depend on latitude for their timescale, the dry season lasting usually from June to September, although that is not to be relied upon.

I stayed in the Hotel Americano, a decaying pile that had seen better times. It must have been quite a grand place in the 1940s, with its enormous entrance hall with the high ceiling, and the squeaky leather sofas. Long tiled corridors led to further inner courts lined with wooden balconies, opening on to tobacco-stained rooms with fading paper and old pictures on the walls. Mine had a rather incongruous black-and-white photo of a Bavarian castle. The window opened on to the backyard of the hotel, where the staff hung out their washing and men walked about in nothing but a towel around their waists on their way to the showers beyond the washing lines. My bed was a worn-out mattress on a metal frame, reminding me of an old hospital bed, but although the individual parts of the room were run down, the place had a certain seedy appeal. I stayed only two nights; enough time to collect my things, make phone calls and send off some important letters. Trujillo was the last place I would visit where the postal service was almost certain to function reliably until I reached the jungle town of Iquitos, over 1000 kilometres downriver from Balsas.

Back in Cajamarca, I went to collect the result of my pregnancy test, and found to my disappointment and relief that I was not pregnant. The physical strain of the journey had disrupted my

149

body's rhythms and given me a marvellous freedom from my periods. What with my boyish appearance and this new freedom, my temporary transformation was complete, and it hardly seemed that I was a woman at all.

4
Amazonia

Last Days in the *Sierra*

The truck dropped a couple of passengers off at Balsas bridge, where the Marañon sped by below, a wide, fast river now. A couple of sun-weathered women were selling tropical fruit on the roadside, and I bought some ripe papayas for my lunch. To reach Balsas itself was about a twenty-minute walk, I had been told, and I heaved on my rucksack, and set off down a dirt track leading through a banana plantation. There was a dry heat down here, but sweat was soon pouring down my chest, and the rucksack weighed heavily on my shoulders.

Balsas was set close to the riverbank, a long succession of adobe houses lining its one road. Corrugated iron and tiles replaced thatch for the roofs, but there was nothing else very remarkable about the village. I stopped to eat a papaya and ask the way to the house of Eugenio Tirado, the local *alcalde*, or mayor.

Señor Tirado's home was set deep among plantations of bananas and cocoa. The house had two storeys and a walled yard in front, a hammock strung up in one corner, and an adobe ledge running around the whole courtyard, providing ample shaded seating. Señor Tirado was in the middle of mending his saddle when I arrived, in preparation to take some cattle to the market in Celendin, a day's walk away. He was all dressed up for the occasion, wearing matching jeans and jacket, a fresh white shirt, and a beautiful felt cowboy hat, and although very smart, his expression lacked the self-assurance of officialdom. He was clearly in a hurry, fiddling anxiously with his saddle, and shouting instructions to his attending sons. He looked up questioningly when I stepped into his yard, but when I explained myself as best I could and showed him my official introductions, he put down his work and kindly gave me an hour of his time.

We set about discussing which route I should take to reach

153

Lonya Grande, writing down the names of the local *tenientes*, or elected representatives, whom I was to approach at each stop along the way. Meanwhile, one of his daughters was sent to gather up some ripe mangoes, and I was presented with a whole bowl, their tangy scent permeating the air deliciously. It was agreed that I should borrow one of his donkeys to carry my rucksack, and a young boy called Nelson was to accompany me to my first destination along the Marañon. This done, Eugenio got back to his preparations, and I was left to explore his lands a little.

His wife and another daughter were busy packing boxes full of mangoes and wrapping up bunches of green bananas for the market. It was sticky work, and the daughter set a few dried cow pats alight to keep the insects away. Wrapping the bananas was quite a complicated business, involving stacking bunch upon bunch tightly into a compact barrel shape on top of a large fan of banana leaves, under which was what looked like a giant tennis racket. Once the bunches were about a metre high, another racket and leaves were laid on top, and, gently, the two were pulled together with strong fibre rope, until the fruit inside was firmly in place. The long leaves were then tucked in around the circular edges, and the whole packet tightly wrapped with more string. It was an ingenious way of packing these delicate fruit without adding any extra weight for the pack animals, yet at the same time giving them ideal protection from the sun and bruising. After the best mangoes had been boxed up, there was still a great mountain of them left, and we spent the rest of the afternoon eating one fragrant mango after another, fingers and faces stained orange and yellow from the juices.

Once dusk fell, the whole family gathered in the home courtyard, waiting for the evening meal to cook. Eugenio's wife lit a fire outside and spread dried cocoa beans on to a flat clay pan for roasting. The family grew coffee as well, but that was far too valuable to consume themselves, so they drank fresh chocolate instead.

We were still in the Andes, but life here was very different to the high *sierras* of further south. The mountains were lower, the canyons even drier, and the main crops were coffee, cocoa, bananas, mangoes, citrus fruits, avocados, and the infamous coca. Potatoes were no longer the staple diet in these parts, but rice from the northern jungle, and green plantain bananas, boiled or fried just like the mountain root crop. *'Disculpe la pobreza,'* (Excuse the poverty) said one of the daughters during our meal of banana soup and hot chocolate; how could I convince her that, for me, this was one of the most memorable, not to mention delicious, meals of the journey.

Early next morning ten-year-old Nelson was found, and Eugenio's spare donkey was loaded with my rucksack and a present of fruit for his colleague in Longblanc. The boy was clearly not keen to be lumbered with a day's walk on my behalf, and I tried to cheer him up by admiring his handling of the donkey. He forged on ahead in proud silence, but his curiosity soon got the better of him, and we had lively conversations about everything from difficult donkeys to what England was like.

An hour or so later I suggested we go for a swim. The path so far had been following a narrow ledge just above the river, and every now and then, pristine sandy beaches appeared invitingly in the river bends. I was keen, but Nelson could not swim, and it took some time before I could persuade him in. He watched uncertainly as I dived into the water, but once he saw me splashing about he could not resist it, and stripped down to his pants he jumped in. The pool was a small backwater, formed behind a particularly large sandbank, and was quiet and cool. Afterwards, we sat on the sandbank, drying in the afternoon sun. A river snake lay coiled in the shade nearby, but on closer inspection we found that it was dead, teeming with ants and flies. I was glad we had not seen it when we had arrived.

My association with Nelson was, however, short. Only an hour after our swim, he decided that he did not feel like walking any further and steadfastly refused to continue, deaf to my cajolery and even threats. We stopped at the last homestead before the track left the river for the hills beyond, and Nelson tried to persuade me to wait here, until someone could be found to continue with me the next day. I would have none of that, though, and left him behind carrying on alone.

The path to Longblanc was very clear, I had been assured, so I was reasonably sure of not getting lost. As I was leaving, a donkey driver passed by heading in the same direction, with a group of three donkeys, and I brought up the rear with mine. As we walked on through the afternoon, I had time to reflect on the virtues of my old donkey; these ones were excruciatingly slow, and we seemed to make little if any progress. We were following a small canyon leading away from the Marañon, and the hours crawled by monotonously, the green heights beyond never seeming any closer. Occasionally my companion offered me the use of one of his animals, and the afternoon was at least broken up with periods of riding. The donkeys were covered in nothing but thin blankets, and I had to shift constantly from one buttock to the other to avoid the bony spine in the middle, but it was a welcome change from brooding about my blistery feet.

We made such slow progress that, by the time we had reached the green foothills of the higher altitudes, it was already nearing dusk and my intended destination was at least another two hours away. Unfortunately, the donkey driver's path now separated from mine, and I faced the prospect of trying to find my own way in the dark. He assured me it was not difficult, and with that we shook hands and said goodbye. My path now followed a steep zig-zag through thorny bushes, and I herded Eugenio's donkey up ahead of me, hoping that we could perhaps move faster now.

The donkey, though, had other plans, and we had barely zig-zagged twice before he did a sudden U-turn and galloped down the hill in the direction of the other donkeys. I shushed and shouted at him to stop, but he was off at full whack and out of sight within moments. The only good thing was that he had not decided to head back towards his home: that way a whole day would have been lost. As it was, I knew he would slow down once he reached the others, and I panted along the trail after him as fast as I could. Sure enough, I found him about half a kilometre ahead, and after saying goodbye again to the donkey driver, I headed off in the opposite direction, this time leading the donkey by a rope.

He broke loose at almost the same spot as before and off he went. I tried to catch him by running straight down the hillside to cut him off, but instead collected a handful of thorns as I grabbed on to anything I could find while I rushed down the hillside. It seemed I would never make it to Longblanc now. But I stubbornly refused the donkey driver's kind invitation to stay at his place and, just as it was dark, I managed to make it to a large farm, set on a wide ledge under the trail for Longblanc.

The main building was a long, single storey, looking much how I imagined a Mexican-style *hacienda*, with a covered porch

156

running the whole length of the house. As I arrived, everyone was seated on the porch after the day's work, and at least six pairs of eyes watched me approach. I explained that I was on my way to Longblanc, and that the donkey was Don Eugenio's.

I was soon sitting among the three families who lived here, sipping fresh lime juice in the flickering light of oil lamps. Three brothers ran this place, each of their families living in adjacent large rooms in the main building. At one end was the kitchen quarter, and I went to sit with the oldest wife, who was making soup over the open hearth. She too had a raised cooking area, just like Vilma's, and I settled in to watch her cook over the wood fires as we talked. She was a large woman in her early forties, but her fleshy sunbeaten arms were still smooth, and her face had not lost its beauty: she had chestnut-coloured eyes the shape of almonds, and large brass ear-rings dangling either side of her face, giving her the look of a gypsy. We laid a long wooden table with tin plates and spoons, and everyone was called in for supper. Over the soup, I explained to one of the men that I was travelling through this area to learn something of the local agriculture, and he promised to show me around the plantations in the morning.

This region of the Alto Marañon, between Balsas and Bagua, was the exact location of the coca plantations that the general in Lima had warned me about. The main area for coca growing in Peru is the Huallaga valley, further east, but this farm had large coca fields as well, and the eldest brother showed me around the following day, explaining that in this region it was not illegal for him to cultivate coca. That, in fact, the whole enterprise was under government control. What kind of control was that, I asked; to which he replied that government agents visited his farm regularly to buy up his crop and check that he was growing no more than the official limit. It seemed to me that this was getting in on the action rather than control, but when I enquired about it in Lima I was told that, in buying the coca themselves the government was trying to keep order and control in the trade, and that most of what they bought was used in the medical industries. Well, that was their story. Back at the farm, my host went on to say that, unlike many other crops, coca could be harvested three times a year, and kilogram for kilogram, it fetched just over three times the price of coffee. The government had a hopeless battle on its hands. What farmer was going to

157

cultivate coffee and cocoa when faced with the temptation of a coca crop and all its advantages? We wandered about the plantations and examined the leaves and berries of the coffee bushes, ate some of the sweet green oranges, and finally came through the tall sugar-cane fields, and past the cane press back to the house.

The press was an enormous contraption comprising three large tree trunks, trimmed and plated in a mixture of copper and gold. The three trunks stood in a row, bound together by interlocking spikes, a wooden clockwork of wheels attached to their base. The whole stood on an elevated platform, so that oxen could push a great wooden pole round and round to turn the trio of barrels and crush the rock hard cane poles of all their juice. A great vat stood beneath to catch every drop for making molasses and chunks of compressed sugar. The man told me proudly the press was over a hundred years old and still working perfectly.

Eugenio's donkey had only been given to me for the first two days, after which I left him with a friend of his along the way. It had been extremely generous of him to entrust me with his donkey for nothing in return, but he was the exception; after that, cash had to change hands with everyone I met that week. The contrast with the earlier part of my journey in the mountains was dramatic: without maps and a donkey to carry my gear, I was completely dependent on other people, who were not always inclined to help. I could understand their reaction; they had fields and plantations to attend, and I had to pay a high price to persuade them to lose a day's work. And, of course, they knew I was helpless without them, which bumped the price up every time. If it had not been for my rucksack, a young boy could have been sent with me; but Nelson's behaviour had made me distrust young guides and my seventeen kilograms of gear needed a man to carry it. My dependence depressed me, and I was glad that I had experienced the generosity I had at the beginning of my trek, rather than the conniving I met with now.

Moments stand out from this part of my journey, most notably walking through my first cloud forest. With each day the Andean landscape was gradually transformed into thickly forested foothills, the paths softer and muddier. The horizon was no longer dominated by grey mountain peaks or brown cliffs, but by the unending green undulations of valleys, and the milky sky by great banks of rain-stained clouds. Mists rose from the warm and humid vegetation in the mornings, and sometimes rain would pelt down in heavy drops, reducing the paths to red mud shutes, threaded with a tangle of roots to trip and slide over. Generally, though, the trails were easier to walk on, the gradations less steep, leaving behind the stony ledges and steep gravel paths of the mountains.

The first time I stepped into the shadowy twilight of a real cloud forest, I could hardly believe I was there. It looked very similar to how I imagined a jungle: furry lianas hung from the trees, green and dirty red epiphytes wound round branches and boughs, the undergrowth was thick with curly fern plants, and the ground was covered with layers and layers of rotting leaves, all shades of brown decay and ribbed with the trails of insects. Enormous spider webs were suspended delicately over bushes or between trees, and white spindly tufts sprouted from the tree-tops, rather like old man's beard. Unlike the steaming lowlands of the Amazon basin, the cloud forests clung to slopes, some 1000 metres, some 2000 metres higher up, and were cool and misty, like their name.

The landscape was changing before my eyes and each day brought more and more new plants to wonder at. I wish I had had a botanical guide with me to find out the names of some of them; as it was, I only remember the trees whose fruit I ate for the first time. The most abundant wild fruit tree was known locally as *chirimoya*, and grew a large fruit the size of a grapefruit and the taste of vanilla. Its skin was green and tough, similar in texture to a breadfruit; inside the flesh was soft and white, with lots of shiny brown seeds the size and colour of lychee kernels. Another fruit was the *guaba*, which hung from a large tree in long hard pods that looked like overgrown green beans. These could be split open lengthwise, and inside were large, plum-sized seeds, covered in sugary white pulp that could be chewed off. There were the *cocona* bushes, with smooth golf balls of fruit, the colour of rosy lemons, and with a bitter-sweet flavour, that was excellent against thirst, either raw, or boiled and cooled into a delicious drink. There were plenty of other citrus fruits, oranges, lemons, and limes the most common, but other types too that I had never tasted, like the enormous sweet lemons, peeled and eaten just like oranges, their segments watery with only a hint of lemon flavour, enough to refresh a dry throat.

My progress was rather slow over this period, as I could never persuade anyone to accompany me much further than a distance they could easily return from in one day. That did mean that daily hikes were not very tiring, and there was more of the day left to talk with my hosts, although the fact that I was using my official papers and staying with the local *tenientes* made for rather a different relationship.

In the Central Andes, I had been travelling alone, like any Peruvian wanderer and, although I had undoubtedly been an outsider, I was nevertheless treated well and people were mostly friendly and open with me after the first shock of meeting me. Now, though, documents and money came between us, and made the relationship much less open. My hosts were on guard and concerned to make a good impression, while at the same time intent on securing as much money as possible for whomever was found to escort me further. Our conversations were hampered by a quicksand of leading questions. Other things probably came into play as well, such as the region's close links with the eastern coca fields, and people may have suspected me of being a government agent. Far-fetched it may seem, but it was no more unlikely than the villagers of Pumpa thinking I was a *Sendero*: any stranger, especially in these parts, was to be suspected, and a foreigner was even more suspect. A couple of times I was surprised by questions that were obviously designed to expose me as a mineral prospector. What was the price of gold these days, and, how much did metal detectors go for, were both questions thrown casually into a conversation one afternoon. So thinly disguised were the questions that I laughed in response, but I did not enjoy being the object of so much suspicion.

There was one notable exception to the cagey treatment I met with, and that was in a small village called Tactamal. I arrived there on the sixth afternoon of walking, and found Don Juan, the *teniente*, already quite drunk at four in the afternoon. His house was on a muddy bank overlooking the grass square of the village and a wide set of stone steps led up to the entrance. On these steps Don Juan and his friends were celebrating the sale of their latest coca crop, and the purchase of a beautiful golden stallion, who was grazing nearby.

Juan was a good-looking man in his early thirties, sitting bare-chested with a bottle of beer in his hand. There were three others as well, much more drunk, one a young *muchacho* with a bulging moneybelt tied around his waist. He was the first to greet me, swaying slightly as he shook my hand, his eyes half shut with drink. A bottle was pressed into my hand and we spent the rest of the afternoon in circular conversations that inevitably came back to who I was, where I was going and how lovely my eyes were; it was all good humoured, though, and I bided my time to ask Juan for help with the next day's hike. He was more in control of himself than the others, and eventually I managed to get through to him what I needed. I showed him one of my introductions and they all hung over each other's shoulders as it was read out loud.

'You are a writer?' asked the young gun. 'I too am an artist,' he said, and proceeded to recite some treacly love poems he claimed for his own. Love crashed over bodies like waves, rosebuds were red lips and eyes stars: he crooned and leered closer, his alcoholic fumes biting my nostrils. His name was Ricardo, and the money around his waist was from the sale of his horse, and from drug debts he had been collecting in the region. He was only twenty-four but, he confided, had lived a lot. He had run away from home at fourteen and worked the streets of Lima and Bogota, getting in with the drug gangs and learning to shoot and pilot small aircraft. Eventually he had got a job as a minder with one of the cartels, occasionally flying shipments of coca paste from Uchiza in Peru to Colombia. $2000 a flight, he told me, and bought another round of beers. He was quite unsteady by this point, and, as he made to pay, wads of stacked 10,000 Inti notes fell all over the ground. The others scrambled on their knees to collect them for their rich friend, while he sat back smiling, drunk and powerful.

'I would escort you myself,' he said. 'But what will you give me in return?'

I was dressed in my only pair of trousers and a long-sleeved shirt and my hair stuck filthily to my scalp, but the game was on and, however unresponsive I was, he continued unabashed to make love to me in front of his appreciative audience.

'Ah, Natascha, I am so sad. If only I could come with you to Balsas. But I would lose my heart, and then what would I do?'

I appealed to Don Juan in his official capacity as *teniente* to find me someone responsible for tomorrow, but he just nodded and did nothing. All I could do was to sit it out and see what came up in the morning. By nightfall many of the villagers came to join the party, and the drinking and smoking went on long into the night. The men brought out their pouches of dried coca leaves and giggled delightedly when I accepted a handful for myself. Women in Peru don't normally chew coca, but as a foreigner I could afford to break that rule, my *macho* behaviour suiting my clothes. I said I wished I could have my own *cal* bottle, and Ricardo gave me his, a fine gourd, shaped like an hour-glass, fitting neatly into my palm. For me this bottle symbolized life in the Andes, and I was very pleased to have it, especially because it was a very personal gift, each man making his own bottle from a chosen gourd; there are no market stalls where they are sold.

My stay at Tactamal was also the only time I came even remotely close to an unpleasant experience with a man. The sleeping quarter at Don Juan's was a large dormitory under the roof, where his whole extended family slept on mattresses lined up next to each other on the wooden floor. I was shown to a spot next to his three young children, who laughed and whispered excitedly, but eventually dropped off, as I did soon afterwards, sleepy from the beer and the late night.

Hours later I awoke when an arm slid gently around my waist and, thinking it was one of the children, I settled against it, enjoying the human warmth. My body froze, though, as I realized suddenly that the arm was far too heavy to belong to a child, and that there was a man lying behind me. His groin nudged me surreptitiously as I stared into the darkness, trying to decide what to do. I chose to go on the offensive. We were surrounded by many sleeping bodies and I spoke loudly, hoping someone would wake up: 'Don't molest me please,' I said, and the arm retracted like a frightened snail.

Nobody woke up, the body did not go away, and the arm came creeping back again and again. I got up eventually to find my torch and confront my assailant, but the body immediately crept away into the darkness and I had no way of finding him. I slept fitfully after that, my dreams disturbing. In the morning I got a nasty shock when I realized that the groper was the children's uncle, who had seemed so pleasant the day before, the only person not to drink at the party, and who had seemed rather shy

162

and serious. I had assumed that it must have been the arm of the amorous Ricardo, and to discover that it was this quiet man that I had hardly spoken to was somehow much more sordid. I recognized him by his wheezy cough, the same as that the body gave when it slunk off. He avoided my eyes when we met at breakfast, but I said nothing. There was no point: I needed the family's help.

From Tactamal it was only another two days' walk, the first an easy couple of hours to Camporredondo, and the last a long, ten-hour day to Lonya Grande. The final day's walking was a glorious climax to almost three months of making my way through the Andes, and I enjoyed every minute of it, my spirits soaring with the pleasure of successfully completing the first phase of my journey. There were many people making for Lonya Grande because it was the time of the coffee harvest, and mule trains were leaving daily for roads to the coast. The terrain was creased with the last outcrops of mountainous rock and tight gorges through which rivers ran towards the Marañon, and the craggy switchback trail made for a tough day. But I was totally fit by now, my leg muscles steeled, and I kept up effortlessly with the *arrieros*, dodging among loaded mules and donkeys. Men whooped and whistled at their animals, and great swirls of dust came up in the wake of pounding hooves on the sunbaked track. A party atmosphere pervaded the day, my companions also in high spirits; soon they would be delivering their cargo to the coffee depots and there would be money to blow on booze before heading back home. They cheered and shouted across the gorges to drivers lagging behind or way ahead, and one man tossed me an orange from his saddle as I jogged alongside. *'Tu eres muy varonil,'* I was told once more, and took pride in the compliment.

   At last we joined a dirt road and the Marañon came into view in a wide gorge below. A small gravestone stood lonely by the wayside, and one of the men told me it marked the spot where a muleteer had been shot dead by bandits the year before: killed for his coffee. I was reminded once more how cheap life could be here, and of my own good fortune that had let me get this far. The most dangerous part of my journey was now over, and my mind filled with visions of the new world I was soon to enter. I finally walked into Lonya Grande as the sun slipped beyond the horizon. It was 24 June, a Saturday, and ten and a half weeks since I had first set off from Huaraz.

The River

From Lonya Grande to Bagua was an easy journey of twelve hours made in the back of a pickup truck. The *camionetta* kept overheating and coming to a grinding halt at the slightest hill, but nothing could bother me that day and I knew that we would make it to Bagua sooner or later. I was in a haze of contentment, still unable to believe that the walking had really come to an end, and that soon I would be in a completely new world. The truck bounced so much as it went over pot-holes that we in the back had to hold on tight not to fly straight over the edge. It was like being on some mad fairground ride, and the young fruit merchant and I, the only passengers, were being thrown constantly against each other and bouncing apart again.

By the time we finally arrived in Bagua, our mutual ordeal had made us allies, and I gladly accepted his offer of showing me the best place to stay. Many of the hotels did not have running water, but the Hotel Azul did, and that is where we went. We arrived late, around 11 p.m., and the only rooms left were doubles, but I decided to trust my new friend, and we took a room together. He had told me he was also a lay preacher, which eased any suspicions I might have had. In the morning I went to buy fresh bread and made us tea on my camping stove by way of thanks for his help. Later, when I left to find a truck for Immasita and the Marañon, my friend thanked me for trusting him, and I was glad that my experiences of the previous week had not marred my good faith in trusting strangers.

There was supposed to be another pickup leaving for the jungle riverpost of Immasita by late morning. I found it already parked at its regular street corner by 9 a.m., but it was hanging on for more passengers to make the drive more profitable. I joined the others waiting, a group of mission nurses, fruit and

165

fish merchants, and labourers returning home from work on the coast.

Bagua was only a small town on the edge of the Amazon forests, but it was a central traffic point for anyone travelling on to either the northern or south-eastern jungle, and had grown up around the hotels and trading such a junction spawned. The town spread out in a grid of ugly concrete bungalows, the walls peeling and stained red from the frequent rain on the mud roads. It was a muggy, humid place, only about 800 metres above sea level, the sky above opaque with grey clouds, and a fine film of sweat sealed my skin as I sat by the roadside, my eyes heavy in the dull light. A couple of hours went by before the driver had gathered enough passengers, and I spent the time writing in my diary.

Looking up, my eye caught the headlines on a local newspaper, which spoke of bombings in Huaraz. The town was still the focus of a bombing campaign, and a number of hotels and tour agencies had been dynamited. The direct result, reported the papers, was an 80 per cent cut in tourism in the area. The region's economy was almost at a standstill, and the normally busy Mountaineering Week, in early June, had been very subdued in the face of a feared *Sendero* assault. Only a short time before the event, a 24-year-old British tourist, Edwin Bartley, was shot dead in the valley, when he was found in a council building in Olleros during a terrorist attack on the place. I thought of Americo and his family; there was no way of finding out whether they were safe or not and, as usual there was nothing to do but hope for the best, something which, thankfully, was almost natural to me by now. Peruvian fatalism had rubbed off on me, or perhaps it was my own new peace of mind, and I found it easy not to worry about things I could do nothing about.

At last the pickup driver had crammed enough cargo and passengers into his vehicle, and I left Bagua, this time sitting on the front seat, shielded from bumps and rain. Within a short space of time, the countryside metamorphosed from brown shrubland to cane fields and rice paddies, and the first tentacles of green forest reached towards us. The track followed the Marañon for a while, and I willed time to hurry on to the following day, when I would finally get on to my first rivercraft.

I had an invitation to stay with some Jesuit missionaries

downriver from Immasita, which lessened the fear of not knowing where I was going or how I was going to travel. My only worry was whether Padre Pancho remembered inviting me. We had met by chance in Lima when I first arrived, and I had been impressed with his practical knowledge about conditions on the Alto Marañon. His patch was the entire northern region of the department of Amazonas, a jungle area of several hundred square miles, whose rivers he had travelled for the past twenty-five years. He would be the perfect host to advise me and help me acclimatize.

That was tomorrow; now I was packed tightly on the front bench of the pickup with the driver and another passenger. By late afternoon we passed the last village before Immasita, and stopped for a meal. The driver had stopped many times along the way to pile on more passengers, and I was amazed to see at least fifteen people spill off the back, when there had only been a handful before. There was no longer any room to sit, and everyone in the back had been standing for the last three hours, holding on to the railing welded around the edge.

As we sat eating boiled rice and beef stew, another potential passenger came ambling up. He was a giant man with a neck like an ox and a body to match. How he was going to fit into the back I could hardly imagine, and I dreaded to think how the axles would cope with his weight: he must have weighed at least twenty stone, if not more. The other passengers looked at each other in disbelief when the driver accepted him, but the man was a well-known fish trader who paid good money, so he and his fish baskets were coming along one way or the other. In the meantime he joined us eating and ordered a double plateful of beef stew and beers all round. No wonder the man was popular. He was known as *el gordo*, or the fat one, and in spite, or perhaps because of his immense ballast, he ended up a real asset for the rest of the journey.

The road got progressively worse and worse the deeper we got into the jungle, and rain soon turned it into an almost impassable mire of red mud. The truck got stuck again and again, and whenever this happened, everyone yelled for *el gordo* to get off, which he usually did and, what is more, put his whole weight behind pushing the truck out of the mud. The driver also had a man in the back who was hired specifically to dig mud away from the wheels, and as the earth turned into thick soup, the

167

poor man found himself knee-deep in the stuff again and again. We were getting stuck every couple of kilometres at one stage, and a number of passengers had to help out with the digging. No one complained; this was a normal jungle journey, and having to dig mud, change wheels, or push vehicles was all a predictable part of it. In Europe this kind of journey would have surely met with demands from the passengers for their money back, but here they took it all in their stride, working almost as hard as the driver to get on with the journey. I could see now why he had waited so long to gather enough fares: the life of his trucks must have been very short.

In the end we made it to Immasita by two in the morning, having left Bagua at roughly the same time the previous afternoon. Everything was in darkness, so the few of us who remained slept in the truck until dawn, and I fell asleep with the fresh images of purple and pink orchids imprinted on my brain. The road had been nothing but a muddy gash in the jungle, and these precious flowers had stood out from the exposed green banks that formed on either side in beautiful relief.

I woke at dawn to the sound of an engine starting in the water. The others had told me there would be boats leaving for Santa Maria de Nieva in the early morning, so I jumped out of the truck and reached the river bank just in time to see two motorized long-boats heading downriver. Would there be others? I asked some men nearby, but they shook their heads and said maybe not for a couple of days. A metal speedboat was moored among some dugout canoes, and I asked who the owner was: it would be a matter of minutes to reach the other boats in that, if we set off straight away. The owner was a fat Indian man in red football shorts, who was observing me with a calculating eye. He would take me for 10,000 Intis, he said; an outrageous sum (he could have bought two and a half gallons of petrol for that). He had me at his mercy, though, and all I could do was appeal to his gallantry. We knew each other's game, and I managed to talk him down to 5000 Intis. After a hurried goodbye to my companions in the truck, I dashed off with my rucksack, slid down the mud bank and landed in the speedboat. The boat's metal nose rose high as we sped down the river, and large waves piled onto the banks. It was a strange start to my river travel. As we flew around a bend in the river, we passed an Indian couple, the man in shorts, the woman in a traditional Indian tunic of brown woven cloth, poling a small balsa raft at the slow water's edge. The surface area of the raft was that of a large table and there was nothing to hold on to other than a contraption of bamboo poles, tied together at the centre for securing bags; the large waves sent them bobbing up and down on their frail craft. My chauffeur was an Indian too, but he had chosen another world, and he sped past them without so much as a look. I was grateful to be getting a lift ahead instead of being stuck in Immasita, but I could not help wishing that my introduction to the river had been different.

Another bend in the river revealed one of the long-boats cutting smoothly through the water, not far ahead. My taxi swerved alongside in a last flourish, and once I had established that the boat was heading for Nieva, I climbed onboard in mid-stream. The boat sat deep in the water from the weight of its cargo, but there were plenty of places to sit as there were only four others aboard; it had wide bows and was about ten metres long, with a small engine at the back and half its length covered by a tin roof to give shade from the sun. For the moment, though, it was still early in the morning and warming rays had not yet penetrated the clouds. The damp air was cold, and the chill wind on the boat made for a clammy couple of hours. Each of us huddled out of the wind as best we could, sitting in silence until the day woke up. An Indian man stood at the bow, holding a wooden pole, which served as an aid to balance as well as a tool to head off floating trees and submerged obstacles. He wore nothing but shorts and a thin cotton blanket wrapped around his shoulders, and goose-pimples puckered his skin. Now and then, he would indicate to the helmsman to steer more to the left or right, expert at recognizing underwater hazards by the swirls of the current on the water's surface. On one occasion he lifted his pole right up and smashed it into the river, but he missed his aim, and a large snake wagged through the water towards the riverbank.

I felt full of wonder and strained to see and feel and hear everything about me, my ears full of the sounds of churning water, but my eyes scanning the river and banks for new images. The Maranon was about 100 metres wide, and I could see the riverside clearly, distinguishing tangled jungle from the occasional field of cultivated banana trees or yucca bushes, where long bamboo houses on wooden stilts stood at the tops of the mud banks. I sat quietly on the boat, agog with new sensations.

After a couple of hours, by which time the sun was pounding down, the boat pulled over to pick up more goods and take on two more passengers. They were a young Indian couple: he again in shorts, his wife in a sky-blue cotton dress, stretched tightly over her pregnant body. They were both very beautiful, but quite different to the Quechua Indians of the Andes. They had wide, high cheekbones and almond-shaped eyes, which gave them something of an Asiatic appearance, and the woman's skin was more the colour of golden sugar than the coppery shade of Quechua people. They spoke to each other in a soft tonal language that sounded very soothing and gentle to me. It was probably one of the languages of the Aguaruna and Huambisa tribes that are the traditional inhabitants of the Alto Marañon, but my untrained ear was unsure.

Shortly after boarding, the woman unpacked her palm-leaf hamper, and laid out fire-roasted yucca and boiled eggs on a bed of green banana leaves. She peeled the eggs and the brown bark off the yucca, and I tried not to look too hungry. She then broke off parts of both her foods and distributed them among the other men and, after a moment's hesitation, she even offered me some, and I accepted gratefully. I had never eaten yucca before, and she explained to me in lilting Spanish, that it grew underground, just like potatoes, and could be cooked the same way. With a sprinkling of salt, it tasted delicious, and my stomach filled, I settled down to gaze about the river while the others slept through the afternoon.

We arrived in Nieva by late afternoon. It was a small settlement on the mouth of the river of the same name, and its mainly wooden houses clustered on the curve of land that formed at the confluence of the two rivers. Sodden logs lay implanted in the steep mud to make climbing the bank easier, but it was still tricky and I was relieved not to slip in front of the small crowd of onlookers that had gathered to meet the boat. Did anyone know where Padre Pancho lived? I enquired, and was directed towards the main square and the church above. The land rose steeply

170

soon after the riverbank, and the mission stood overlooking the settlement beyond the church. More mud steps and then concrete ones led up to the church entrance, and alongside was a tropical garden that stretched back towards the mission bungalows, where I found Padre Pancho having afternoon tea on his verandah. My trousers and boots were covered in mud from my two-day journey, and as I walked on to the swept terracotta tiles, I felt self-conscious about my filthy state. Did he remember me? I asked, holding out my hand. I need not have worried. He recognized me instantly, and I was invited to sit down while another *padre* dashed off to get another cup. Padre Pancho stared at me in disbelief as I slid off my rucksack, and admitted that he had never expected to see me here. So many people said they would come, but none of them ever did, and he chuckled to himself as he poured out more tea. He was a jolly man in his early sixties, with a curiously squeaky voice that sounded as if it had never quite finished breaking; as he spoke, and especially when he laughed, high squeaks escaped from his throat, and it was impossible not to laugh with him. His face was the mottled brown of a white man who has spent his life in the tropics, and his thin grey hair was combed neatly away from a handsome Castillian face. In his right hand he held a black wooden staff with a silver handle, and as he strode about with his pot belly and funny voice, he looked like a dashing little count in a comic opera.

As soon as I had had something to drink, he got out a map and made me show him where I had come from. I traced the 1000 kilometres or so that I had journeyed from Chiquian, and he gasped in open-mouthed astonishment. *Incredibile! Que brava!* (How brave!) he gasped, and made me promise to tell everyone all about it over supper. The reception was a little overwhelming in its welcome, but it was wonderful to have arrived in the jungle, and as the sun set I was shown to a room under the church roof, where a fresh bed had been made and the wire-netted windows looked out over the river.

As I cleaned up for supper, I pondered the fact that I had entered a very separate and secluded world from the one that was all around. However, if I was going to have to be dependent on others, I could not do better than this mission. Padre Pancho was my only contact until Iquitos, and how the journey would continue and how much I was going to learn about Amazon life depended a lot on chance and meeting the right people at the right time. My greatest wish was to spend some time away from the main river, staying at an Indian settlement, but I knew that the likelihood of that happening was small. Understandably, I had met with closed doors on this subject, and even though I had spoken to the Indian-run organization AIDESEP in Lima, I had been given no more than an assurance that I was welcome to try my luck once I reached their territories. It was up to me to make contact there once I arrived. The Aguarunas and Huambisas, whose territory I was now in, are the most highly organized native group in Peru and are dominant within AIDESEP; it was therefore a positive step to have spoken with their representatives in Lima, but it ensured nothing more than that no word had gone out against me here. I would have to play it by ear from now on; perhaps somewhere between here and Brazil I would get my chance.

The *Padres* and the Pongo

My four hosts at the mission were Pancho, Pacho, Pocho, and Carlos, and there was a touch of the Walt Disneys about them as they went about their business at the mission. Pancho and Pocho were very keen gardeners, and when free from their pastoral duties, either one could be seen sweating away in the sun, cutting back grass with a sickle, or gathering fruit from the nearby lime grove. One afternoon I came upon Pancho hacking away at the undergrowth, dressed in ample yellow shorts, an old vest, and a red baseball cap, and I could hardly believe this was the same man I had seen holding mass the night before. Pocho was the only *hermano* (brother) among the *padres*, and sitting next to him at a meal you would never have suspected that he was a Jesuit missionary. His nails were permanently black from working in the woodshed, building boats, and he ate his meals with uninhibited gusto, gesticulating with his fork to make a point, and depositing debris freely about the table. During the evening meal, the *padres* always listened to the news on long-wave radio and, while the others hung on every word from the outside world, occasionally exclaiming in agitated agreement or disgust, Pocho was happy to ignore matters that did not concern him, and frequently got hissed at if he spoke over the radio. Their manner with each other was mainly calm and tolerant: they had all known each other a long time and accepted each other's differences in the same way a family would, and the atmosphere at the mission was easy and good-natured.

As a guest I had nothing to complain about: I had a room with a beautiful view, my own shower and flushing toilet, and generous meals were provided three times a day. I was free to wander about the gardens and animal sheds, read books in the study, or join in during church services, as I pleased. One thing rankled, however; I was unequivocally excluded from the visits to and work with the native Aguaruna settlements. Pancho once commented pointedly that he did not like being observed any more than the Indians. Nothing more was said, but I knew better than to ask for something which I sensed met with disapproval.

I knew it was a vain hope to think Pancho would allow me to accompany him; my personal desire to see what an Indian village looked like and perhaps learn something of the life style there was selfish. It was so tantalizing, though, to be so close to the forest and yet so completely without it. As I stared across the riverbank and into the endless jungle beyond, I felt as if I were looking at a wall without a door.

Nieva needed no more than a morning's stroll to get to know it: there was a concrete main square, which doubled as the local football pitch, below the mount on which was the mission. The largest building was a two-storey concrete municipal building, which also housed the local bank and market hall; for the rest, wooden stalls and stilted houses huddled along the bank for another 150 metres. There were a couple of bars, one of which was called Bum Bar, where men drank beers at bare wooden tables as the day wore on, traders most of them who, bereft of any but a few customers, did little other than drink and doze insensibly in their doorways. Inside, their wives stood swatting flies from great tubs of rancid olives or rearranging their one shelf of tinned sardines and sacks of rice and pasta.

Nieva was a very quiet place. One day I went to the market in the municipal building, but found it completely empty. Not a single piece of fruit was to be found anywhere: where was the fabled richness of the jungle? Where the pineapples, papayas, bananas, and other delights? People did not grow papayas around here, I was told, and it was the wrong time of year for pineapples. Didn't these things grow all the year round? I wondered; to which someone replied that the locals preferred to buy tinned goods flown in from the coast than be bothered with growing their own food. Sobered by disillusion, I enquired about fish more cautiously, and was hardly surprised when I found that most people preferred to buy tinned fish than spend hours on the river. I remembered *el gordo* and his salt fish, and finally realized why he was prepared to make such arduous journeys into the jungle: here he could sell his fish for four times the coastal market price.

Most of the inhabitants of Nieva were originally from the mountains or the coast, and knew very little about the jungle around them. Nobody went into the forest if they could help it, and they only left the village for long-distance journeys back 'home', or for business. At first sight it was difficult to see why these people had come to settle here at all. Of course, the answer to Nieva's origin lay with the mission. The modern town of Santa Maria de Nieva had only been established for some forty-five years. The settlers scattered around the region had been drawn in by the mission's school and medical post. Traders had soon followed, and the Banco Minero had opened up a branch to buy up the local river gold. Now the place was a firmly established community, creating its own life, quite apart from the mission.

The local bank was the clue to the original attraction the town had for settlers: the Marañon is a gold river, and, from Chagual onwards, lone gold washers can be seen sifting sludge through makeshift sieves. It is backbreaking, monotonous work, but occasionally a man will sift out a gram of gold dust or even a rough clump mixed with other metal, and it will fetch a good price at the bank. While I was in Nieva, a gram of gold was selling for between I/35,000 and I/42,000, depending on its purity, which was a small fortune, when compared with the highest daily wage a local man could earn: I/4000. The villagers may have appeared to be impoverished, but most of them had plenty of money and despised the produce of the forest; they had cash to buy whatever the traders brought them, and the fact that they were a captive market and had to pay outrageous prices did not seem to bother them. One morning, a boatload of watermelons was brought in; unbelievably each one of them was on sale for around I/7000.

Nieva soon palled, and I began to make enquiries about boats that were leaving. There was, however, a mighty obstacle in my way, just a few kilometres downriver, and since the Maranon was high with rain-swelled rivers from Ecuador, it was impassable.

The barrier was the great Pongo de Manseriche, last watershed before the Marañon spreads out and flows on for another 900 kilometres, to become the vast Amazon river itself. The Pongo is one of the largest, and most famously dangerous, set of rapids in

175

South America, and I knew it would be hard to persuade anyone to take me through it. Traditionally, the Pongo is a natural barrier between the Upper and Lower Marañon, and traditionally the people on either side have always been quite separate. To the west lies the Santiago river, a large tributary of the Marañon and the main artery of Aguaruna-Huambisa territory. To the east stretch the flatlands of the lower Amazon basin itself, and many different tribes once inhabited the banks of countless tributaries on either side of the main river. Not only the people, but also the landscape is distinct: the western forests are spread over the last outcrops of the Andes, with sizeable hills protruding above the green horizon. The higher altitude makes for a slightly cooler climate and, most importantly for humans, the jungle is almost free of mosquitoes and their associated diseases. No one bothers with mosquito nets in Nieva, and sunsets can be enjoyed without having to hide from the dreaded insects that haunt the rest of the Amazon basin; once past the Pongo, mosquitoes and *zancudos*, small biting flies, would be a daily menace come nightfall.

For the moment, however, I was still preoccupied with trying to find someone, anyone, who was prepared to risk his boat and life shooting the Pongo. Pancho advised me to get a lift in the *hydroavion* that was shortly expected from Iquitos; but I was intent on continuing my journey by water. I felt it would have been cheating to go any other way, and, as usual, I found the dangerous aspect a trifle: not because I am brave, but because my will to go was stronger than my fear.

One of the men I spoke to about shooting the Pongo was the local *alcalde*, who was an eloquent Aguaruna Indian, very conscious of the duality of his position as an Indian and as a representative of Peruvian order. Clearly it was a local victory for the Aguarunas to have penetrated the national system of representation, and yet it put the *alcalde* himself in an invidious position, incapable of pleasing the two interests whose symbol he was. On the one hand, he was responsible for keeping local order and representing the interests of the *mestizo* settler community; but on the other, he was concerned for the protection of Indian lands and about the fight against central government's policies of Amazon development, which particularly affect the basin's marginal areas, such as the Alto Marañon. He gave me a copy of the government's most recent legislation on Amazon development, and it made depressing reading. The most futile

176

and destructive element of the new law related to the attempt to attract agricultural settlers, offering them financial incentives and land in a development programme that was unoriginal and short-sighted. I was not surprised that Lima's government officers had been concerned about bad publicity: with the best will in the world it was very difficult to find anything positive in the new legislation. Neighbouring Brazil is an example of how ineffective such a policy of settlement has been, leading to the senseless destruction of the Amazon forest. Peru is only just beginning to attempt Amazon development and the destruction is, as yet, nothing like that in Brazil. The future looks bleak if the government cannot be persuaded to commit to other projects; although, ironically, the country's state of emergency is one of the most powerful obstacles to any of the government's programmes being realized. One can only hope that by the time democracy and order are restored in Peru, its politicians will have been persuaded to research more positive options for the Amazon territory under their jurisdiction.

The *alcalde* had the use of the local trading co-operative's speedboat, and he offered to take me through the Pongo for nothing more than the cost of the gasoline, which I would pay him in American dollars. All we needed to do was to buy the gas and wait for the river to subside. It seemed an excellent arrangement, and I told the *padres* of my good fortune, pleased to have solved my problem without resort to their time and experience.

It was then that we discovered there was no gas in all of Nieva, and that we would have to wait for a new shipment from upriver. No matter, the shipment was expected any day, and indeed arrived the following morning. I went to find the *alcalde*, but he was busy with other duties that day and also pointed out that the river was still too high. Two more days passed, and I realized that my friend in the municipal building was avoiding me. Another day passed, my enquiries met with evasive answers and awkward smiles; the *alcalde* was clearly regretting he had ever made me any promises, and instead tried to persuade me that I should get a boat to the Pinglo military camp, which was just before the Pongo, and ask them to find a passage for me.

That, however, was an option I had every intention of avoiding. Here in Nieva I was safe and well provided for. Pinglo, on the other hand, was nothing more than an army barracks on a

177

mud bank, riddled with bored soldiers. If I were to be stuck for any length of time, Nieva was by far the better place to be. I did not give up hope.

There was a trader who was said to be waiting for the river to settle, before leaving with goods for Iquitos, so my chances of a lift were still strong. The lower the river, the less turbulent the rapids, absolutely crucial, even in a motorized boat, to run the Pongo with the least danger. The *alcalde* was not convinced that the water levels were low enough, and he was not going to risk something happening to me or to the co-op's boat. I should stop being so pushy; I would wait and be patient.

The sixth day in Nieva was a Sunday, and I decided to relieve the monotony by joining the local school children on a visit to Padre Carlos, who resided a short distance up the river Nieva, where he tended a botanical park. A small crowd of us waited for a man to pick us up in one of the local dugouts, into which we piled, the girls screeching as the canoe wobbled in the water. Planks were wedged in at intervals along the dugout, and we squeezed together, three or four to each one, trying not to slip on the slimy wooden bottom. There was a small engine at the back, and we set off making easy headway against the current. The engine was cleverly adapted for use in local conditions, its propeller shaft about three metres long, so that it could be tilted almost horizontally to work in the shallow water of smaller tributaries and near the riverbanks. For the moment we were on a steady course in the middle of the river, and the *peque-peque*, as it is known locally, chugged swiftly up the Nieva, not much narrower but quieter than the Marañon. The banks appeared to be uninhabited on this lower stretch, and the branches of large trees hung over the water into a tangled undergrowth.

The *pacela* was only a short journey away, and we were soon clambering up the mud bank to the Padre's haven. The children went off to spend the day with their Sunday school teacher, while I went to have tea with Carlos in his bamboo house. It was raised slightly off the ground, and the wooden platform was divided into a walled room and a covered, open-sided space where he had a writing table, and a hammock slung between two corner posts. The roof was a traditional thatch of woven palm leaves, whose fringes hung low to create the maximum amount of shade for his open work space. It was a beautiful home, with just a few simple conveniences, such as a gas cooker, a raised bed and book shelves, and I understood why Carlos preferred this to the mission bungalows in Nieva.

He was a blond Cuban in his early forties, who had spent most of his life here, studying the region's flora and fauna with the local Indians, recording traditional names and characteristic properties. His park spread out over a number of acres located between two streams, and within this space, he had cleared parts of the forest to make room for trees and flowers collected from all over the Alto Marañon. The area aimed to show as much as possible of the region's plant variety in one accessible place and it was rich with plant species, and especially in Amazon fruit trees. Carlos took me on a guided tour, and although I could not remember the names of all the plants he described, it was a wonderful experience to be guided around his forest and swept up by his obvious love and enthusiasm for his work. I recognized some of the plants from the Balsas area, including the many varieties of citrus, and also the cacao pods, coffee and cocona bushes, guaba, papaya and banana trees. Most plants, however, were completely new to me, the most memorable being a tree whose brown fruit grew straight out of the trunk, hanging on a short stalk, and looking rather like smooth, elongated kiwis. Another tree was hung with Christmas baubles of green, spherical fruit on long threads. Many of the trees and bushes were not in fruit at this particular time of year, and I got only a small glimpse of the variety the park had to offer. It reinforced the concept of the jungle, not as a paradise of edible, available fruit, but a place of seasons and locations, fruits never growing in one convenient spot, but spread all over the forest, to be searched out at the right time, making the traditional diet of the Amazon Indians a seasonal one, with only a few staples such as fish and yucca, which can be cultivated in cleared jungle areas.

I felt close to the forest for the first time, even in this cultivated place, and it was easily the happiest day of my first week in the Amazon. During the afternoon I spent many hours talking with Carlos about his work as a missionary: how he saw his role regarding the Indians, and to what extent the mission got involved in disputes over Amazon development and local interests. The Jesuits had originally been in the vanguard of the

Spanish Conquest and were an important force in colonizing remote areas and pacifying the Indians, although this was admittedly only during the initial phase. Their active part in the creation of the Spanish empire and the subjection of indigenous peoples changed soon after the first century of conquest, and by the eighteenth century, their role had already changed significantly from the breakers to the protectors of the Indians. Once the Indians had been gathered in the *reducciones* of the missions, Spanish colonial authorities saw them as a good source of slave labour and, when the missionaries took a stand against the proposed enslavement of their flock, they soon found themselves the target of violent opposition. This, and their skill in developing rich farming estates on many of their mission lands, and acting as money lenders to the colonial administration, gave the Jesuits the reputation of dangerous rivals for economic and political power, and they were eventually expelled from the new empire. They have long since returned and their history continues to be inextricably linked with the fortunes of Spanish and Portuguese imperialism in South America.

Carlos did not mind my questioning in the least, and went on to explain that he saw his duties in a more pragmatic context than those of traditional missionaries. His was not the role of gatherer of souls, nor that of imposing a Christian God on the Indians, but rather of showing God's existence and love through creating a caring community. The *padres* never imposed their religion on the native settlements of the region, visiting them only if they were invited to do so, and when they did, they used both Spanish and Aguaruna to conduct religious ceremonies, and important occasions such as baptisms and funerals were adapted to include traditional Indian rituals as well. Robes for mass were decorated with Indian designs, and often the ceremony was conducted by an Indian catechist. On local issues they steered clear of partisan involvement with any interest group, but they did play an advisory role and certainly argued the issues with the government representatives of their department and in Lima.

These men were very different from my preconceptions of missionaries as destroyers of local culture and identity. After spending a week here, I began to believe that if they were going to be here at all, they had the best possible attitude and played a vital role in helping local communities to self-determination, while also carrying out important botanical and scientific studies.

180

I still could not reconcile myself to the necessity of their presence in the first place, but I had learned that their position and their influence here were more complex and vital than I had presumed. Even the highly organized Aguarunas are only just beginning to learn the convoluted rules of dealing with the government and securing their rights, and they need all the help they can get. It seemed to me that the oldest missionary orders, such as the Jesuits, have the most humane approach to their work, and are the least self-seeking; while the numerous modern sects operating in the Amazon have often been well documented as brutal and destructive proselytisers, wreaking cultural devastation wherever they go. I would soon get a chance to meet someone who played a role in this part of the missionary movement and, in his case, my prejudices were only confirmed. For now I was full of admiration for my missionary hosts, and for Carlos in particular.

Meanwhile I was no closer to leaving Nieva and, by the following Monday morning, I decided I was going to continue my journey one way or the other. It had been very interesting spending time with the *padres*, and I was grateful for their generous hospitality, but now it was time to move on. Pacho had radioed a mission situated on the Santiago river, and the sisters there had said the river was quite low, which meant that there was a chance the Pongo would be passable. After breakfast I went down to the waterfront and, sure enough, there was a man leaving for the Santiago by *peque-peque* later that morning. Hope bubbled up inside me and I asked him about shooting the Pongo, but was unable to get a straight answer out of him. I offered him good money, and in the end we agreed that if the water levels at Pinglo, on the mouth of the Santiago, were low, we would go for it; if not, I would be stuck at Pinglo. Now I was beyond worrying about that and I knew only that I was going. I hurried back to the mission for quick goodbyes, cleared my room, packed my rucksack, and returned to the boat to wait for our departure. The man was not leaving straight away, but I was not going to miss this boat, so I sat there together with an Indian mother and child, happy to be on the move at last.

Rain began to pour as we set off up the river, and I hid under my plastic poncho, wondering what was coming next. An hour later the weather had cleared and the boat pulled up at Pinglo military camp. A small shack, like a bus shelter, stood overlooking the confluence of the Santiago and Marañon, and anyone passing had to check in at the post or be pursued by angry soldiers. It must have been a miserable job being stationed here for a year or so, but Peru has a longstanding territorial dispute with Ecuador, and the military checkpoints along the Marañon fortify the country's claim to the region. South American maps still reflect this dispute and, depending on where they were made, show the Peruvian-Ecuadorian border to be either on the Marañon itself, or a line through the forest that begins 200 kilometres north of Pinglo, and cuts diagonally north-east towards the river Putomayo, which forms the Colombian border. The disputed area is a vast chunk of Amazon jungle, and it contains Peru's vital petroleum extraction sites. Therefore all tributaries coming down from Ecuador have military checkpoints to stop potentially hostile forces entering the region. I had been dreading having to check in at Pinglo; it mattered little how many official recommendations I had, if the local captain did not feel like letting me pass, there was nothing I could do about it. The border dispute and the onset of the *Sendero* attacks rendered any stranger the subject of a great deal of suspicion, and I could only hope the captain was in a good mood this morning.

The three of us from the boat climbed up to the shack, and stood in line to hand over our documents. Two boy soldiers with machine-guns slung across their chests stood guard nearby. My turn came, and to my great relief, I was not asked to explain myself beyond saying that I was a tourist who had been visiting Padre Pancho and was now on my way home to Iquitos. The captain was convinced of my harmlessness; perhaps he thought I was a lay sister.

The day was looking good, but now came the difficult part: I had to persuade the trader to make a detour down the Pongo for me. A wooden post the other side of the river showed the river to be at fourteen metres, and my man now decided this was too high. I had no idea whether it was or not, but I did know that the sisters had thought it was low enough, and I made a big show of outrage at his renegation. We argued on the bank while the Indian woman retreated into the dugout under the shade of her black umbrella. I was desperate not to be left there, and eventually I drew the captain into the argument. This man had pledged to take me through the Pongo, I told the captain in my best distressed tone, and now he was going back on his word. How would I continue? The captain came out of his shack, more for the entertainment than out of concern, and together we studied the measuring post. Even he agreed that the river was low enough to pass the Pongo; if the river was between twelve and fifteen metres he said, it was possible to attempt the rapids. My man was not to be persuaded and talked of two German kayakers, who were reputed to have drowned the year before. An hour went by and still he had not left, but neither was he agreeing to take me onwards. His engine was not strong enough, he said, but plainly he was just too scared to go, and I sensed that it was pointless trying to argue any further. He wanted my money very much, but the truth was, he had never shot the Pongo, and now that it came to it, its fierce reputation over-whelmed him. Another boat pulled up, the helmsman of which had just been to scout the entrance of the Pongo, and according to him it was passable. His boat was shaped like an elongated rowing boat, about five metres long, and he had a strong engine at the stern. It looked to me as if nothing much could go wrong in that, and even better, the young man on board was someone I knew from afternoon chats around Nieva's shops. He was on his way to collect some school children from beyond the Pongo and, to my great relief, he let me join him on his journey. I had been prepared to pay a small fortune for my passage: now I was getting a free ride. My gamble had paid off.

As we approached the Pongo, I was a little bit nervous, mainly at the thought of losing my rucksack and my notes. I had put myself in the hands of fate and my companion's river skills and there remained nothing but to sit tight. I sat on a plank in the middle of the boat, while my rucksack was wedged under a seat at the front, although I would have preferred to have it within grabbing distance. But it was too late now. The water ruffled up around us, and I could hear a distant rushing noise, rather like the one you hear from a conch shell, held close to the ear. We rounded a bend into a narrow gorge, lined with high rockface on either side. Suddenly we were going much faster and the boat bobbed up and down on a hundred currents. There were strange, smooth sheets of water, surrounded by angry white swirls, each one representing a dangerous current beneath. We came through the first stretch, and the river was fast but steady. Was that it? I asked my friend, almost disappointed; he laughed nervously and told me that was just the beginning. He stood up to check the waters ahead, and suddenly we entered an even tighter passage of sheer cliffs and slippery boulders, and the waters went mad. There were currents pulling in all different directions: at the centre, there was a strong diagonal pull towards the left, while directly in front of the rockface, the water seemed to be flowing upstream instead of down. We rode on the ridges of enormous waves and edged around great whirlpools, the engine going full blast to counter the concentric pull. It was all a matter of a few, swift minutes, and we were spat out the other end, passing one last giant whirlpool, whose awesome mouth gaped as wide as the boat itself, looking as if it went right down to the riverbed. I shuddered to think what would happen if one were sucked down into its depths; sometimes boats get caught in these whirlpools and spend days going round and round until they are either dragged under or pulled out by another boat in an extremely dangerous rescue operation. Almost a hundred years earlier, Fritz Up de Graff came this way, and wrote about a giant whirlpool at the mouth of the Pongo; perhaps the very one I saw. He had seen a 150-foot tree caught up in it, swept around a few times, and then forced up into a vertical position before being sucked straight down the watery hole in the middle.

It was only afterwards that I fully understood the deadliness of the rapids I had just shot but, having made it, I was exhilarated. It was 3 July, my father's birthday, and I wondered what he would have thought of the Pongo. The wait had been worth it: I had come through the dreaded Pongo de Manseriche, which only a handful of foreigners have ever done, and I felt privileged to be among them.

Shattered Nerves

8 July 1989

I have escaped from a cesspit of intrigue and madness. It seems already as if the last few days cannot have really happened, that it was all a bad dream, a nightmare.

That was the entry in my diary that day; it took another week before I felt able to write again, by which time I had travelled almost 1000 kilometres to Iquitos.

Once through the Pongo, the first significant settlement is Saramarisa, which is where I arrived at mid afternoon. There was a small crowd gathered on the grassy pitch of the village green, watching two *gringos* building a balsa raft, which stood half-finished on one side, surrounded by planks and tools and a large heap of drying palm fronds, intended for the roof. It was a sophisticated version of the simple craft I had seen near Immasita, and the two men were hammering busily, paying no attention at all to their amused audience. I had already heard news of two crazy Germans building a raft in Saramarisa, and I had been looking forward to meeting them, and perhaps catching a lift downriver.

For the moment I needed to find somewhere for the night. In the crowd was a European couple with a young baby, missionaries I guessed, and I decided to ask them if they knew anywhere I could stay. Happily a brief conference of looks decided them on an invitation to their home, and off we went.

Bodil and Manolo were Pentecostalists from Sweden, although Manolo was in fact Spanish. The mission was located a few

185

kilometres downriver, and only accessible by boat. It seemed a shame not to be staying close to the village, but there would be plenty of time to meet the raft-builders the following morning. The small metal speedboat was similar to the first craft I had travelled on, but with an enormous engine, and we speeded downriver breathtakingly. The cleared patch of the mission came into view and Manolo swung the boat round in a great curve, but misjudged the distance and almost beached us on the wooden jetty. Bodil, with the baby in her arms, gave her husband a quiet reprimand, and he laughed, embarrassed. He was the same age as me, although his beard and sturdy body made him look much older. Bodil was in her early thirties, with a lovely face that reminded me of old-fashioned drawings of Little Red Riding Hood. She spoke with a Swedish sing-song and her Spanish came out softly, in contrast to her boisterous husband, whose words tumbled over themselves in Spanish rapidity.

The mission was built a little way back from the river, set in a meticulously kept tropical garden. Red-flowering hibiscus bushes were dotted about a neat lawn, palms stood pruned, and the tall poles of six papaya trees stood to attention overlooking the river. As we arrived, a large German Shepherd dog tore at his lead and barked himself hoarse. The house itself was a two-storey wooden chalet, and looked odd here in the jungle. Inside were luxuries unheard of in Amazon homes: carpet and linoleum on the floors, two tiled bathrooms, a kitchen with every electrical gadget imaginable, and, of course, a private generator to supply them with electricity. It was a Western dream home, and when supper was served, the illusion continued: hot chocolate made with fresh milk, home-made bread and butter with paté, fresh vegetable soup, and delicious brownies. The food was a joy to my taste-buds, especially the bread and butter, which I had not eaten for months. Where did all this food come from? I asked, and my hosts explained that most of it was flown in from the United States and Lima. They were even able to make radio contact anywhere on the planet; while the immediate world of the jungle was kept at a safe distance, the forest behind fences and the people upriver. Bodil, Manolo, and I had very different attitudes but they did not stand between us, and we enjoyed each other's company.

Early the next morning, Manolo drove me back up to Saramarisa to wait for any boats that might be heading downriver. The two *gringos* were already hard at it, working on the skeleton of poles that was to support the roof and walls of their raft. One was a tall man in his mid thirties, wearing a kind of pirate cap made out of cloth around his head; while the other was an old man in his sixties, sporting an Aussie hat without the corks. They looked like eccentric travellers and I set out to get to know them. The old man was in charge and bossed the other around grumpily, but he took little notice, his only response to roll another cigarette. They spoke a hilarious mixture of English and German with each other – the old man had lived in Australia for the past thirty years – and I laughed till my sides ached listening to their banter. They enjoyed having an audience, and relentlessly flung insults at each other, pulling faces behind each other's back to the delight of the children and the other villagers alike. Lunchtime saw us the best of friends, and I was formally invited to join their expedition. I accepted, making a mental note to myself to find out more before I made up my mind, but for the moment happy to join them in their lodgings in the village.

Saramarisa was a populous but small collection of wooden shacks on stilts, which had sprung up fifteen years earlier to service the needs of the nearby Petroperu station. It was a dilapidated, dirty place, with putrid swamps underneath the houses, where rotting food and rubbish was thrown from the kitchens above, to await the annual rains that washed it away.

The two Germans were staying in a fine, two-storey house, built high off the ground, and with spacious rooms inside. It too had bubbling green slime underneath it, as I soon found out when I needed to go to the toilet: a slippery line of planks led under the house and out to the back, where a rickety ladder leaned against the stilted privy, below which was the remains of a bush, festooned with excrement and bits of toilet paper. The house belonged to a handsome *mestizo* woman, who lived here with her five children, her husband away working at the oil stations. She was cutting up a fresh pineapple when we arrived, and I was soon sitting around the table, eating fruit, and welcomed as a new member of her extended family of foreign guests. The atmosphere in the house was very friendly, and I felt it would be good to spend some time here.

After lunch, the younger German and I went off to find the local police captain to get my name added officially to the expedition documents. The captain was visiting town from his

187

usual office at the oil station, but he had brought his pad and rubber stamps, and between us, we composed the new document.

My new friend played the clown, even with the captain, and very effective it was too because, in spite of his gravity and starched uniform, the captain could not help smiling at this ridiculous *gringo*, and consequently he did not bother to ask who I was and where I had suddenly sprung from, and I was thus formally entered in the expedition documents and given permission to travel freely in the Peruvian departments of Amazonas and Loreto. I already had permission to travel there, from Lima, but it could do no harm to have it from the local authorities as well. We all went for a beer to celebrate, and I came away with an invitation for lunch at the captain's headquarters the following day. It was an excellent start, and I spent the rest of the day back at the raft, a new member of the circus.

We laughed a lot that afternoon, making fun of ourselves as great explorers and mixing English, German and Spanish into an endless patter of silliness. Jokes apart, I was let in on the general plan for the expedition, and had time to reflect that, although the two were fun for a while, I was not sure I could spend any length of time on the confined space of a raft with them. I had been travelling independently for four months by now, and I was not about to join a group unless the people were right and the project similar to my own. Their plan was to spend about a month travelling up the Santiago, staying with Huambisa Indians and looking for lost Inca ruins before heading towards the Atlantic.

Listening to their talk I felt they were neither particularly competent nor informed about the regions they planned to journey through, and I began to wish I had not been so quick to accept their invitation. By the time we packed up for the day, I had come to the conclusion that they were a dangerous combination of gung-ho adventurers and selfish opportunists, their interest in the Indians and the forest merely an exotic backdrop to their fantastic delusions. My suspicions were confirmed when the old man confided that the real reason for their journey was to look for El Dorado and its fabled gold. He had a map that someone had given him twenty years before, which was supposed to show the way to a cache of gold treasures, untouched by human hand. This sounded like Hollywood to me, but the old man was completely serious and made me promise not to tell a soul.

The following morning I had decided that I wanted no part in their harebrained scheme and that, in any case, they were going too far in the wrong direction to suit my purposes. How would I tell them I had changed my mind? It was an awkward moment I decided to postpone till I had plucked up enough courage.

Instead, I kept my date for lunch with the captain at Petroperu's *Estacion 5*. Closed off behind high wire fencing and armed guards, the workers of the oil station lived on a man-made island in the middle of the forest. They had their own runway to fly personnel and provisions in and out from the coast, and lived in air-conditioned bungalows with every convenience, from showers to videos. As at the mission, the food was excellent, and I gorged myself on steak and roast potatoes. Little wonder that I had not seen many Petroperu workers in Saramarisa: there was nothing but women the men could not get at the compound, and even they were said to be flown in occasionally, highly paid to service all the stations along the pipeline in one convenient airlift.

On the way back from the station, I encountered a local prostitute, an Indian transvestite, who was waiting for a lift as we passed in one of the oil trucks. The driver slowed down to allow her to jump on, and at first I thought it was just her clothes that were rather unusual for these parts: her bare feet were squeezed into patent leather high heels, and she was carrying a white plastic handbag to match her white halter top. Shiny black hair hung down her smooth back, but the shoulders were too broad, the legs too muscled, and the truth dawned on me by the time she jumped off again. The driver said that s/he was a very popular local attraction; she, or he, seemed sad to me and symbolized a prostitution of both sex and culture. This was the ultimate Amazon development. Saramarisa's underside was as rotten as the earth it stood on.

Another *gringo* who was preparing to leave shortly was William C. Townsend, son of the founder of the notorious Summer

Institute of Linguistics (SIL), for more of which, see 'Is God an American?' He was also preparing a craft on the village green, only his was a large boat with room for ten people and six weeks' provisions; he had hired Saramarisa's top trader to fix up a boat for him, and everyone in the village was laughing behind his back at the outrageous money he was paying. We all spent time on the green, and it was only a matter of time before I got chatting to him. I was tempted to try and join his trip; I had read so much about SIL, and this seemed a unique opportunity to observe the machinations of the organization at close quarters. William was not a working member of SIL himself, but he was obviously indoctrinated with his father's militant missionary philosophy. He had grown up a mission kid in Peru and spent a long time living with Indians as a child. He was now in his early thirties, and returning to visit *curacas* (the tribal headmen) along the river Morona, who were about to hold important meetings with chiefs from all over the region. He was an amiable enough man, but his ideas were completely up the creek.

'You like clean bathrooms and toilets don't you? Well, all I want to do is help the Indians have these things too. Just as Jesus purified us by bringing Christianity to mankind, I want to show the Indians how to live a more hygienic life with better housing designs.'

He said this with the sublime self-assurance of the righteous, and if I disagreed, it was only because I did not understand.

Perhaps I do not understand, but I will never cease to be amazed by people who think they have a right, God-given or otherwise, to change other people's beliefs and way of life, and I knew that if I spent any length of time with him, his God-squad talk was bound to drive me mad. More importantly, association with anyone from SIL was not likely to be productive when attempting to visit an Indian settlement. I abandoned that option and, the second evening, I told the Germans that I had changed my mind about joining them; at which, to my enormous relief, they did not take offence. We drank a couple of beers and a small bottle of rum before heading back to the house, toasting each other and wishing good luck all round.

Over supper I mentioned my conversation with William. Among other things, he had told me some rather unpleasant personal details about our hostess, which I thought was indiscreet of him; and before I knew where we were, a full-scale row had erupted about whether or not she should be told what was being said about her. For me it was out of the question to hurt her feelings by passing on insulting rumours, but the others insisted that it was my duty to tell her, and that if I didn't they would. I refused to repeat what William had said, and the row finished with the two men leaving the dinner table, our hostess and I left to stare at each other in embarrassed silence. The row had taken place in German, but she knew that we had argued and that her name had cropped up a lot. She sat in baffled silence, and I tried to pretend it was nothing important, and wished that I had not opened my stupid mouth in the first place.

In less than forty-eight hours, the two men and I had gone from being friends to enemies and I was quite worn out by the pace of it all. I tried to calm down, it was only a silly disagreement, surely nothing worth fighting about, and when the others returned to the house, I tried to be conciliatory, and even apologized for upsetting them. Instead they were on the warpath, and with breathtaking logic had decided that I was trying to sabotage their expedition. They began to threaten to set the captain against me, making sure that no one would help me travel onwards, and I could not believe their vicious talk and the anger in their faces. I can only suppose it was the alcohol we had drunk earlier. The old man, in particular, got it into his head that I was out to use them to find the gold for myself and that I wanted to trick him out of his secret map.

Nothing I said seemed to make any difference, so I retreated to our joint sleeping quarters upstairs, ignoring their ridiculous rage. The old man followed close behind, however, and insisted I show him my copy of the document the captain had written for me. I got it out to reassure him that it gave me no rights to his expedition, but then he wanted to destroy it, and I refused to hand it over. It was a useful document, and anyway, it was mine and not his.

'Give me the document,' he shouted, and made a grab for it.

The room was only just wide enough for the three beds, and as I dodged with the paper in my hand, I fell back on to one of the beds. Instantly the old man jumped on top of me, tearing at my hands, banging my back against the wooden wall, until finally I let go. Our bodies untangled, he set a match to the document, and stamped the remains into the floor.

'There,' he said. 'Now we are quits.' My shoulders were aching from being flung against the wall, my head was spinning in shock, and meanwhile the old man's friend stood by and watched it all.

'Why didn't you help me? You saw what was happening.'

He shrugged his shoulders and said he wasn't the boss. It was another game for him, but it had turned nasty, so now he was keeping out of the way.

Our hostess had remained downstairs, but now she had had enough and told us all to go to bed. It was the only thing left to do. As I lay down under my mosquito net, an arm's length away from the old man, I still could not believe what had just happened, and I brooded long into the night, figuring the sudden horror of it. I hate arguments and loathe physical violence even more.

In the morning I woke up tired and tense, determined not to stay in the house any longer, and to leave Saramarisa as soon as possible. As I dressed, the old man came up behind me.

'Why did you look through my papers during the night?' he asked in a low, threatening voice.

'What?' I said, unprepared for this new assault, my first reaction to shrug him off, sick as I was of the whole performance. I angrily told him not to talk rubbish. He was deadly serious, though, and began to shout at me to pack my things and get out at once, and that if I was calling him a liar, he had a good mind to punch me right now. I could not believe it. *What* was going on? Perhaps he had gone mad. It was preposterous. But no, he had seen me with his own eyes, looking through the papers under his bed. I forbore to point out that I had not known where his papers were, and that I would not have been foolish enough to look through them while he was in the room.

He stormed downstairs with a great wad of papers and handed them over dramatically to our hostess, who was trying to cook breakfast. She spoke neither German nor English, but the old man gave her a grave speech in English about how I had searched his papers, and could she please lock them away in a safe place. Mystified, she turned to me, and I had to translate what had just been said. It was crazy: suddenly I found myself in the role of the devious enemy, accused and condemned without redress.

I was in a helpless state of shock, my mind a defensive blank, and although I kept reminding myself of my innocence, I was completely incapable of defending myself, or explaining the

192

situation to our poor hostess. The old man's paranoia disjointed my own sense of reality and I became disorientated and panicky, unable to make sense of what was going on. I tried hard to catch my breath and stay calm, but it was not easy; I could not bear to be accused of something I had not done, and something which I thought despicable.

Leaving the house was easy. I packed up my rucksack and went looking for the Swedes, explaining that three guests were too much for the local woman. They took me back without further question and I said nothing of my experiences.

The next morning Manolo returned me to the village, as he had on the first day. A local Petroperu launch was leaving on a supply journey to Saramuro, halfway to Iquitos, and to my immense relief the captain let me hitch a lift. They were not leaving until midday, so I went back to the house in the village to say goodbye to the woman who had kept me for the previous two days.

She was still confused about what had happened, and asked me not to think badly of her house, nor to believe the gossip around the village. She had guessed that William had said some bad things about her, and told me there was a lot of bad feeling between them because her cousin had been engaged to him, but had left him for someone else. I was sorry for the way things had turned out, and wished above all that I had said nothing, feeling that the subsequent events had been my fault to a certain extent, although I could never have imagined the consequences.

Perhaps I should have kept away from the Germans in the first place; I had been prepared to use them, to put up with their half-baked antics in return for a free ride to places otherwise inaccessible. My attitude had been selfish and was perhaps a lesson in getting on under my own steam and creating my own opportunities. At the time the experience bowled me over, and it was all I could do not to crack up. Gone was my cherished sense of inner peace I had nurtured in the mountains, back was my mistrust of others and all my old cynicism.

Saramarisa suddenly epitomized corruption and decay to me: the forest that had been burned down to make way for the oil station and this cesspit of a village; the rotting slime under the houses;

193

the Indian transvestite; the rumours people spread about each other; the lack of care for the environment and for other people.

The Amazon was a disappointment: not only had I failed to get into the forest or meet its people, but I had experienced the worst moments of the journey so far. My illness and the risks taken in the mountains were as nothing compared to the strain of the last two days. Most depressing of all was the difference in my relationships with people: in the mountains, the *campesinos* had welcomed me with kindness and generosity, never asking for anything in return. We shared our food and I felt that, even in the brief moments we spent together, we acknowledged each other as individuals and enjoyed meeting. By contrast, during the first two weeks in the Amazon, almost all my relationships were based on money. I was trapped in a dependence on others, whose willingness to help was usually directly linked to the size of the payment I made. I could do nothing, go nowhere, without help from someone else; each advance I made the result of haggling, persuasion, and elaborate games of double-bluff: it was very frustrating indeed.

Back at the village green, I talked to some of the villagers while I waited for the launch. There were more people there than usual because a corpse had been fished out of the river, his eyes eaten away, his legs cleaned to the bone and the rest of him crawling with worms and fish. A body did not last long in the Amazon; what was left of him was put in a blue plastic bag. He had been a soldier from Pinglo, and we waited for the army helicopter to come and collect him. Two other soldiers arrived by boat to identify the body, and when the helicopter finally arrived, they put the body on a plank to carry it over. But the plank was too narrow, and the body flopped on to the ground twice, the plastic contorting into macabre shapes as it slipped again and again into a crumpled heap.

Rest in Iquitos

The journey to Saramuro on the powerful Petroperu launch was scheduled to take one day. Instead the engine broke down, and we spent three days drifting slowly downriver, in between short bursts of the motor working at half throttle; the first day we made it as far as San Lorenzo. On board with me were seven men: the captain of the launch and the Petroperu workers who were transferring to other stations along this section of the pipeline, which runs parallel to the river. We did not speak during the first day's journey. I was in no mood to talk to anyone, and was also uncomfortably conscious of my solitary state amid all these men.

By the time we all climbed on to the river bank at San Lorenzo, the atmosphere had lightened a little, and I joined in, helping to carry valuables to the nearby guesthouse. It was an attractive wooden house, which had U-shaped wings built towards the back, where one tiny room backed on to the next, cubicle-fashion. There were no windows, but a wide section connecting the walls to the roof was made up of wire netting, providing a constant breeze in the otherwise baking heat of the rooms. The netting also gave us some protection from the plagues of *zancudos*, the biting flies of the sticky tropics which leave an itchy blood blister. The blisters leave ugly marks once scratched open and I could never resist picking at them, my elbows and hands rapidly becoming a mess of welts.

The men found a local woman who they persuaded to cook us supper, and while we waited, we drank *cano de azucar* (cane rum) outside the riverside bar. We did not talk much. The men were not sure what to make of me, and some had seen me having lunch with the police captain, and treated me with restraint, just in case.

We finished our meal in the growing dusk, and I left the men to continue drinking. I was worried that they might leave me

195

behind in the morning, and I wanted to be up early to ensure against it. Sleep was difficult, though, since my recurrent diarrhoea made a fresh attack and, as I prepared to visit the toilets for the umpteenth time, the men returned from the bar, drunk as skunks. I stood behind the locked door of my room, waiting for them to disperse, but two hung about just outside my door, crashing around, laughing and groaning, repeating monosyllabic utterings to each other. I could hear one of them relieve himself on the lawn and, as I was by now close to bursting myself, I could wait no longer, and hearing one let himself into his room, I decided to come out. A dark silhouette stood swaying an arm's length away, but I made a dash for some nearby bushes, squatting in the darkness, hoping he would not come over. He did not.

But when I returned, the captain grabbed me by the arm; I was not paying for my passage downriver, and he thought perhaps I would do him a different favour. This time I was far more aggressive than I had been in Tactamal, and shouted at him so loudly and suddenly that he let me go immediately. He managed to mumble a surprised apology before I slammed the door in his face. He was not to know that I was much more humiliated by having to empty my guts within his earshot than by his clumsy advance, and when I had calmed down, I almost giggled at the thought of his sudden fright. The incident broke the tension within myself, and I felt easy for the first time since leaving Saramarisa. In the morning we continued our journey as if nothing had happened.

The Marañon snaked onwards in a sedate but powerful flow, and now many large islands obscured its true breadth. There seemed no obvious way to recognize which was the main stream of the river, and which a tributary heading off in the wrong direction. Sometimes the river dissolved into what looked like a large lake, especially if tributaries flowed in on a curve, and then only an expert navigator could know the way ahead. The banks, meanwhile, were an endless monotony of shrubland and secondary forest, with the odd dense patch of reeds in the water where the current was weak. Very few people seemed to live along this stretch of the Marañon, but the forests nearby had obviously been cleared or cultivated at some point in the past, and what I saw was not what you might call jungle. There was little wildlife to be seen. We were unlikely to see very much in the daytime anyway, and were too far from the banks to get a close look at the river fowl. Green parakeets screeched overhead sometimes, but that was about it. There was more wildlife on the launch: some of the men had bought presents for their families. One man had a red-breasted parakeet, which sat miserably on the floor of the cabin, detesting the noise of the engine, and squawking madly if anyone tried to pick him up. We gave him a plantain banana to pick on, but he seemed to have lost his appetite. Another man had a tiny marmoset on a lead, that scrunched up its nocturnal eyes in the blinding daylight, covering its furry face like a frightened child. The men thought it was funny to set it on deck, and see it trying to scamper for a dark corner until it was dragged back by the lead around its waist. It made me cringe, and eventually I asked what kind of a *macho* it was who tormented defenceless animals. They only laughed in awkward embarrassment; I was embarrassed too. I knew it was ridiculous to make a stand with these men: they would not change their attitudes because of my 'foreign' sentimentality towards animals, and the marmoset was only left alone for the moment. It would soon be the plaything of the man's family. This was the reality: there was no wildlife to be seen, but it could still be hunted down and brought out, either for eating, decoration or entertainment. I am not sure whose fate was worse: the parrot's, the marmoset's, or that of the land turtles, who slid up and down the floor on their backs. They were for eating, their beautiful armour to be discarded like cracked nutshells. There were plenty of jungle animals: there were the rolled-up furs of Amazon jaguars, cured skins of boa constrictors, and knives with handles made of lizard claws. The jaguar skins sold for I/15,000; worth $5 at the time. Five dollars for the life of one of the Amazon's rarest and most beautiful animals, soon to be another statistic on the list of extinction.

On the second day we stopped briefly at Barranca military camp for the standard checking of documents. It was early evening and the sun set in a red blaze, setting the river a-glitter as each little wave cast its reflection. I wanted to photograph it, but the men insisted I put my camera away as we were approaching a military installation, where photographs are forbidden.

I wished I could have taken a shot of the scene at the camp. The soldiers had evidently just had their evening meal, and about a hundred of them were picking their way down the red clay riverbank to wash their aluminium food trays. All of them were dressed in immaculate sea-green trousers, their chests covered only with white vests, and most seemed barely old enough to be there. Some looked no more than fifteen years old, and I was reminded of the sad stories I had heard of young boys, especially Indians, conscripted against their will. Once stationed in one of these camps, they are waterlocked prisoners for a minimum of two years. Some try to escape, but strangely, many Peruvians cannot swim, including those born on, or near, the Amazon, and often they drown in the attempt. Perhaps that is what had happened to the soldier who had been washed up in Saramarisa. The looks on the boys' faces as they watched us leave were saddening; not one had spoken while we were there but their eyes said everything.

We made it to Saramuro on the third day. There was nothing much there. It was a small settlement of wooden houses next to the fenced-in compound of the Petroperu station. My lift was over, and we parted, the men went to the station and I to the village to find out about the next boat for Iquitos. The jungle city was another night and day away, close in local terms, and I knew there would be plenty of trade and passenger *lanchas* passing by. One was expected that very afternoon, bringing plantain and other goods from the river Pastaza, which flows to meet the Marañon from the Ecuadorian border. I settled down in the shade to doze away the hours of waiting, glad not to stay the night; I had no desire to make conversation and hang around these gossip-ridden settlements. I craved the anonymity of Iquitos, where I could get a hotel room, go to restaurants and watch the crowds, alone and unknown.

The *lancha* was a stumpy little boat, with an iron base, no more than fifteen metres long and five wide, with a cramped, two-storey cabin built on top. The lower deck was mainly taken up by the cavernous storage space, where there was just enough room for three hammocks to swing in between the plantain, petrol barrels and pig-pen. The only light that came in was through the cracks in the plank walls and the doorway at the stern. Directly next to the storage space was the engine room, which roared and shuddered with bone-rattling ferocity. A small stove and toilet were set close to each other at the bow, and the negotiation of anything in either was severely hampered by the vibration of the engine. The upper deck was luxurious by

198

comparison, with cabin doors and railings painted white, and a pleasant, windless gangway in which to while away the long hours. Up here there was no smell. Down below, the sweet smell of plantain was tainted with petrol fumes and the sourness of pig shit and poultry droppings. The boat owner and his two Indian mistresses were installed upstairs, and I was in a hammock below. I was free to wander, though, and I spent the daylight hours sitting on the upper gangway. The open deck area up top was crammed with palm baskets full of chickens and ducks, covered in green palm fronds to protect them from the sun. The heat shut them up for the most part, but at feeding time they exploded into life, a flurry of feathered bodies scrambling for the corn.

The boat owner was a wrinkled, white-haired man with a plump belly, who spent most of his time being pampered by one or other of his mistresses. In his cabin was an Aladdin's cave of goodies stacked and crannied away: tobacco, shampoo, plastic plates, chewing-gum, anything, in fact, that the inhabitants along the river might want to buy. There was nothing to drink on board, but he was selling bottles of Coke for I/5000. The normal price was I/1000, but who cared when you had a dry throat? He was a very rich man, and I saw him counting neat stacks of bank notes, ready to be deposited in Iquitos. When his girls were not attending to his pleasure in the cabin, they shared a hammock on deck, sleeping or putting make-up on each other, their lovely golden faces looking like those of naughty children: garish red lipstick smudged around their lips, their eyes heavy with baby blue eyeshadow and black mascara. I wondered about them and where they had come from. Was this a better life than before? Here they were with one man, for the moment, provided for and safe.

We reached Nauta, on the confluence of the Ucayali and Maranon, at dawn. From here on, the river is known as the Amazon, and as the sun edged its way over the fluid horizon ahead, I felt elated and happy to be here after all. We were heading directly east into the sunrise, and the whole river was a wonderland of colour and light. Banks of mist hovered at the water's edge, and a couple of dugout canoes appeared through them, their occupants paddling slowly against the current. The moment lasted only a few minutes before it was dissipated by the white light of morning. My spirits remained high, though, and I looked forward to our arrival in Iquitos.

We still had most of the day before we reached port, but somehow the hours passed quickly, and by late afternoon the outline of the city came into view. The helmsman picked his way among the channels that formed between vast floating lawns of tangled weeds, until we nudged out into the main waterway approaching the harbour and its floating slums.

Long before we reached dock, large motorized canoes came out to meet us, and the boat was soon crowded with women market traders, bulging out of their overalls, and heaving off the best produce before it even got near town and the competition. Each of the women had a male assistant, and once they had argued out the price of their plantain, the man was quickly ordered to heave the goods on to her canoe floating alongside. By the time we reached the harbour itself, the storage hold was already half empty, but even so, as soon as the *lancha* came to a standstill, the decks were awash with people pushing and shouting. Wads of money were flick-counted with expert speed, ducks and chickens were plucked out of their baskets by whatever part of their bodies came to hand, a pig was sent squealing over the edge, flopping painfully into the bottom of a waiting boat: it was mayhem, and all the while the old man was upstairs, counting his growing pile of money.

I handed over my own contribution, and hopped onboard a river taxi to reach dry land and walk into town. My first shower in a week awaited me, and I hurried past rotting piles of discarded vegetables to find *La Pascana*, one of the cheapest places in town, but highly recommended by other travellers, where I intended to stay.

I liked Iquitos from the moment I arrived. It was a crumbling mess of concrete new and colonial old, the waterside market was filthy and the prices outrageous, but I enjoyed the atmosphere of melancholic decay that hung about this once beautiful city. During the rubber boom, at the turn of the century, its grand mansions with their Portuguese tiles and iron-wrought balconies must have looked splendid; now their cracked and rusty facades stood neglected amid the hurly-burly of modern streets. Iquitos was a faded photograph of its former self, when fortune seekers mixed with wealthy merchants, and the streets were paved with nothing but red mud. I think perhaps that I imposed my own romanticism on the place, but I was in the mood.

I spent the first day or two just wandering about the traffic-choked streets, and the evenings eating expensive meals in the city's many and varied restaurants. There were lots of Chinese restaurants here: a colonial legacy. A meal of fried greens and mushrooms with noodles was delicious after months of potato and rice dishes, and I ate as much as I could, although I knew my guts would revenge themselves. I got sick soon afterwards and even developed a fever which kept me to my bed, but it was worth it.

On the main square, there was a bar that sold freshly-made fruit juices – no doubt from dirty water – and I made a point of drinking at least two every day. The pineapple ones were the best, with a wonderful fruity froth on top, and another good one was papaya juice whisked with egg and rum. All the upsets and disappointments of the past week were soothed away, and my good faith and confidence gradually returned.

My most important contact regarding a journey into the forest to an Indian settlement was here in Iquitos, and the local FOPTUR office helped me make an appointment to see him. He was the Franciscan bishop, whom I was hoping might be persuaded to authorize a visit to a remote Franciscan mission on the rio Napo. This mission, I had heard, worked with Kichwa Indians, who were not acculturated to an advanced stage and would therefore be particularly interesting to visit. It was a long shot, but it was all I had, and I went to my meeting, desperately willing it to go well.

The bishop listened politely to my tenuous explanations for wanting to visit the Napo mission, only to tell me that torrential rains had turned the entire region of the Upper Napo into a disaster area. Crops were ruined, people without food, and the mission was virtually cut off because the only hydroplane had broken down. It was a bleak picture and my heart sunk.

The bishop had other things on his mind, and I felt guilty about pushing my point, but I was clutching at straws. We looked at a map together, and finally he pointed out a small place called Pebas, where he said the local sisters might be able to help me visit Bora Indian communities along the rio Ampiyacu. He

201

was going there himself in the next couple of days, but there was no room on his boat, so I would have to make my own way. It was not much, but at least he had pointed me in the right direction and for that I was deeply grateful. Pebas lay twelve hours downriver, not far away, and in the right direction for the rest of my journey. I thanked the bishop for his time and advice, and made straight for the port to enquire about boats for Pebas. There were none for a couple of days, but I had a plan, hope, and plenty of time.

In the meantime, I made friends with some of the residents at *La Pascana*. The rooms were arranged on either side of a private garden with a bed of flowering shrubs and circular covered benches, where guests could sit in the peaceful shade. It was very pleasant, even though the rooms were separated by very thin walls through which you could hear absolutely everything going on in the entire hotel.

Across the flower bed from me were three Canadian college boys on their first journey abroad and I enjoyed their company and some good laughs over fine food and cold beers. Another guest turned out to be an English botanist from Kew Gardens. I had seen him smoking leaves in a strange contraption in the garden, and wondered what he was up to. When we finally got talking, he explained that he was drying the plant samples he had collected in the forest. His name was Terry and I told him about my own project for getting into the forest, only to discover that he was familiar with the Boras and the rio Ampiyacu. He had spent some time there, studying the forest and staying in the house of an Indian botanist from the local Bora community. Terry generously offered to introduce me to his Indian colleague, so that I might get an introduction to stay with his people. I could hardly believe my good fortune.

After many delays and false starts, I eventually got a passage out of Iquitos on the *Juliana*, the same boat that Werner Herzog had used for his film *Fitzcarraldo*. She was a marvellous old riverboat with almost all her original features. The walls of the white hull were drawn right up to the floor of the upper deck, and inside was the noisy storage, where third class passengers shared their hammock space with trade goods and animals. Above, there were two rows of private cabins in polished wood, while the open deck astern was the place for second class passengers to string up their hammocks.

202

On arrival, there were just one or two here, but by the time we came to leave, the deck was festooned with colourful hammocks, strung next to each other in parallel lines, over each other, under each other, anywhere there was space. Lying in my hammock was like being in a suspended sardine can, with someone else's feet in my face, another body bumping mine the other side, and yet another hanging directly overhead. There were at least two hundred passengers onboard, and almost as many friends and family crowding the banks and the boat for their farewells. Men and women shouted last messages to each other, argued over how to arrange luggage or tie knots for the hammocks, children cried, and the engine rumbled below.

It was already dark by the time we left, and rain began to pelt the *Juliana*'s leaky roof. A full-blown tropical rainstorm ensued and large drips began to spot the passengers on the open upper deck. Great canvas flaps were quickly unrolled from the roof and tied along the railings, but helped little against the drips coming from above. I had my plastic poncho with me, and lay there happy and dry, soaking in only the bustling atmosphere of the boat: I was on my way.

Hours passed before we left port and I had time to reflect on how Peruvians always seem to be ill-prepared for their climate. Affordable covers are available to virtually anyone in the market. Yet people will do almost nothing to change the course of fate, whether it's the country falling to pieces, getting wet in the rain, or having things stolen from them. The latter is a classic example of the problem.

Many a time, I sat waiting in bus stations, and there would be pick-pockets and thieves operating among the passengers. The long-term passengers usually had time to spot the thieves, but would say nothing. They would watch something being stolen from the very next person in silence, and yet if that person jumped up and noticed, they would be the first to commiserate and agree that the thief was a scoundrel. At first I thought this was outrageous hypocrisy. But it isn't. It's just a part of this national character of fatalism, which creates a terrible inertia and makes it almost impossible to take an active part in forming events. Things just happen, but it would be a mistake to think nobody cared.

Visiting the Boras

The *Juliana* stopped outside Pebas at dawn, and a couple of boys in canoes came to taxi passengers ashore. I was the only one getting off here, and I felt distinctly vulnerable and self-conscious as I was paddled away under the staring eyes of the boat behind me and the villagers ahead. The storm had cooled the air considerably, the morning was grey and the air clammy.

From Terry's Bora friend Guillermo, I had an introduction for Pebas as well as for further upriver, and it was not long before I was having tea and bread at Lola's. Her home was a single-storey wooden house, set on a concrete base on the ground. Pebas was an outpost of 'civilization', with municipal offices, a police station, mission, and school. Only the houses built on the regularly flooded mud of the riverbank were built on stilts. The rest were either entirely made of concrete or like Lola's house. There was no running water, but a generator provided electricity in the evenings, when it was working. And though there was no piped water supply, Lola still had a ceramic toilet perched over a trench in the back garden. It was not much, but it was a big improvement on the stilted arrangements used by settlements upriver. I stayed the night, and in the morning, I persuaded the local sisters to let someone take me up the Ampiyacu in their boat. It cost me a fortune in gasoline, but it was the only way to reach my destination. No one travelled beyond Pebas apart from the Boras themselves, or the occasional missionary or anthropologist.

The journey upriver took three beautiful hours. The Ampiyacu wound north into the forest and, for the first time, I was treated to the sight of Amazon kingfishers, flocks of lemon-yellow butterflies that fluttered through the air like showers of confetti, and most exhilarating of all, the sight of the giant Morpho butterfly. Its wings are a metallic azure blue, and it is about the size of a woman's hand, much too large to fly gracefully; it is majestic, though, and its halting flight is captivating.

We passed two villages, my heart beating faster each time at the thought that we might be there, and at last we arrived at the traditional thatched and stilted houses of Brillo Nuevo. The village was arranged in a single row of houses along the bend of an oxbow lake, the remains of a loop in the river, which had been cut off once the water's flow had washed away the separating earth. A wide, grassy bank stood between the houses and the water, creating a spacious promenade which was very attractive. At either end of the village, a cluster of houses were built into a clearing of the interior, with a large village green and the school one end, and the communal meeting house, the *maloca*, the other.

Beyond the village, a wall of forest stood in protective embrace, with a few footpaths leading off to the villagers' *chacras*, the clearings where they cultivated their crops of fruit and vegetables. In former times they would have cultivated coca too, but now, this near to the Colombian border it was prohibited, and as if to assure anyone who might come to check up, the village sign proclaimed *Brillo Nuevo – Vida si, coca no!* (Life Yes, Coca No!)

I had an introduction to the *presidente* of the community, Leonidas Lopez, and the boatman pulled up at the far curve, outside his house. A small group of people were standing around a large upturned boat that was being prepared for the water. Now they all turned to see who had arrived, and feeling even more self-conscious than the day before, I carried my rucksack up towards them.

Leonidas came forward to shake my hand, while someone else hauled off my rucksack and the large sacks of provisions I had brought as a gift. I explained briefly the purpose of my visit, and handed him Guillermo's letter. He was a grave middle-aged *mestizo*, with a short, stocky body, and a handsome face that glistened in the sun. He wore jeans and a shirt, and looked just like any other settler I had seen so far. On first glance, the appearance of the other men, women and children was familiar, although their faces were recognizably Indian, with high cheekbones, full lips and straight black hair.

I was ushered into the house, and Leonidas' Indian wife came to shake my hand with a broad gold-capped smile. She was a corpulent woman, whose flowery dress strained around her middle, but her face was as fresh and beautiful as that of an

205

eighteen-year-old, and her smile and charcoal-coloured eyes exuded warmth and generosity. I felt instinctively comfortable with her, although I knew it would take time before she felt the same around me. For the moment she just hid behind her beaming smile, and went off to make tea on her open hearth at the back of the house.

In the meantime, I was introduced to the *curaca*, the traditional head man of most Indian communities, and he shook my hand, swaying slightly. He was drunk, and a green stain of coca rimmed his mouth. I tried not to let my distaste show, but I took an instant dislike to the man, which was reinforced when he took me aside and asked what I was going to pay him in return for staying here. It was obvious that he felt in competition with Leonidas, who was the elected head of the village, in charge of Peruvian order; while he was the traditional head, elected for life and responsible for the community's tribal customs. I was eager not to get caught between the two interests, nor fuel any trouble, so I explained that I had brought many provisions, fish hooks, and medicines for the house of my host, Leonidas, which I had been told was the proper thing to do. He would have to talk to him if he felt there was a problem. The *curaca* dropped the subject, his concentration drifting, but with a new burst of energy, he insisted that I come to see the *maloca*, which it was his honour to live in as well.

The *maloca* was a large, open-sided roundhouse, about twenty metres in diameter, covered by a steep roof of intricately woven palm leaves. The thick supporting beams of the structure were decorated with ancient geometric patterns in black and white, very simple and beautiful. To one side stood the twin barrels of the *manguare*, the talking drums which traditionally called the people together when there were meetings to be held or news to be relayed. Now, the *curaca* told me, they were rarely used and many of the younger generation do not understand its language and cannot play the instrument. I found the *maloca* a wonderful place, though, where the spiritual atmosphere of a great cathedral was mixed with the down-to-earth feel of a home. The *curaca*'s family hammocks and sitting logs dotted the whole area, fires smouldered under blackened cooking pots, and a tame parrot and midget monkey teased each other across the ground; and yet it seemed also a good place for contemplation and for celebrating special occasions. I shook the *curaca*'s hand and thanked him

206

with suitable humility for showing me this sacred house, and promised to visit his family soon. I sensed that he enjoyed my deferring to him in this way, and I was glad to be able to soothe his pride a bit. I treated him with the respect a woman was expected to show men, especially him, and left him reassured that I appreciated his importance.

The Boras originally came from the Colombian forests, further north, where the majority of the tribe still lives. They were quite numerous, but many were enslaved by the *caucheros* (rubber tappers) during the rubber boom, and of those a great number died. The invaders were called *balleadores* by the Indians, meaning shooters, and even today the phrase is still used, although the killing stopped long ago.

The Boras were dispersed all along the Amazon waterways during their slavery, but a few generations ago, the survivors came together in communities along the Ampiyacu, where they have been ever since, trying to re-establish their tribal culture. Ironically, a family of SIL workers has been largely responsible for bringing the communities back together, and they have lived and worked among them for the past thirty years.

The tribe's cultural disintegration is therefore well established, with not only the replacement of their religion with the evangelical gospel, but Peruvian officialdom only three hours downriver, and a village school run on national curriculum principles. Traditional woven cotton has long been replaced by cheap synthetic fabrics brought back from Iquitos, plastic bowls replace gourds, and battery-powered radios are one of the most prized possessions.

One of the most positive projects is the bi-lingual system of education in the local school, where children are taught both in Bora and Spanish. On the other hand, that is as far as the cultural recognition goes. The Peruvian flag flies outside the school, and the annual calendar is peppered with national holidays, celebrating such events as the birthday of Peru's liberator, Simon Bolivar, or independence from Spain, but there are no holidays of Indian origin. Newly transcribed Bora is taught but there are no Bora books to read, as like all Amazon languages, it is an oral language, and the people's history, myths, and ideas are not yet in print. Important tribal knowledge used to be passed from one generation to the next during festivals, where the young asked the elders about the Bora past. During these story-telling sessions, the elders would relate their *historias* of times past, of wars and migrations and famous ancestors. Now, the school is the medium for education, and the subliminal message of this marginalization cannot help but have a profound effect on the children. In spite of the undoubted good intentions of bi-lingual education, the contents of the curriculum and the limited place of Bora culture and language within it, indelibly marks that culture and language out as peripheral. Most of the information they learn in school is irrelevant to their lives if they choose to remain in the community; they are better prepared for national service, which seems a rather small bonus. If they choose to leave the community for money jobs in Iquitos, their education gives them even fewer advantages: entrenched racism means that Indians are not generally considered employable for anything other than manual labour or, if they are lucky, as tourist guides, where they are expected to act the exotic, ignorant Native.

The Boras still retain their traditional skills, though, of architecture, agriculture, cooking, and craftsmanship. The wooden houses are still built to ancient designs on raised platforms. The art of palm leaf weaving is still the basis of roof construction, and other than the plastic bowls and metal cutlery, cooking is still centred around a wood-fired hearth, and food is processed and cooked the same way it always has been. They do eat the occasional tin of sardines, but their diet is mainly made up of the crops yielded from their slash-and-burn farming, and from plants gathered in the forest and animals hunted and fished over a wide radius. Unlike the river settlers who live off an excruciatingly boring diet of boiled rice and plantains, the Boras cultivate a varied diet from their difficult environment, through knowing how to work it and where to look for food. They eat domestic chickens, fowls and pigs; they hunt turtles, boar, deer, capybara (a giant rodent), snake, and tapir, to name but a few; cultivate yucca, corn, sweet potato, beans, squashes, plantains, nuts and berries, pineapples, papayas, cocona, and many other seasonal fruit, unknown to outsiders. Throughout the seasons, the community enjoys an excellent diet, and when times are lean, there are always the two staples to fall back on, plantain and yucca.

Yucca is a surprisingly versatile plant. There are two types: one can be boiled, fried or roasted, just like a potato; the other kind is known as *yucca brava*, and is poisonous when raw. This type is rasped and soaked, so that the poison can be squeezed out, and then dried into a rough flour that is used to make *cassave* bread; or it is fried loose, to be used on many dishes, rather like parmesan.

To drink, there are any number of juices made from boiled fruit, or there is the famous *masate*, made from masticated yucca, which is left to ferment for a couple of days, to be drunk mixed with water. Great tubs of this slightly alcoholic liquid are kept in every house, to be offered to guests. It is always made by the women, and they are in charge of serving it as well. To a Western taste, it is disgusting, reminding me of regurgitated bile. But if mixed with sugar it is not too bad.

The traditional festivals are still held as well as the Peruvian ones, even if unmarked by the calendar. This is when the *maloca* becomes the focal point of the community, and the entire village comes together to celebrate important occasions, such as the completion of a new house or a particularly good harvest or hunting expedition. Sometimes an entire neighbouring village is also invited, a time to strengthen relations and show potential brides to each other. Traditional songs are sung, plenty of food and *masate* is laid on, and the elders chew coca and tell stories. Villagers are called to the roundhouse by the drumming of the *manguare*, and the older generation can still recognize their names individually, from the tone and length of the beats. In former times, the Boras used to paint their bodies for these festivals: intricate black geometric patterns, covering every part of their bodies, from the face down. These days, they only paint their faces, but the songs and dances are still the same, slow, repetitive choruses to a regular drumbeat, occasionally accompanied by rattles and flutes as well.

Leonidas played me some tapes of the last great festival, and the songs reminded me of the chanting songs of North American Indians or Australian Aborigines. I found it hard to listen to, as they did not have any recognizable tune, but there was a mesmeric force in them, the entire village singing in unison, two groups facing each other in a kind of shuffling dance, while some of the men wear clusters of dry nutshells around their ankles to underline the rhythmic stamping of their feet. It would have been wonderful to take part in such a traditional celebration, but

209

they do not take place very often and when they do, they are spontaneous events, the occasion decided upon by the *curaca*.

On the second evening I was asked to explain the purpose of my visit to the assembled elders of the community. While the dozen or so men gathered in Leonidas' house, I waited nervously in the kitchen, trying to think of something to say that did not sound ridiculous or trite. Now that I had to justify myself to the people who mattered, I suddenly became unsure of the sincerity of my interest and intentions.

I reminded myself of the years I had spent reading about the ecology and the history and culture of the people of the Amazon; of my concern for its destruction and commitment to the Indians' rights to their lands and to self-determination. I had been genuine about it, hadn't I? I was well informed of the issues and the realities; so what was I embarrassed about? I could not get away from the fact that my good intentions still did not give me any right to come and stay here. I was hoping to write, and share my experiences with others, perhaps bring the reality of the situation closer to those who do not have a chance to see for themselves, and dispel a few myths. I intended to present a realistic picture, not a romanticized or exotic version, as so often seen in the media. But all these assurances to myself did not stop me feeling like the nosey outsider that perhaps I was, and I took my place among the circle of men, more nervous than before any examining board I had ever faced.

I explained that I was travelling along the entire Amazon river, to learn something of the landscape and people, of history and the way of life. That I was here on my own initiative, and not hired or paid by anyone. I told them about walking in the Andes and how much I had enjoyed it, and that now I was hoping to learn just as much in Amazonia. I was especially interested in coming to Brillo Nuevo, because I wanted to find out what a traditional community was like, as well as to see the forest, which you could not do from the main waterway. When I returned to my own country, I was going to write about my journey and what I had learned. In particular I intended to show a realistic picture of a modern Indian village trying to live in today's world, and the difficulty of combining the traditional with the external way of life. I said that I knew how they resented the insulting way they were portrayed as naked *Indios* by tourist agencies, and that I hoped to redress the balance in my own account. In return for their hospitality, I had brought bread, salt, sugar, and other provisions, as well as medicines, which I hoped the community would find useful.

My speech was short, and afterwards there was silence for a minute as they digested it. All the while I sat there feeling like an idiot. Everything I had said seemed a feeble excuse for inviting myself into the village. Why on earth should they let me stay, let alone feed me and show me around?

The elders, however, were pleased. They made jokes about me in Bora and laughed amongst each other before telling me it was fine to stay if it pleased me. They would do their best to help me find out whatever I wanted. We shook hands and the audience was over.

Over the next couple of days, I took tentative strolls around the village and passed most of the time with the many members of the Lopez family. Leonidas was usually outdoors, working on the boat, but there was his wife, two daughters and one husband, a son and his wife and child, and two adopted girls, whose mother had left them to live in Iquitos. Gradually, I had conversations with all of them, and we got to know each other.

Hernan, the twenty-year-old son, was a joker and we got on almost immediately. At first he played the Indian tour guide with me, a job he had held briefly, and his first words to me were:

'Hey, Miss, you wanna guide? I show you the jungle?' It was humiliating to be treated like a camera-clicking tourist from Iquitos, but I knew it was fair enough. Thankfully, he soon dropped his pose, and we talked to each other on the same level.

My Spanish was now quite good, and we had animated conversations about everything from forest plants to his parents' disapproval of his marriage to a *mestizo* girl from outside the community. He was to be my ally in breaking the ice with the others. Once he formed a good impression of me, his mother and sisters became much more open.

It took a few days, though, before we felt easy with each other, and I found it frustrating. Being an outsider among a close-knit

211

family was an emotional strain. It is little fun eating by yourself but, at first, I was always served food separately from the rest of the family, and what was worse, before anyone else had eaten. I wanted to ask them not to bother with this, but I was not confident that they wanted me around during mealtimes. It was the time when all the family came together and talked and joked with each other, a private moment, when everyone was off-guard. Their excessive hospitality seemed like a barrier. Often when our eyes met, we would smile warmly at each other; but this hardly ever led to a conversation in the first few days, and I felt isolated. I hate being a guest. I did not want special treatment that set me apart. What on earth did I expect? Here I was, turning up uninvited with a load of food, and in return I wanted to be friends and find out all about them, immediately, in ten days! It was absurd of me to expect anything more than courtesy, but I was childishly disappointed. I felt like the new girl in the school with whom nobody wanted to play. My vanity could not bear the thought of their identification of me as one of the 'jungle tour' *gringos* from the tourist boats.

The tours did not reach as far as this village, but the next one down got weekly visits from a luxury boat based in Iquitos. Every Wednesday, the Bora villagers dressed up for the tourists, sang and danced in traditional style, and then flogged them as many artefacts as possible. It was demeaning; but the tourists brought in money which the community would otherwise have no access to, and provided funds for expensive gasoline to make journeys to Iquitos and purchase basic provisions they did not have, like sugar, salt, cooking oil, and soap. I wondered if the only way they could cope with the contradictions in their life style was by closing ranks behind a smiling wall of hospitality. I knew all I could do was be patient, and hope that I might glimpse just a little through their defences.

Left to my own devices, I decided to explore the surroundings. Leonidas said I could take one of the small dugouts on to the river, and I set off round the continuing curve of the oxbow lake. Out of sight of the village, I felt more at ease, and once I had paddled a good distance, I stripped off my clothes and dived into the cool water. Dugouts lie very low, and when I came up from the dive, I saw that my clothes had been tipped into the river. There was nothing for it but to spread them out on the canoe and dry them in the sun, while I waited naked, hoping no one would come. Most of my body had not seen daylight in months, and it was good to feel the warm sun on my skin. My shirt dried quite quickly, and I had just put it on, when an Indian came paddling by, on the way to his fishing lines. He giggled and said hallo without stopping, and I did too. If nothing else, I could make people laugh. Hernan had promised to take me canoeing the next day, so I turned back, feeling happier for having felt water and sun on my bare skin. The river could wait.

Contradictions

'I hate anthropologists,' said Hernan fiercely. I was taken aback by the anger in his eyes. At the time, we were paddling on the peaceful Ampiyacu, kingfishers were skimming the river, and the forest was reflecting off the smooth water in perfect symmetry. I had been telling him how I felt, and he had been reassuring me that nobody resented me, that they believed I was genuine. This naturally led the conversation on to feelings about outsiders in general, and Hernan had a lot to say on that subject:

'They do nothing for us. The only one who benefits is the anthropologist, who goes back to his job at university and writes clever books. A Bora person isn't like some animal to be studied in a zoo! We want to study you, they say. But they're not interested in us how we are now. Only in our past and how we used to be. They contribute nothing to our present state of being. But we tolerate their presence because it's not the Bora way to show our disapproval. We keep it to ourselves and let the anthropologists stay in our homes. We're hospitable people, but inside we feel differently.

'In the neighbouring village, the people present a false picture for the tourists. Women dance half-naked, something they never do at a traditional festival. They sing songs and sell them things, and after a couple of hours the tourists go away again. Our community wrote a letter to the others and the tourist agency, condemning what they were doing, but they still go on selling themselves. They don't even get paid very much.

'I too, used to work for a tour agency, guiding people on forest walks. But I got sick of being the token Indian, wheeled out when anyone wanted to see a real *nativo*. The only time I went along with it, was when King Juan Carlos of Spain came to Iquitos. His boat was surrounded by armed guards and no one was allowed on the boat except crew and invited guests. I went

214

to that, but only because *I* wanted to meet Juan Carlos, not so that he could shake hands with an Indian.'

It was humbling hearing Hernan speak, and it forced me to re-examine my own motives for being here. Was I not using them just as much? I also planned to write a book. Was a personal desire to learn about forest life enough justification for being here? In the end, each case has to be judged individually, and in my case, it seemed the villagers of Brillo Nuevo had accepted me, perhaps for the very reason that I was here under my own steam, not part of a tour nor any official investigative body.

I had to admit to myself, that given the choice, I would have chosen to visit a less acculturated village; however, Brillo Nuevo was probably more representative of reality. Most tribes in Amazonia are changing rapidly under the influence of the outside world, and most have permanent or semi-permanent contact with non-Indians. As Hernan said, people should not impose their preconceptions on the Indians, but see them as they really are: people trying to retain their cultural identity, while living in the modern world of money, schools, and gasoline. It is unfair and wrong to search for an ideal of innocence, of prehistory, in the Indians, and it only insults the Amazon people of today, who are having enough difficulty establishing a sense of pride and self-respect in the context of their present lives, without being treated like picturesque relics of the past. There is nothing romantic or exotic about their lives, and outsiders who would wish them more 'primitive' are imposing their own imagined reality, rather than recognizing real people, like themselves. I was grateful for Hernan's openness, and promised myself that I would look to see what was there, and not for what I wanted to find.

It was my fifth day at Brillo Nuevo, and the family had stopped only smiling at me all the time, and we talked instead. We 'children' played around, swinging in the hammocks, slung between posts in the house. The age range, from the adopted girls to the eldest daughter, was from eleven to twenty-seven, although most of us were over eighteen. They loved to laugh and make jokes, often making fun of each other with a dry humour that stuck pins in anyone who got above themselves.

215

They tried to teach me Bora, which was good for a laugh. I could not get near the language at all, because Bora is a tonal tongue, which operates rather like morse code. Meaning is inferred from the length and tone of sounds, which makes it almost impossible to recognize 'words' as such. The school books, which transcribed Bora, indicated these long and short sounds by printing the same letter about five times. 'House', for example, was something like *aaaaaha*, with an upper inflection at the end; 'us' was *ughugh*, going up at the end as well. But my favourite was 'no', which was *tsa*, nice and short. I dislocated my throat trying to make the correct sounds, the others rolling around laughing, watching my face contorting itself as I tried to say the simplest things.

Stephanie, the mother, was heading for the *chacra* that afternoon, and I was allowed to accompany her. She had been going every day, but I had not had the courage to ask if I could come too, and it had not crossed her mind that I would want to. We set off, up past the *maloca* and along a narrow path through the forest, which was secondary, not virgin jungle. Most of the area within an hour's walking distance of the village had at some time been cut down for cultivating yucca or other plants. There were no giant trees and, apart from the many birds and butterflies, there was no wildlife.

The *monte*, as the wild forest was called, was at least a couple of hours' walk away, and any hunting entailed a minimum journey of three days to get far enough into the jungle. I yearned to go on one of those hunting trips, to get a feel of the real forest. Hunting is men's work, though, and my short visit was not long enough to convince anyone that I had the stamina to come along.

One of the youngest girls was also with us. She was a sturdy fifteen-year-old, who seemed to do most of the cooking and work around the house. Stephanie told me she had run away to Iquitos and got in with a bad crowd, and now she was entrusted to Stephanie's care to teach her better ways. The poor girl worked hard, first up in the mornings, cooking, cleaning, washing clothes in the river, tending crops; but she was not mistreated and seemed to accept her role in the family. She carried a large rattan basket, made of woven palm fibres, for collecting fresh yucca. The headband for carrying it was broken, so she chopped down a certain thick-stemmed plant, that looked like an overgrown weed to me. The girl cut it with her machete, and pulled long

216

strips off the length. Then she rasped the best strip smooth, and produced a new band for the basket, strong as any rope.

Stephanie and I left her to dig up yucca, while we went to weed a pineapple patch, or rather, Stephanie weeded while I watched. Wielding a machete is a skilful business and I was not much use except for company. The patch looked like an overgrown clearing to me. The climate and environment does not lend itself to the neat fields of more temperate regions. Everything grows so quickly in the heat and humidity, that any cultivated area is soon smothered in creepers, grass, and the fresh saplings of trees and bushes. The only way a crop has space to grow is by constant weeding, but the undergrowth is only ever thinned out not eradicated. The pineapples, which sprout up in the middle of a kind of cactus plant on the ground, are quickly hidden by the tangle.

We were not there long before the sky turned a milky grey and large raindrops started to fall. We just had time to shelter under a banana tree before the rainstorm began in earnest. Stephanie cut some broad banana leaves from the tree, and we huddled up under their floppy protection, giggling at each other's bedraggled appearance. It did not last long, only about ten minutes, and afterwards the air was alive with the sounds of excited birds. The branches of a tree nearby were bent under the weight of hundreds of small birds, pillar-box red with black feathers on their heads and wings. From a distance came a hollow sounding 'tock', which I was told was the call of a toucan. On the open patches of steaming mud flocks of butterflies came to suck the earth, and every leaf and bush dripped with raindrop prisms reflecting the new sunlight. I felt as exhilarated as the birds as we slipped and clambered back home over soaked logs and squelching mud.

In the evening, fresh yucca was boiled in preparation for the making of *masate*. The soft vegetable was pulped in a large wooden trough by the aid of a flat piece of rounded wood with two handles on it, which Stephanie held upright, swinging it through the white mash. She sat on the ground in front of the trough, her powerful arms working up and down as fast as pistons. The girls sat around also, chewing mouthfuls of yucca which they then spat back into the trough. They laughed shyly at me, expecting me to be disgusted. They offered me a cup from a tub already made. Its white, slimy texture made my stomach turn, but I sipped it slowly and tried to get used to its sour taste. I had to say I did not like it, but nobody took offence, and I was glad I had tried it.

28 July: Peruvian Independence Day, and a strange time to be in Brillo Nuevo. It is a perfect example of the dual lives of the Boras, lost rather than caught between two worlds. On the one hand, as Peruvian citizens they take pride in playing their part in the national celebrations: parades, flying the flag, and making speeches about freedom from servitude and Spanish rule; yet at the same time, the Peruvian flag and this particular holiday stand for everything that has led to the Bora's near annihilation. There is something unnatural about all the Peruvian flags hanging outside Brillo Nuevo's thatched wooden houses.

Worse is to see the children marching around the village green with carved guns, in preparation for the time when they will do their national service. All Peruvian schools are keen on military orderliness, and I had often got the impression, especially in the *sierra* and *selva*, that it is more important to have a spotless uniform than to have done any homework. School work itself is highly ritualized and compartmentalized, with the emphasis on neat copying of texts or pictures, and learning things off by heart to repeat parrot-fashion for the teacher. The children are drilled from an early age, and by the time they get into the army, they know all about saluting and goose-stepping. The Bora children know their parade formations better than the old dances.

To see the president and *curaca* of this community making speeches about being freed from slavery made me cringe. The preparations for the big day were taken seriously. I think the Boras, in part, have genuinely accepted their Peruvian identity, and as such they can speak with pride of their national history and the country's fight for independence. They are not Peruvians at all, though; they have never shared the benefits of independence. Only at the turn of this century they were being hunted like animals and enslaved by the rubber barons. Are they thinking about that today? Or about the fact that no self-respecting woman will go out with a *nativo*; no well-paid job ever comes their way; and that the government still feels free to appropriate

218

their lands. Perhaps to think of all that would make life unbearable. And it would make today's celebration impossible.

There are times when anger wells up. Young Bora men make snide remarks about visiting *gringos* taking photos of Indians, or ask white women if they would like to sleep with a real native. Perhaps the usual opaque hospitality, the courtesy without familiarity, is the only way for the Indians to keep their self-respect. They are very proud: it is a brittle pride born of a deep pain, of loss, and of survival as reflections of their former selves on the margins of 'their' country, Peru.

I was glad to be here on this particular day because it raised so many contradictions. Seeing the youngest children re-enacting the story of the conquest was too sad for words. Five-year-old Bora boys, dressed up as *conquistadores*, tied two Indians to a stake, while the other children whooped and shouted before the two prisoners were shot to death and fell dramatically to the floor. '*Viva Peru!*' they shouted, and everybody clapped.

The whole community had gathered in the school and around the green and the day had started off with parades and the ceremonial hoisting of the national flag, and now there were recitals and more speeches inside the school.

It seemed a good time to slip away and take unobtrusive photographs of the village and *maloca*. I had not used my camera at all so far, and although Leonidas had given me permission to take photographs today, I still felt it was better to do it while no one was around to take offence. I wanted especially to take pictures of the *maloca*, and I walked along the grassy promenade, past the row of raised houses, each one adorned with the red and white flag of Peru. Up past Leonidas' house and towards the *chacras*, the *maloca* stood silent.

The only person there was the *curaca*'s ancient mother, peeling the bark off fresh yucca. She took no notice of me, engrossed in what she was doing. We could not have talked; she was too old to have learned Spanish, a true survivor of a former age. She had been the wife of Mibeco, the last chief of the Boras under the old system, but he had been dead a long time. Now she lived on in the sacred *maloca*, cutting a sad and lonely figure, sitting in the great emptiness of the roundhouse. Independence Day certainly meant nothing to her.

*

219

The day after the big celebration was very quiet. Like anywhere else, everyone had drunk too much and stayed up long into the night, dancing at the school disco. It was a lazy day.

Hernan and I decided to go looking for palm hearts in the forest. We picked our way through the undergrowth beyond the *chacras*, and Hernan chose a slim-poled palm among the trees. Its silvery-grey trunk was smooth and no thicker than a man's leg, but it stood close to a number of other trees, and in order to give it room to fall, Hernan had first to chop down four other trees in its immediate vicinity. He swung the axe in great arcs from over his head, and the thud of its metal cutting the wood reverberated around the forest. Soon he was pouring with sweat, while I sat and watched, the useless *gringa*; we laughed and parodied ourselves as white lady and Indian warrior.

At last there was space for the palm to fall and, after a few strategic blows, it keeled over, taking branches and smaller trees with it as it slowly crashed to the ground. Underneath its crown, there was a thickened green band, which held the palm's heart. From there sprung the new leaves and at its centre it was a soft, creamy white. The head of grown palm fronds was quickly chopped off, and the delicate fibres inside the heart were soon exposed. The centre was made up of layer upon layer of wafer-thin strips, which could be peeled off individually. There was only a very small amount, and we did not even eat it all; by itself, it tasted little better than the best leaves from a salad. We left the slaughtered palm to rot among its four companions on the ground, and headed back for a more substantial lunch. Five trees wasted. Palm hearts are considered a delicacy; in Iquitos tinned ones are an expensive shop-bought luxury. There must be few delicacies whose extraction is more destructive and wasteful.

In the evening music was played in the *maloca*, as if the celebrations of the day before had been the official version, and today came the community's own party. The whole Lopez family came along after dark, as well as many others, and we listened to a handful of men playing deerskin drums and bamboo flutes. The scene was lit by the flickering light of a few kerosene lamps, and there was something very solemnly festive about the place, like a church filled with candle light. Here, though, people did not sit in neat rows, but swung in hammocks or chatted to each other, sitting on long logs on the ground. The children ran about, playing tag, and hiding in the shadowy edges of the open circle of poles. Somebody played the *manguare* drums, as if to call more villagers into the magic circle, and a few shy couples shuffled in a dance to the rhythmical music of the hand drums. The *curaca* was in good form that night, and he pulled me up to dance with him. He was much friendlier now, and he swung us around the dirt floor, showing off to everyone.

It was just over a week since I had arrived in Brillo Nuevo, and I felt happy and at ease. In only a short time, I had learned a great deal and even broken through the hospitality barrier that isolated me so much at first. Hernan's friendship had allowed me much closer into the family, eating and laughing with them, and discovering at least a fraction of what it meant to be Bora. It seemed an awful lot to me, and I treasured the time spent here, even if there was so much more I could have learned. I was sad not to have experienced the true jungle of the distant *monte*; I did not get the chance to find out what being in a tropical forest was like, nor see much of its flora and fauna. I did see another side to Amazon life, however, other than the one I had found along the Upper Marañon, amid the sleazy *pueblos* there. The settlers could learn a lot from the Indians, especially with regard to food and the environment, which they viewed only as a potential source of petroleum or gold.

People had come for the festival from all over the region. One of the guests was the agent for the Indian co-operative, which sold traditional craftwork and artefacts in Iquitos. He came to visit every three or four months, and each family in the village contributed items for sale. Leonidas had three jaguar pelts and one boarskin to send off, Stephanie had made a string hammock out of grassfibres, and all the women and girls between them had made about fifteen crocheted shoulder bags, dyed in attractive shades of brown, blue, purple, and maroon.

The hammock was an excellent piece of work, beautifully woven out of hundreds of pieces of string, strong enough to hold one, or even two people. It had taken three months to make but its price in Iquitos was I/15,000; which was just under four dollars at that time. It was nothing for such highly skilled work, but the community's bargaining power was low. The agent bought their work directly. If someone from the community went to Iquitos, the things could be sold for more in the markets, but a large chunk of the profits would have to go on gasoline, travel, and living expenses; hence the arrangement with the co-operative.

221

Wispy horse tails of freshly collected grass hung drying on posts around the house, and I had a go at trying to split some into fibres. It looked easy. All you had to do was rub one end between your fingertips, then hold the other end on your knee, while pulling the grass into two equal strips. It was surprisingly difficult, though, and I fiddled ineptly with one piece of grass, while Stephanie split one after another. I gave up and tried my hand at rolling string out of the fibres instead. A small ball of string lay on the floor, and I decided to add a few more lengths to it. For this, you needed to rub the string up and down your thigh with the flat palm of your hand, careful to keep up a regular rhythm to ensure smooth string. New fibres need to be introduced at regular intervals, and this way you can make an endless piece of string. I was useless at it. For one thing, it was quite painful, as the tiny hairs on my leg got caught as I rubbed the fibres up and down, plucking them out as if I were pulling off a plaster. I could not make my palm rub the fibres in one smooth action, and they quickly knotted themselves up like so much matted hair. It was embarrassing not to be able to do something which looked so easy, and I quickly lost patience with it and retired to a hammock, where I began to crochet, which I knew how to do, and after completing a few rows of a bag, my self-esteem was restored. Given time, I could learn to make string, I insisted to the others, and they smiled big grins and agreed that of course I could . . .

It was my last night in Brillo Nuevo. The following day I was to return to Pebas with two canoe-fulls of others, who were heading home after the festive weekend. It was a Sunday, and I decided to go to the mission church mass. I had not had anything to do with the American missionary family who lived here; I was not interested in them, and they were not interested in me. Their house and church were built some way from the village, and I had not occasion to see them more than once or twice.

That night there was the promise of a video after the church service, and all the children of the community were raring to go. Hernan commented that on other Sundays they stayed away. Padre Pancho had used the same trick in Nieva, showing Walt

Disney cartoons after the Sunday service, and they captivated everybody.

The Brillo Nuevo church was small and wooden, with rows of benches inside which tonight were crammed full. There was a short sermon, given in Bora by an Indian acolyte, and then the highlight of the evening began. The generator rumbled into action in the darkness outside, and the video screen on the altar came to life. There were excited squeals from the youngest children at the front, and the grown-ups crowded in, standing at the back. The film was the story of Christ's life, from his miraculous birth until the crucifixion. The actors were mainly white, a few looked like Arabs, dressed in Biblical robes, playing out the story in the dramatic settings of the desert and the ancient cities of Israel. It was an exciting story, and the Bora children were glued to the screen. Everybody was glued to the screen. It was the only time they got to watch television. Leonidas and Stephanie were deeply religious; but young people, like Hernan, were less reverent, and privately mocked this white religion, and dismissed its relevance to them. It was ironic: the Boras owed the missionaries so much. They helped to bring these communities back together, and the Indian bi-lingual teachers are trained at the SIL headquarters in Pucallpa, their travel and living expenses paid for. There were many painful contradictions in Brillo Nuevo; yet it was the happiest place and the truest community I encountered in Amazonia.

Slow Days to Belém

Back in Pebas, the distant sound of engines woke me at dawn. I had come down from Brillo Nuevo the day before, ready to leave for Brazil on whatever boat was going. Lola accompanied me to the river to help secure my passage, but the vessel we found was the three-deck luxury tourist boat, on its weekly trip down the Amazon. It does not normally take casual passengers, and it was moored well away from the jetty, alongside the swampy bank upriver, so that local people could not board. We stood there, wondering what to do. It could be a few days before another boat heading east stopped off at Pebas, and I was impatient to go. I had fulfilled my hope of staying with a traditional community away from the main river, and now I was eager to continue on to the Atlantic and the end of my journey. There were still over 3000 kilometres to go. I decided to try my luck.

In order to get near the boat, I had to pick my way down the steep and overgrown riverbank, and then wade through a tangle of reeds growing in a bog of soaked earth. Before I even got within talking distance of the boat itself, I saw the crew waving their fingers at me, as if to say 'no way'. I smiled broadly, and ignored their signals, asking instead where they were bound. Leticia, they said, which was perfect for me, since that would get me as far as the Brazilian border, and within stepping distance of boats for Manaus.

Now the captain himself came to the railings and joined the crew in trying to turn me back. There was no space on the boat, they shouted, and anyway, the owners of the boat didn't allow passengers who weren't part of the tour. Only a couple of metres of sludge and undergrowth separated me from the boat railings, and I began to pick my way forward, my feet sinking deep in the mud, and my rucksack threatening to unbalance me at any moment. I prayed that I would not slip right now, a spectacle in the mud for all to see. A small crowd of crew and passengers had gathered on the decks to watch my antics, but as long as I did not fall, I felt I still had some dignity.

I made it close enough to climb over the railings. The captain came forward to bar my way, saying the boat was absolutely full and there was no space for me. I smiled my friendliest smile, telling him that Leticia was just where I wanted to go and, as it happened, I had a hammock, which if he would just let me string up somewhere, I would be fine. You don't understand, said the captain, shaking his head, this was a luxury liner, not a normal passenger service, so they couldn't have me putting up a hammock in the gangway. Yes, but I really must travel today, I said, getting a little nervous. Perhaps we could talk on the boat? handing an obliging crewman my rucksack across the watery gap between the sludge and the boat. The next minute I lunged for the railing and climbed aboard, leaving an unfortunate brown trail on the pristine white of the boat's side.

I stood on the polished gangway, soaked in sweat from my efforts so far, and my legs and boots covered in mud. I beamed at the captain and held out my hand. It's no good, said the captain, smiling by this time at my flagrant persistence. Even if I did have a hammock, there was no food for me. Everything was tailored for the exact number of *paying* guests. Oh, I said, that's fine. I can do without food for two days, just as long as he'd take me. He laughed in my face, saying I couldn't possibly not eat for two days. Of course I can, I replied cheerily, and explained that I had been travelling for many months now, and was well used to the occasional hardship. He wasn't convinced, and again repeated what he had already said at least five times, that there was no room. I, in turn, repeated my answers, smiling all the while, trying to communicate to him that I knew I was asking the impossible, but he in his munificence could help me out, if he really wanted to.

Finally he said he would have to radio Iquitos to get the owner's permission. At this I became a little nervous, and pulled out my trump card, showing him my official recommendation from FOPTUR; I told him that I was researching a tourist report, aided by Peru's tourist board, and that he really shouldn't stand in the way of my work. As a matter of fact, I lied desperately, the FOPTUR office in Iquitos had told me expressly that I could travel on this boat. The perplexed captain went off to radio his boss.

225

The boat's well-dressed guests had been watching this little scene from a discreet distance, their faces betraying their incredulity. I tried to look confident, as a handful of young Brazilians came over to chat with me while I waited for the captain. They seemed unusual passengers for such a boat, dressed in flip-flops and shorts, and I found out that they were members of a football team from the Brazilian border town of Tabatinga, returning victorious from a match with the Iquitos side. They commiserated with my predicament, and generously offered to share their food with me for the day and night it was going to take to reach Leticia. They also told me they were paying $20 each for their passage, and I decided to offer the same to the captain, if he would take me.

He returned a short while later, and said that if I really didn't mind not having anywhere to sleep, nor any food, I could come along for $60, but that was definitely the bottom line: if I couldn't pay, I should get off right now. I put on my most crestfallen face, and began to explain desperately how hard up I was, and that I could not possibly pay $60, quite apart from the fact that it seemed an outrageous price, given the conditions I was going to travel under. The guests are paying $250 dollars each, he said coldly.

Things did not look good at this point. Hanging around in Pebas, though, possibly for days, was to be avoided if at all possible. There was nothing to do here. I did have one more card to play: another of the men who had ambled up to talk to me, a more conventional passenger than the footballers, also happened to be from the Ministry of Tourism. I latched on to him straight away, showing him my papers and explaining my position: I certainly was not going to pay $60, and knowing how much the footballers were paying gave me some leverage. My kind friend did have a word with the captain about this and, lo and behold, the price was grudgingly dropped to $30. What was more, a crew cabin was found in the bowels of the lower deck, and I was invited to eat with the other guests, who had far more food than they could manage. All this goes to show that anything is possible in Peru, and nothing should be taken literally. Disconcerting at first, it makes for miraculous possibilities, which I found an exhilarating challenge every time they presented themselves.

I enjoyed the luxury of good food, while the boat ploughed on through the muddy waves of the Amazon. The banks were now so far away that only the haziest outlines were visible, and there was more water to be seen than land. It seemed to me that the tourists were paying an awful lot of money for four days of food and an unchanging view. There was a short stopover at the Indian village beyond Pebas, and a shopping trip in Leticia, but that added little more than expenses to the existing fee of $250. Some of the passengers seemed to think so too, and I almost felt guilty for taking a cheap ride. Nobody seemed to resent my arrival, however, and I was treated more like a tour diversion than a freeloader. A group of finely manicured American ladies even told me that they had rooted for me when I had climbed on board, hoping the captain would give in. One lady from California was so concerned about my unkempt state that she insisted on giving me a whole toilet bag full of expensive shampoos and face creams.

The following day the boat moored on the Peruvian bank, across the water from Colombian Leticia and, while the tourists were ferried off for a shopping spree, the football team and I were taken to neighbouring Tabatinga, in Brazil.

From there it was only a two-hour ferry ride to the small town of Benjamin Constant, where passenger boats left regularly for Manaus.

'Welcome to Brazil,' said a handsome border official in jeans and an open shirt. Loud music blared from the roadside bars, and down by the harbour a whole flotilla of brightly coloured river buses stood waiting for customers. There was one leaving for Benjamin in ten minutes, and as I stepped on to the plank leading to its deck, my Brazilian friends waved goodbye with their shiny brass football trophy.

'This is so civilized!' I wrote rather prissily in my diary. I was only a few kilometres downriver from Peru, but the difference was marked. The river was the same; but this was a different world. My first impression of Brazil was of a bright and happy place, where people wore loud colours and went about to the constant sound of lively music blasting out from every shop and market stall.

I spent one night in Benjamin Constant, waiting for a ferry of the same name to take me to Manaus, and the little town was in

227

complete contrast to any settlement I had encountered in the Peruvian Amazon. I was struck by its cleanliness and friendly atmosphere. Walking around its sleepy streets, I had much less a sense of being a *gringo*, and of being watched with beady eyes as a potential source of income. My normally combative haggling was unnecessary in the market here, and one stallholder even recommended someone else's stand for cheaper cigarettes.

In Peru, a small town like Benjamin would be standing in mud and garbage; in Brazil the streets were paved, and pretty wooden houses lined their path, rubbish bins in front of neat garden fences. If I sound a little too excited about cleanliness, I can only say that the surprise of it made it all the more memorable. There were letter boxes too, indicating a postal service that even reached these smaller places, unheard of upriver in Peru: Iquitos was the only place where you could be almost certain to receive post. Brazil is clearly a much richer country than Peru, and I doubt that the differences are more marked anywhere than along the Amazon border region.

The *Benjamin Constant* was a large, three-deck ferry boat, painted white with dark green railings. The decks and cabins were in polished chestnut-coloured wood, and a long wooden table stood on the second deck for serving meals for the passengers. As with the smaller *Juliana*, third class passengers were in hammocks on the lowest deck, next to the engine room and the cargo; the second class was in hammocks on the upper deck, and the first in the cabins built to the fore and on the third deck. It was a beautiful boat, a ship really, and the decks soon filled up with the usual tangle of hammocks, everybody jostling for the best positions and building small stategic mountains of luggage. Some people chained their bags to the supporting poles on deck, but most just kept a careful eye open. We were going to be travelling for four days to Manaus, and there was little danger of theft at this early stage. Running water, toilets and showers, and even loo paper and soap were all provided free; the whole passage, including the meals, cost just $33. Upriver, this would have been a luxury boat reserved for rich tourists; here it was just one of the better passenger boats, and I was glad to be travelling downriver in style.

The journey to Manaus passed in tranquillity, with nothing to do but eat and sleep, or chat occasionally with the occupants of neighbouring hammocks. Meals were served in three shifts at the long table and, if you wanted to, you could eat at all three sittings; it was hardly necessary, though, as the portions of rice, beans, and meat or fish, were very generous. We even got coffee afterwards, sweetened into a sickly syrup. Unsweetened coffee seemed to be unavailable in Brazil, and whenever I asked for it I was met with complete incomprehension.

The river was so wide now that it was almost like being at sea, sky and water all that the eye could see. The Brazilian Amazon is vast: people arriving from the Atlantic say it is impossible to tell when the mouth of the river is reached, until almost 160 kilometres inland, when ships pass close to the giant island of Marajó or dock at the city of Belém.

The *Benjamin Constant* docked at the port of Manaus on a Monday morning. The harbour was teeming with men hustling for cab fares, stevedores unloading gaping cargo holds on to the jettys, and clutches of vultures which picked at the remains of someone's catch in the tidal mud. The city's skyline had been visible for at least half an hour before we had arrived, and the metropolitan atmosphere engulfed us as we stepped ashore.

Manaus is the largest city in the Amazon, a hybrid of old and new, choking with cars and factories, and with one tax-free shop next to another. Its duty-free status has made it into the commercial centre of the north Amazon and there is nothing you cannot buy here. Electrical goods and watches seem to be the most popular items on the streets, and vendors crowd the pavements, their wrists dripping with fake Rolexes. Gold jewellery, perfumes, and luxuries from all over the world lure from every shop window, and travel agents ply for customers on every corner. Jungle tours promise exotic adventure for $100 a day, tempting tourists to fulfil their dreams with appetizing photos of verdant foliage and colourful parrots.

For me, though, Manaus was a dirty city with smelly slums and frantic consumerism. There was very little that was attractive to see: its most famous landmark, the stuccoed opera house, was obscured by restoration scaffolding. One day was enough in the concrete jungle, and the inflated prices of hotels and restaurants soon sent me packing.

*

There are no direct boats to Belém; instead one makes a two-day journey to Santarém, halfway, and then it is another two days from there. In between the two journeys there can be anything up to a week's wait before getting a connection onwards, and the entire journey can, in practice, take many days. It was a prospect I did not relish, having just spent four days lying in my hammock.

Delay was intolerable to me now. I had been travelling almost continuously for four months, and was looking forward to the journey's end. I was exhausted, mentally rather than physically, and my energy was low. All I could think of was arriving in Belém, and knowing that my journey was over. In the face of this, I decided to fly to Belém, which in terms of a journey from the source to the sea was a cop-out, I suppose. On the other hand, there is nothing of note about river travel between Manaus and Belém, and I saw no point in being bored on a principle. My only regret is that I could not fly during the daytime and see Amazonia from the sky; but all the flights went in the middle of the night, as if the airlines deliberately do not want to give anyone the view free.

I arrived bleary-eyed at 4 a.m. in the city of Belém do Pará, on Wednesday, 9 August 1989. It was still dark, and the small airport was hardly more awake than the arriving passengers, but I felt a surge of excitement. This was it, the end of a journey that had started in the tense city of Lima and the even more dangerous Cordillera Huayhuash, on the other side of South America. I could barely believe it was the end, and I knew it would take a couple of days to sink in fully.

For the moment, I concentrated on catching a bus to the city centre, and checking in for more sleep at the Hotel Central, on the Avenida Vargas. Months later, I was pleased to read that the Victorian traveller, Lizzie Hessel, had stayed there in 1897, almost one hundred years earlier; although she found it lacking – the toilets did not work – and moved elsewhere. Margaret Mee, the well-known botanical artist, also stayed here, on her first journey to the region, to depict Amazon plants, in 1956. She recalls it as 'simple', but I thought it wonderful. Its decor was 1930s, and my mind peopled it with the Hollywood film stars of the era. My third floor room was furnished in plain but elegant furniture, the chest of drawers topped in grey marble, and an old fan whirring away in front of a framed mirror. Green peeling shutters kept out

230

the sun, throwing striped shadows across the bed made in white linen, but letting the street sounds filter through from below. It was a beautiful room to wake up in, and by late morning, I was refreshed enough to explore.

Belém is a more attractive city than Manaus, with many of its Portuguese colonial buildings still standing, and its ancient harbour and market very much as they have always been. There is a cosmopolitan air to the streets, and a certain sophistication generated by the elegant nineteenth-century buildings, such as the Teatro do Paz and the beautiful Mercês church. I climbed a cobbled street to reach the old fort overlooking the small harbour, where wooden fishing boats stood aslant on the riverbed, their owners selling their catch direct from the decks. Looking out to the horizon from the battlements, there was water, water, everywhere: a fifth of the world's fresh water pouring out into the Atlantic at a rate of 7.5 million cubic feet every second. The mouth of the Amazon is so vast, that it covers roughly the same distance as that between London and Paris; yet at its headwaters in the Peruvian Andes, you can leap across the water in one bound.

I felt a tremendous sense of joy to have seen the river grow from a mountain stream to this great giant of an Amazon. We had known each other a long time now and, although there were some miserable moments, most of the journey was a dream come true, unexpected in its development, but fulfilling nevertheless. I learned to love not just the river and the land it flowed through, but also many of the people along the way. The journey taught me more than I could possibly have imagined, and in particular, to know myself better. I was filled with a greater sense of my own abilities and, liberated by this achievement, felt at peace for the first time. This journey was unique, and if I never achieved anything else, it would always remind me that I can hold my own in the world.

What struck me most was that I had done what I set out to do: it was a staggering thought. If I had known how tough it was going to be, I would never have tried; but as I had come through, I felt like jumping up and down and shouting it out to the world. Standing alone among the fort's old guns was a lonely anticlimax. It was hard not having anyone to share my joy with, and it was the only time I truly wished that I was not alone. I paced the streets of Belém, feeling like I was about to explode.

One morning, as I walked along the busy Avenida Vargas, two Indian men, dressed in nothing but shorts and beautiful feathered crowns, came walking through the crowd of office workers. They marched along the pavement barefoot, and they seemed oblivious to their surroundings, walking briskly with intent expressions on their faces. I turned to gaze in wonder, as their backs disappeared into the crowd, long black hair swinging to the rhythm of their bodies: they were an apparation from the world I had never really entered.

After a few days I phoned England and spoke to my brother. It was comforting to hear his voice, but also made me feel sad, magnifying my loneliness in Belém, on the other side of the world. I treated myself to an outrageously expensive meal to make up for it, and gorged on good food and wine at my table for one.

Last Words

Things never turn out as you expect them to. When I first set out on this journey, I thought that Amazonia was going to be the highlight of the expedition. All my sights were trained on the time when I would travel on the river itself and learn about the forest and its people at first hand. More than anything else, I wanted to know what it was like to be in a jungle, to see and feel and hear a world I knew only in my imagination.

I never imagined the reality of walking through the Andes, nor had a clear idea of what the mountains and their inhabitants would be like. And, in the end, it was the months spent in the Andes that gave me the greatest pleasure. I found a landscape and a people that I learned to understand and care for, and without having done any hiking before, I discovered that I love to walk. It proved to be a very educative time for me personally as well: discovering things about myself that were not always attractive, but which now, at least, I could try to improve. In the loneliness of the mountains, I also faced the insignificance of my own life on this earth and, for the first time, I understood that life is not made special by achieving ambitions, but by sharing the experience with others. Easy to say, but for me, it took this journey to learn and believe it. I do not know if it will be any easier to change my solitary nature with this realization, but perhaps there is a better chance than before.

By contrast, the tropical Amazon part of the journey proved to be much less rewarding, and often extremely frustrating. Apart from the obvious disappointment of never having seen what I regarded as the 'true' jungle, it was very hard indeed to find myself so dependent on others, when I had been so free in the mountains. The endless hours of inaction and waiting, the boredom of downriver travel, the depressing sense of being an outsider: all this taught me that getting into the forest is a

233

separate expedition in itself, which was good to know for the next journey, but helped little at the time.

In a sense, however, I am glad to have had the experiences I did, because whatever I thought I knew about Amazonia in theory, I had no idea of the difficulty of life there. Only a desert could be less yielding: one could easily starve to death in a jungle.

The most valued lesson I learned, though, was to recognize the reality of the Amazon Indians trying to live in the no-man's-land between traditional cultures and the encroaching twentieth century. I caught myself wishing for something else, a romantic idea, a beautiful tradition, man in harmony with nature. It was a false image and one which should not be perpetuated as it denies indigenous peoples the respect and autonomy which are theirs by right; and allows their own government and those in the West to continue to exploit, neglect and, ultimately, negate them, their history, their present identity and, most importantly, their future.

As far as I know, I am the first woman to follow the Amazon from any of its headwaters to the sea, alone. I admit I like that idea. What would give me far greater pleasure, though, is if my story encourages more women to fulfil their travelling dreams.

Many women still assume they could not possibly go on solo expeditions, as if being female is supposed to disqualify you, when in fact, nothing could be further from the truth. A woman travelling alone has many more advantages than disadvantages: she poses no threat to anyone, and people are therefore much more open and ready to trust her enough to invite her into their homes and lives. They are also more likely to offer help; even to the extent of being over-protective, which is a more common occurrence than hostility. The woman on her own travels more safely through sensitive border areas or war zones, less likely to be treated with suspicion than a man. Officials usually treat women better than men and, although there might be terrible exceptions, they are exactly that – exceptions – and should not be held up as spectres to scare women off.

You do not have to be incredibly brave or strong to travel alone to remote areas. You do need to be knowledgeable about the country, well prepared, and well equipped. It is a myth that men are safer travelling alone than women: they may be stronger physically, but they do not have better wits than women and, nine times out of ten, danger comes from ignorance, a lack of communication, or awareness.

Many people, both men and women, do not travel alone to other countries, possessed by a fear of otherness, of difference. They imagine themselves isolated in an alien place, by an alien culture and its people. Cultures differ, but people are not foreign when you speak their language. Even basic knowledge of a language makes an enormous difference, and in remote regions it is essential. Best of all, it provides the chance to get to know and understand another culture at first hand. To understand the conflicting economic and political interests, and historical legacies which compound the problems of the Third World, we must learn to recognize, respect, and celebrate the otherness of people on our planet, and realize our aims and needs in common. Ecological realities force this fact in our faces with even greater urgency. Amazon Indians are not somehow less concerned about their homes, families, and their way of life than ourselves. The poor in South America have no less need of food, clothing, and self-respect. If more people had a sense of our common identity and interests, governments might be forced to look for solutions with greater sincerity, or lose the next election. It is hard not to sound naive. All this has been said before, yet international co-operation is still only marginal on any government's agenda; the work is left to charities and aid agencies. There is a reality gap between what is said and what is actually believed. A good way to change that, I believe, is to travel. Break down the barriers and, women especially, find out that you can do whatever you put your mind to.

*

After reaching Belém, I made my way back to Peru via the Brazilian coast, flying from Rio to La Paz, and then continuing overland. I took it easy, meeting up with friends in Salvador and spending a few days indulging myself on the sandy beaches of Bahia. In Rio I was ready for some flashy nightlife, but had to make do with more bars instead, as I had neither the money nor the clothes to show myself in any club full of beautiful Brazilians. I also developed a mysterious blistery skin infection, which spread from the end of my nose across my right cheek. The only thing I had to treat this with was the remains of the donkey's cream, which unfortunately was white; wherever I went people stared at the white blotches on my face, doing nothing for my vanity.

I arrived back in Huaraz in early September. It was a homecoming eagerly awaited on both sides, and everyone at Hostal Huascaran gave me a warm welcome. Much had happened in the intervening months, to me and to them, but it soon felt as if I had been there all along. Americo and I still felt great affection for each other, although the uncertain times Peru was going through had put a damper on our exuberant plans for a future together.

The summer of 1989 was a very bad time for everyone in Huaraz: the *Sendero* violence and assassinations drove away the tourists, leaving the town without its main source of income, while rocketing inflation made money almost irrelevant. By the time I returned, gas and kerosene had been rationed or were unavailable for over a month, and the family was reduced to cooking over open fires in the back garden. There was no bread because there was no flour, and food prices were five times higher than they had been five months previously. The future looked very bleak.

It was no time to be thinking of personal lives, and Americo now had more important things on his mind. I, in turn, had had plenty of time to think about how I felt, but the completion of my journey had brought me no closer to knowing what I wanted. I had had months to wonder what it would be like to make my life in Peru, and although I was very tempted, I could not get away from a nagging feeling that it was too distant from my own culture. I knew I could easily assimilate, but the other side of the world seemed too far from home. To my unpleasant surprise, ambition also still reared its ugly head. Chasing my dream had brought a certain kind of peace, but I still wanted the fulfilment of work, and there were few opportunities for me in Huaraz.

Emotionally I was torn in all directions, and it was impossible to think straight. My mind was full of doubts and confusion. I tried to write them out in my diary, but to no avail:

236

It's just impossible to say what the future will bring. I don't feel I can promise Americo that I'll come back; perhaps it's just my craving for security, but I don't feel that I can leave Europe and the opportunities I might have there. In May I wrote that ambition is a sterile thing, that it shouldn't get in the way of personal happiness with others, that we're too much alone even without the exile of ambition. I crave a life and work of my own, although the idea of having a family is one I love. Could I stand the constant invasion of privacy and personal thoughts, though, which having a child would invariably entail? One of my friends said she thought of motherhood as a kind of slavery and I can see her point.

Americo and I spent three weeks together, enjoying the last of the Andean summer and walking in the mountains. We went on a four-day hike, something we had not had a chance to do alone before. Americo took an old pair of boots and got terrible blisters, which was ironic, him being the mountaineering guide.

A few days before I was due to leave for England, we went to our favourite restaurant to eat grilled rabbit. Suddenly the lights went out, which was the usual prelude to a bomb and, five minutes later, a loud explosion ripped through the streets. As soon as the light had gone, the manager pulled metal shutters over the windows and put candles on the tables; the explosion a few seconds later attracted no comment, no one in the restaurant even stopped eating. Explosions were too common by now to take notice of each one.

Appendices

1: Equipment

I chose all clothes and equipment with light weight and small bulk as my priority, which meant that it was often expensive, but it was worth it in most cases. There were only a few exceptions: my Saunders tent was unfortunately not rainproof; the candle-lantern was useless – I could not see a thing with it; my Survival Shop mosquito net was for hanging over a bed, and was little use over hammocks: I should have bought it in Iquitos; the flexible waterbottles leaked; and I never used my expensive compass, not that I knew how to.

Clothes

For the Andes:
silk long-johns and top
silk headover
two pairs of thick socks
knickers
one pair of trousers
two long-sleeved shirts
one T-shirt
one windproof zoot-suit (doubled as pyjamas)
one down-jacket
one basha (combined plastic poncho and groundsheet)
one pair of non-leather walking boots
one pair of trainers
one pair of gloves

For the Jungle:
one pair of cotton trousers
one pair of canvas boots
cotton hat

And from the Andes:
two long-sleeved shirts
knickers
one T-shirt
one zoot-suit
one basha

Accessories

For the Andes:
one 70-litre rucksack
sun-glasses
sun-cream
one sleeping-bag (capable of standing up to more than −15°C;
mine was not quite warm enough)
kip-mat
tent

For the Jungle:
three bottles of neat Deet (insect repellent)
mosquito net
plastic army hammock

Utensils

multi-fuel stove
two aluminium pots
cutlery set
one-litre aluminium fuel bottle
plastic mug
plastic bowl
Mauser knife
two flexible one-litre waterbottles
compass
headlamp
candle-lantern
two stuff-sacks
rope
large plastic rainsheet for donkey
home-made saddle-bags

countless plastic bags for food
tin-opener
Bio-wash (for body and clothes)
nail-scissors
toothbrush
toothpaste

Essentials

Canon AE1 camera and 28mm lens and 70–410mm zoom lens
about thirty rolls of Fujicolour slide film, ASA100 and ASA400
padded camera-bag
maps from the Peruvian military in Lima
colour postcards of London to give away
English stamps to give away
small photo collection of family, cat, friends, and home
solar-powered calculator (excellent aid to changing money rates)

Papers

passport
vaccination booklet
flight ticket
travellers cheques
insurance papers
recommendations

2: Medicines and Vaccinations

I took a vast number of medicines, most of which I never used and gave away instead. I am glad I had them nevertheless, even though it was a bore to carry them and they cost a lot of money.

Medicines

flea powder (much needed)
antiseptic fluid
a roll of plaster
footplasters for blisters (essential!)
two rolls of bandages
ear-drops
eye-drops
anti-histamine
Tetracycline
thrush pills
penicillin tablets
Lemotol
Paracetamol
Flagyl
Proguanil and Chloroquine
Praziquantel
anti-fungal cream (feet)
water-purifying tablets (ha!)
Aids and Hepatitis B transmission prevention pack: three syringes; ten needles; suture material; drip needle; steristrips; melolin dressings; alcohol swabs
tampons

Vaccinations

Yellow Fever
BCG (widespread TB in the Andes)
Rabies
Typhoid
Tetanus
Polio
Hepatitis
Hepatitis B

3: Costs

The most expensive thing was my equipment; I had nothing in the first place and needed specialist gear. In total, it cost me about £2000 (including camera, lenses and film). I wasted money on many things I never needed, such as webbed belts and pouches, bungees, inflatable travel pillow, mess tins and compass. The medicines and vaccinations were about £100. The return flight was £450. The donkey cost roughly £25, and I had $1200 in travellers cheques for the seven months I was in South America; this was cutting it very fine, in spite of inflation, and I had to have money telexed to Brazil. This is something to be avoided if at all possible: it took me four weeks of hassle and phone-calls to get my money.

4: Organizations

Royal Geographical Society, 1 Kensington Gore, London SW7 2AR

Survival International, 310 Edgware Road, London W2 1DY

Catholic Institute for International Relations, 22 Coleman Fields, London N1

South American Explorers' Club, 1510 York Street, Denver, CO 80206, USA

Latin American Bureau, 1 Amwell Street, London EC1R 1UL

Centro Amazonico de Anthropologia y Aplicacion Practica (CAAP), Parque Gonzales Prado 626, Magdalena, Lima, Peru

El Instituto Geographico Militar, Avenida Aramburo 1198, Lima, Peru (for topographic maps of Peru)

Bibliography

Travel and Nature

Asheshov, A. *The Gold in the River*, London, Hodder & Stoughton Ltd, 1975

Bartle, J. *Trails of the Cordilleras Blanca and Huayhuash of Peru*, Bartle, 1981

Bates, H. W. *Naturalist on the River Amazon*, Dover, 1975

Berwick, D. *Amazon*, London, Hutchinson, 1990

Daniels, A. *Coups and Cocaine*, London, Century, 1986

Donner, F. *Shabono*, Ulverscroft, 1982

Fleming, P. *Brazilian Adventure*, London, Penguin, 1957

Up de Graff, F. W. *Head-Hunters of the Amazon*, London, H. Jenkins Ltd, 1923

Guppy, N. *Wai-Wai*, London, John Murray, 1950

Hanson, F. P. *Journey to Manaos*, London, Gollancz, 1938

Harrison, J. *Up the Creek*, Bradt, 1986

Hatt, J. *The Tropical Traveller*, London, Pan, 1982

Jordan, T. & M. *South American River Trips*, Bradt, 1982

Kingland, R. *A Saint among Savages*, London, Collins, 1980

Man, J. *The Amazon*, Time-Life Books, 1973

Mee, M. *Flowers of the Amazon Forest*, Nonesuch Expeditions, 1988

Morrison, T. et al *Lizzie*, London, BBC Books, 1985

Murphy, D. *Eight Feet up in the Andes*, London, Century, 1985

Ridgway, J. *Amazon Journey*, London, Hodder & Stoughton, 1972

Ridgway, J. *Journey to Elizabeth*, London, Penguin, 1987

Schneebaum, J. *Keep the River on your Right*, GMP, 1988

Shoumatoff, A. *The Rivers Amazon*, London, Century, 1987

Simpson, J. *Touching the Void*, London, Pan, 1989

Spruce, R. *Notes of a Botanist on the Amazon*, London, Macmillan, 1962

Tomlinson, H. M. *The Sea and the Jungle*, Harmondsworth, Penguin, 1953

Ure, J. *Trespassers on the Amazon*, London, Constable, 1986
Wallace, A. R. *Narrative of Travels on the Amazon and Rio Negro*, London, Ward Lock & Bowden Ltd, 1895
Waterton, C. *Wanderings in South America*, London, Century, 1984

History and Contemporary Analysis

Baddeley, O. & Fraser, V. *Drawing the Line*, London, Verso, 1989
Bethell, L. (ed.) *The Cambridge History of Latin America*, Cambridge, CUP, 1985
Branford, S. & Glock, O. *The Last Frontier*, London, Zed Books, 1985
'The Expedition of Pedro de Ursua and Lope de Aguirre in Search of El Dorado', *The Hakluyt Society Series*, Volume 1, number 28
Hemming, J. *The Conquest of the Incas*, London, Penguin, 1983
Hemming, J. *Red Gold*, London, Papermac, 1987
Peru, Paths to Poverty, London, Latin American Bureau, 1985
Lewis, N. *The Missionaries*, London, Secker & Warburg, 1988
Martin, G. *Journeys through the Labyrinth*, London, Verso, 1989
Meggers, B. *Amazonia: Man and Culture in a Counterfeit Paradise*, London, Aldine, 1971
Mendes, C. *Fight for the Forest*, London, Latin American Bureau, 1989
Ortiz, R. D. *Indians of the Americas*, London, Zed Books, 1984
Is God an American?, London, IWGIA and Survival International, 1981

In Spanish

Alegria, C. *La Serpiente de Oro*
Avendano, A. *La Rebelion de Los Mallkis: Medicina Popular Quechua*, Lima, Antawara, 1988
Villarejo, A. *Asi es La Selva*, CETA, 1988
Monumenta Amazonica, CETA, 1988
Ioppe, *Documental del Peru: Amazonas*

Some Peruvian Literature in Translation

Alegria, C. *Broad and Alien is the World*, London, Merlin Press Ltd, 1983
Arguedas, J. M. *Yawar Fiesta*, London, Quartet Books, 1985
Vargas Llosa, M. *The Green House*, London, Picador, 1986
Vargas Llosa, M. *Aunt Julia and the Scriptwriter*, London, Faber & Faber Ltd, 1983
Vargas Llosa, M. *The Storyteller*, London, Faber & Faber Ltd, 1990

249